RAINBOW EDITION

Tell Me How the Sun Rose

Theodore Clymer

Ruth Meyerson Stein
Doris Gates
Constance M. McCullough

Consultants

William E. Blanton

Irene J. Frazier

Milton D. Jacobson

Ken Johnson

Bonnie I. McCullough

Karen A. Scibinico

Roger W. Shuy

E. Paul Torrance

GINN AND COMPANY

Acknowledgments

Grateful acknowledgment is made to the following publishers, authors, and agents for permission to use and adapt copyrighted materials:

Atheneum Publishers, Inc., for "Mechido" by Giggy Lezra. Copyright © 1969 by Giggy Lezra. From *Mechido, Aziza and Ahmed*. Used by permission of Atheneum Publishers.

The Bobbs-Merrill Company, Inc., for "How the Birds Came to Have Their Many Colors," from *The Long-Tailed Bear and Other Indian Legends,* copyright © 1961, by Natalia M. Belting, reprinted by permission of the publisher, The Bobbs-Merrill Company, Inc.

Coward, McCann & Geoghegan, Inc., for "The Great Hunt" by Richard M. Powers. Adapted by permission of Coward, McCann & Geoghegan, Inc. from *The Cave Dwellers* by Richard M. Powers. Copyright © 1963 by Richard M. Powers.

Thomas Y. Crowell for the text of *The Seeing Stick* by Jane Yolen. Copyright © 1977 by Jane Yolen. By permission of Thomas Y. Crowell.

The Dial Press for "Thi Kinh" from the book *The Beggar in the Blanket and Other Vietnamese Tales* by Gail B. Graham. Copyright © 1970 by Gail B. Graham. Used by permission of the Dial Press.

Doubleday & Company, Inc., for the poem "I Go Forth to Move about the Earth" by Alonzo Lopez from the book *The Whispering Wind* copyright © 1972 by the Institute of American Indian Arts. Reprinted by permission of Doubleday & Company, Inc.

Macmillan Publishing Co., Inc., for "Boston Bells," excerpted from *American Adventures* by Elizabeth Coatsworth. Copyright © 1968 by Macmillan Publishing Co., Inc., Reprinted by arrangement with Macmillan Publishing Co., Inc. Also for "How Jahdu Found His Power," excerpted from *Time-Ago Tales of Jahdu,* by Virginia Hamilton. Copyright © 1969 by Virginia Hamilton. Reprinted by arrangement with Macmillan Publishing Co., Inc.

4

son for Elizabeth Coatsworth.

Peter Pauper Press, Inc., for "How the Milky Way Came to Be" and "Nature Cannot Be Changed," both from *African Folk Tales* by Charlotte and Wolf Leslau. Copyright © 1963 by The Peter Pauper Press. Used by permission of the publisher.

The Seabury Press for "The Children of Rain" retold by Elizabeth S. Helfman, adapted from her book *The Bushmen and Their Stories*. Copyright © 1971 by Elizabeth S. Helfman. Used by permission of The Seabury Press, Inc.

Virginia K. Smiley for "The Fuji Stick."

A. P. Watt Ltd, London, for "The Maker of Ropes," adapted from *The Black Monkey* by John Hampden. Used by permission of A. P. Watt Ltd and the author. Also for the galleys of "The Wasp in a Wig" by Lewis Carroll. "The Wasp in a Wig" copyright © Philip Jaques and Elisabeth Christie 1977 Trustees of the Estate of the late C. L. Dodgson. Reprinted by permission of the Trustees of the Estate of C. L. Dodgson, Clarkson Potter Inc. and Macmillan and Co. Ltd. and by courtesy of Mr. Norman Armour Junior and The Lewis Carroll Society of North America.

Illustrations were provided by the following: Angela Adams (348–363); Matthew Annantonio (64–75); Paul Blakey (78–97); Louis Carey (418–456); Joshua Clark (76–77); Patricia Collins (303–311); Dave Cunningham (381–396); Jim Crowell (400–415); James Daugherty (138); Sam Dion (312–324); Len Ebert (12-22, 238–243, 364–371); George Eisenberg (48–61); John Freas (211–213, 244–249); Charles Freeman (294–299); Judy Sue Goodwin (417); Christa Keiffer (399); Harvey Kidder (372–379); Gordon Laite (250–258); Richard Loehle (26–44); Elizia Moon (170–181); Les Morrill (118–128, 201–204); Sal Murdocca (276–283); Jane Oka (380); Marianne Perlack (285); Jerry Pinkney (136–137, 153–168); Richard Powers (336–344); Jon Provost (24–25); Albert John Pucci (260–273); Jim Santiago (63); Miriam Schottland (206–207); Ralph Steadman © The Sunday Telegraph Magazine (144); Karl Stuecklen (101–115); Susan Swan (208–209); Phero Thomas (224–236); Kyuzo Tsugami (188–199).

Photographs were provided by the following: Holle Beldarchiv (328–329); Reproduced by permission of the British Library Board, Additional Ms. 46700, f. 46 v (142); J. B. Collins (118); Charles Michael Daugherty (139); William Finch (286–287, 290–291); Kevin Galvin (116–117, 182–183); Virginia Hamilton (101); Courtesy, Istituto Editoriale Italiano (326–327, 332–333); David Powers/Jeroboam, Inc. (130–135); Nicholas Krenitsky (142); Harry Levy (170); Stephen G. Maka (46–47); Terry McKoy (184–185); Peabody Museum, Harvard University-Photographs by Hillel Burger (214, 218–222); Herb Randle (216–217); Royal Danish Ministry for Foreign Affairs (154); Mike Stammoulis (415); © Jean Vertut, Courtesy, Editions d'Art Lucien Mazenod, Paris from *Prehistorie de L'Art Occidental* (330–331); © Jean Vertut, Paris (334–335).

The cover and unit introduction pages were designed by Gregory Fossella Associates.

Contents

Tell Me
How the Sun Rose

Setting the Pace

In most stories the main characters solve problems of some kind. In doing so, they often learn important lessons, setting the pace for meeting new challenges in the future. The boys and girls in the stories of this unit also face problems. Perhaps these problems are like ones you and your friends are familiar with. As you read the stories, think about how you would act if you were in the same situations.

11

New faces, new places . . . everyone finds the first days in a new school hard. But like Amy everyone has something special to give.

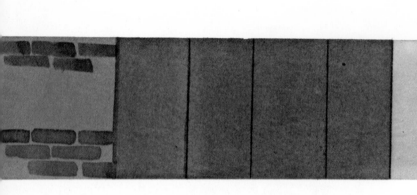

The Friendship String

Amy Spring crossed the school playground, eyes downcast.

"Hi!" she heard close to her ear.

"Hello!" came from across the way.

The "hi's" and "hello's" were not for Amy. She felt alone and lonely.

This red brick city school was so different from the small rambling school on the reservation. There, when she came bouncing onto the playground, friends crowded around.

"Good morning, Amy." She looked up to see Mr. Bates, her teacher. "How about joining in the basketball game?"

Amy wished Mr. Bates wouldn't ask so many questions.

The ring of children stared.

Amy shook her head shyly. "I don't want to play," she said and slowly walked away.

On the reservation no one had to urge her to take part. She was the one who started things, or was always in the midst of them. Here she was like tumbleweed—she didn't belong anywhere.

In social studies class, Mr. Bates said they would study desert country today. He looked at Amy. "It's good that we have a classmate from the Nevada desert. Amy, could you tell me why the land is arid?"

Another question!

All eyes turned toward Amy. Chuck's especially seemed to challenge her. Chuck, who sat right in front of Amy, was the smartest boy in class.

Chuck spoke out. "I know! It's because the storms that blow in from the Pacific are drained dry by the high, cold Sierra peaks. Then the air funnels down the eastern side of the mountains and dries up the water."

He was right again. But Amy was angry with him. He had answered. She had not.

After school Amy went straight home. She no longer waited for her older brother, Ron. Lately he seemed too busy.

Home was different now too. It was a small apartment, cozy with Paiute[1] art on the walls—woven baskets, beaded moccasins, arrowheads. But noisy with the sounds of automobiles, buses, and crowds. On the reservation the air was so clear you could see folds in the mountains miles away. The noises were soft and sweet—the song of a red-winged blackbird, the rustle of reeds by the river.

Everyone else in the family liked something about the city. Ron liked the bright lights. Amy's father enjoyed its conveniences. Her mother liked her new job.

[1] Paiute (py-YOOT)

14

To Amy everything seemed strange and unfriendly.

At supper, Amy's mother proudly told her news. "I passed my driving test today. Even driving down the busiest streets didn't bother me at all."

Amy's father grinned. "I knew you'd get used to it."

He looked at Amy. "How was school today?"

She shrugged and was glad when Ron interrupted.

"Great! In social studies I got a chance to tell about our tribe. Do you know, hardly anyone knows the difference between a Paiute and a Washoe?[1] One of the kids asked what we ate for breakfast. When I said orange juice, scrambled eggs, and toast, you should have heard the class laugh."

[1] Washoe (WAHSH-oh)

Amy put down her fork. "Were they laughing at you?"

Ron snapped a rubber band at her. "No. That's not the way I see it."

Amy's father reached over and covered her hand. "Hewovy"[2]—sometimes he used her Paiute name—"the people here hardly know us. It is hard to get used to new places—but you will."

Ron butted in. "Say, Mom, our whole school is planning a Family Fun Fair. The theme our class decided on is 'Eating Around the U.S.A.' I promised to make some fry bread. Will you help me?"

"You'll be stuck with the fry bread. No one will want it," Amy said.

"No more than the guy who's bringing piroshki.[2]

"What's that?" Amy asked.

"Something Russian. That's what he is. Someone else is bringing matzo[3] balls. We sure all laughed at Marilyn. She's so many different nationalities she's going to bring hash."

"What's the fair for?" Mom asked.

"Just to bring all the parents and kids and friends together so they'll get to know each other better. Nobody's going to make any money. We'll sell the things exactly for what they cost." He looked at Amy. "What's your class going to do?"

Amy didn't know. Her class hadn't talked about it yet.

[1]Hewovy (he-WOH-vee)   [2]piroshki (pi-RAWSH-kee)   [3]matzo (MAHT-sə)

16

Before she went to bed, Amy opened her box of keepsakes. There was the necklace she had made back on the reservation. Maybe she'd take it to school tomorrow, and when they talked about the desert she'd show it to the class. She put it in her jeans pocket so she wouldn't forget.

Next morning Mr. Bates introduced Sharon, a new girl, to the class. Amy could tell that Sharon was scared because she did the same things Amy did. Sharon walked to her desk sort of stiff-legged, not looking to right or left, knowing everyone was staring at her.

While Amy waited for the social studies lesson to begin she fingered the necklace in her pocket. Would she have the courage to tell about it?

But there was no social studies today. "We'll talk about the Family Fun Fair instead," Mr. Bates said. "We need to decide on a theme for our booth."

There were many suggestions, but all were either too expensive or impractical. Even Chuck, who was always bursting with ideas, was silent.

The bell rang.

"We'll continue after recess," Mr. Bates said.

Amy watched the new girl walk across the playground. Groups formed for games. The new girl hung back. She sat down on a bench in a far corner. She looked as lonely as Amy felt. Amy walked toward her.

17

She smiled and sat beside Sharon. "I'm new here too,"
she said.

The girl smiled back. "It's kind of scary, isn't
it?"

"Maybe we'll get over it," Amy said.

She put her hand in her pocket—her necklace! She
slipped it over her head.

18

"Oh, I like that," Sharon said. "Turquoise?"

"No, it just looks like turquoise. It's only corn—the kind that chickens eat."

"I love it. Could I wear it today?" Sharon asked.

Amy was pleased. She put the necklace around Sharon's neck just as the school bell rang.

They walked back into the school—together.

Some of the girls, noticing the necklace, gathered around Sharon.

"Where did you get it? It's so pretty. . . ."

"It belongs to Amy," Sharon said. "She let me wear it."

Even Chuck showed interest. "What's it made of?" he asked.

Mr. Bates hustled the class into their seats, but still the buzz about the necklace continued.

"Amy," Mr. Bates said, "Why don't you tell the whole class about the necklace?"

19

Amy stood, all eyes upon her. Her legs felt wobbly. "The children on our reservation made necklaces like this for our festival last year," she began. Her voice was shaky, she knew.

Mr. Bates nodded encouragingly. "Would you tell us just how you made them?"

That was easy for Amy. "We used plain Indian corn dyed with food coloring. Then we strung the corn together and tied the ends with thin strips of leather. They don't cost much."

"Did you make them to sell?" Mr. Bates asked.

"Yes," Amy said. "Indians from many tribes came together at the festival—even those who had once been enemies. Not only Indians but everyone came. They all wanted to buy a necklace. We called them 'Friendship Strings.' We put labels on them saying who made them. We used our Indian names. Mine said, 'Hewovy'—that means Wild Morning Glory."

Chuck was on his feet. "Got it," he shouted.

"Got what?" someone asked.

"Our theme for the fair—'Circle of Friendship.' We'll make the Friendship Strings. Amy can show us how. Everybody will want one."

Amy tingled with excitement.

The class buzzed.

They discussed their choices.

They took a vote.

CIRCLE OF FRIENDSHIP won.

At home that night Amy could hardly wait to tell the family about the plan to make the necklaces. "I promised to make a list of the things we will need."

"Chicken corn," her mother said. "There's a feed store close by."

"And dye," Ron said. "One package of food coloring goes a long way."

"I've got a piece of leather that will be just right for the ties," Amy's father said.

Amy looked around at her smiling family. Today had been a good day, she thought.

And now she must get busy and make plans for tomorrow.

21

The next day when Amy entered the playground, she heard "hi!" and "hello!"

They were for her.

"Got the list, Amy?" Chuck asked.

"Got everything," Amy answered.

Now she understood. New friends are everywhere. She bounced across the playground.

—*Dale Fife*

What Do You Think?

1. How is Amy like everyone who faces a new place and new people?
2. What do you think helped Amy to make new friends?
3. Tell about a time when you, like Amy, had to face a new situation. How did you feel about it? What kinds of problems did you have to solve? What did you do about them?

Taking A Closer Look

1. How did Amy feel about her new school? her old school?
2. How did Amy act when Mr. Bates asked her to join in on the playground and in class? Why do you think she acted this way?
3. What did Amy's parents like about the city?
4. Why was Amy friendly to Sharon?
5. How is a Friendship String made?
6. What theme did Amy's class choose for the Family Fun Fair?
7. What was Amy's special gift to her new friends?

Putting Ideas to Work

Make a list of other materials you might use to make a Friendship String.

I Go Forth to Move about the Earth

I go forth to move about the earth.
I go forth as the owl, wise and knowing.
I go forth as the eagle, powerful and bold.
I go forth as the dove, peaceful and gentle.
I go forth to move about the earth
   in wisdom, courage, and peace.

—*Alonzo Lopez*

25

Once, as if in a dream, Marra had met a seal named Nerea. Like many dreams, this one had faded by morning. Even the name Nerea was forgotten—until one day during the time of the full moon. What really happened that day? Was Nerea a dream or not? Is the full moon the key?

IS THE FULL MOON THE KEY?

One day during the summer vacation Alison and Marra were at loose ends. They had finished their chores and had no particular plans. It was Alison who suggested a picnic on the Cow and Calves, three small islands not more than forty minutes' row from the harbor. There were usually sheep on Cow Island and they thought there was a ram on Big Calf. They'd see when they got there. There was a small beach on Little Calf which might be best of all. It was scarcely more than a rock where the terns nested, but there were the ruins of the hermit's cabin to give it a sense of strangeness. No one quite knew who the hermit was or how long ago he had built his shelter or when he had died. There were just two walls of beach stones still standing under a single spruce tree. Most people thought he had been a pirate, so now and then children went out and dug for treasure, but no one had ever found a sign of it.

"What I wonder about was where he got his drinking water," someone would say.

"He could have had a catchment at the foot of that cliff," another would suggest, "or there may have been a little spring which has dried up since his time. I've known that to happen."

So there was something rather special about Little Calf even if you didn't believe in ghosts, and the girls told each other that they weren't scared of any old ghost.

"It's never done anyone any harm," said Alison. "It won't hurt us even if there is such a thing."

"No, I don't suppose so, but it is true that people have heard queer noises, and when Jerry Sinclair had been digging there a northeaster came up all of a sudden on the way back and nearly swamped his dory," said Marra.

"Well, we shan't dig." Alison was set on the picnic. The day was mild, with no wind or almost none. "Mother will let us make sandwiches. Why are you hanging back, Marra?"

It was true that Marra didn't feel very eager for the adventure, but she didn't know why. She had often longed to explore the islands but she didn't like to ask Pa to lend her his tender which he left tied up to his float when he took the lobster boat out. Now they would use the doctor's light new rowboat which was waiting at the pier. She didn't even have to ask Granny, who never cared where she was after the work which she nowadays did was finished.

"Scat!" Granny would say when the last chore had been done. "And don't let me see hide nor hair of you until the boats are in."

Granny didn't speak as fiercely as she used to. Sometimes her harshness seemed to be more from habit than from feeling, and Marra had been told by one or two of Granny's friends that Granny even said, "Some ways she's a little like my Aunt Lola."

She didn't say that to Marra and Marra knew better than to expect any kind word from her, but there was a general easing of the tension in the house. The fierce edge of Granny's hatred had worn down to dislike and even to tolerance. Still, Marra asked no favors from Granny and knew she would get none if she asked. But Alison was welcome to use her father's rowboat any time she wanted to, and they would put up the picnic at Alison's.

Still Marra hung back.

Something in her warned her, Don't go today, but she didn't know why. Not today, said her inner self, but outwardly it seemed exactly the right day. Pa had said that morning, "Should have a good day today. All signs point to it." But some sign in Marra didn't point to a good day. Yet here it was nearly noon and it was as fine as it had been at dawn.

"All right," said Marra, still a little hesitantly. "I've always wanted to explore Little Calf, and if we stay late we can come home by moonlight. Moon's at the full tonight."

31

They never reached the three islands. Marra rowed and Alison sat in the stern and handled the tiller. There was no sea running, just enough to bring the little wavelets to flower, and the flock of terns that seemed to follow them for a while seemed like flowers, too, against the sky, or so Marra thought, but Alison only laughed at her.

"We're getting very near," said Alison.

"Don't you want me to take the oars for a while? I'm not as good at rowing as you are, but you must be getting tired."

"I'm fine," said Marra, resting for a minute to turn her head and look at the islands they were approaching. There was Cow Island with a cliff and sheep feeding on the short turf, and Big Calf, and Little Calf circled by reefs. She even noticed the ruin of the pirate's house and some stones by the shore piled for a landing long ago. A glance showed her all this, but what her gaze steadied on was the sun. Surely it was not as bright as it should have been?

"Alison, isn't it cooler than it was?"

"Yes," said Alison comfortably. "It was too hot when we started out. Marra, what on earth are you doing?"

"I'm heading the boat for home," said Marra. "Help me, Alison. The fog is coming in. Look hard at our landing and try to steer for it even when you can't see it. The trouble is that everyone naturally rows harder with one hand than with the other, and a boat like this can be turned completely in the wrong direction in a fog without either of us knowing."

"But I can see our landing perfectly well."

"Now, you can," said Marra. "I hope you still can in ten minutes," and she began to row at a fast, steady pace. She had grown up hearing stories of dories and lobster boats, too, in heavy fogs carried out to sea by the tides. Some had been lost for days and some forever.

"You're making a lot out of nothing," said Alison uneasily.

"I hope so," said Marra. Alison was an inland girl. She might know the dangers of blizzards but she knew nothing of fogs nor of the danger of tides nor of their strength when the moon was full.

Marra went on rowing. Her back was to their destination, but already Cow Island and the Calves were blotted out by a thin veil of fog.

"I can still see the landing," said Alison. Her voice trembled a little, but she tried to hold it steady. Marra's fear had been communicated to her, Marra's courage, too, but she had plenty of her own.

It was almost as if the fog had heard her for now neither she, nor Marra, when she turned her head briefly to check her position, could see the landing on their own island nor its dwelling houses and trees and the fringe of fish houses and piers below them. The white moist presence of the fog drifted all about them, turning the sun into something like a small frantic moon and then wiping it out altogether. Now they moved through nothingness. Even sounds were strange. Somewhere far off a dog barked, a small familiar sound, but they could not tell whether it was ahead of them or to one side.

"Don't row too hard with your right oar," said Alison.

"I'm trying not to," said Marra. "Try to sit just as you were sitting before we lost sight of the landing place."

"I can't be sure!" wailed Alison.

There was a long, long silence while they moved through the dense white cocoon of the fog, and at last Alison said, "Marra, shouldn't we have reached the landing by now?

38

"I think so," said Marra. "I suppose we're going to land in Spain, and won't the Spaniards be surprised?"

If she had hoped to make Alison laugh, she succeeded. Alison gave a little snort of laughter and then, having once opened the door of her silence, burst into tears.

"Don't cry, Alison, don't cry. We may meet a lobster boat or something."

She was much more upset for Alison than for herself. Many people would miss Alison, but no one would miss her, or at least only a little. She didn't think about that, only felt her heart filled with a longing to protect Alison, her first friend. And with the sharpness of that emotion a forgotten memory awoke.

"Nerea!" she shouted. "Nerea! Nerea! Help us, Nerea!"

And almost at once, close beside them Nerea appeared, a gray seal this time with kind, mournful eyes. She nudged against the bow of the boat, turning it. "Don't try to steer, Alison," said Marra. "It will be easier for Nerea if you let her do it all."

The seal gave her a backward look, wise and loving.

"Oh, Nerea, we are so glad that you came!" Marra sighed. She went on rowing, slowly, so as not to get in the seal's way. Then, as the shape of the pier loomed more than life-sized out of the fog, Nerea gave Marra one long, last loving look and disappeared, taking all memory of herself and the rescue with her.

"Thank you," Marra began, but then forgot whom she was thanking. "Thank you, Alison, for steering us so well."

"I don't think I steered well," said Alison uncertainly, but she, too, had forgotten who or what it was that had brought them home. With stiff hands they fastened the painter of the boat to the float and climbed up its short, slippery ladder.

Only when on the pier they almost bumped into the small bent figure in a yellow slicker did they see Marra's granny. But she saw them before they saw her.

"Only a couple of fools wouldn't have known that a fog was coming in," she told them crossly. "The others think you're off in the woods for your picnic. But I knew better. I watched where you were off to from the kitchen window. Now come on up to the house! Come on, Alison, you too. I've got hot chocolate on the stove and fresh beaten biscuits in the oven waiting for you. No use wasting them, now you're here."

Marra was too surprised to answer, but Alison said at once, "Thank you, Granny. We're half frozen."

—*Elizabeth Coatsworth*

42

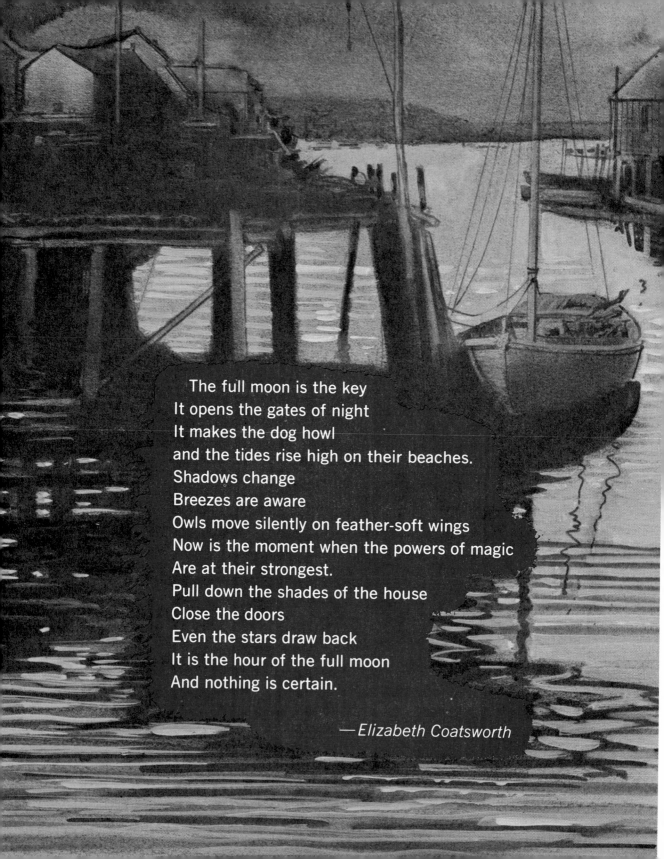

The full moon is the key
It opens the gates of night
It makes the dog howl
and the tides rise high on their beaches.
Shadows change
Breezes are aware
Owls move silently on feather-soft wings
Now is the moment when the powers of magic
Are at their strongest.
Pull down the shades of the house
Close the doors
Even the stars draw back
It is the hour of the full moon
And nothing is certain.

—Elizabeth Coatsworth

What Do You Think?

1. How do you think Marra and Alison were saved?
2. If you were Marra, would you have gone to the islands? Why or why not?
3. Who would you rather have as a friend, Marra or Alison? Why?

Taking A Closer Look

1. What was special about Little Calf Island?
2. How did Marra feel about going to the islands that summer day?
3. Why did Marra turn around before reaching the islands?
4. An artist — in paint or in words — often gives clues to meaning rather than stating something outright. How do the following expressions add meaning and interest to the story?
   a. fringe of fish houses
   b. like a small, frantic moon
   c. dense white cocoon
   d. the door of her silence
5. Why was Marra surprised to see Granny waiting for her on the dock?

NO OTHER SIGN

   At a distance
The restless dunes,
Lonely, desolate, beckon
With their straggly reeds
Given motion
By the endless winds.
The roaring waves
Crash blindly
On the jetty
"Closed until the summer."
There is no other sign of life

—*Javier Honda*

46

47

The Milestone Group

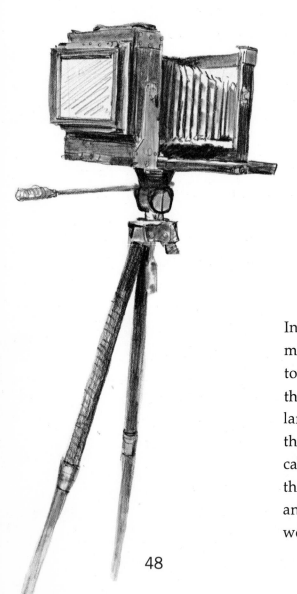

In olden times wooden signposts marked distances from one town or city to another. Later, the miles were marked off by large stones set by the side of the road. These stones were called *milestones*. As you read this story, can you figure out another, newer meaning of this word?

The Plan

Mom seemed quite upset this evening, Lucy decided as she set the kitchen table. She put down four plates and slid four forks toward them. Mom turned from the stove with a steaming casserole in her hand. Lucy stepped back to let her serve the supper.

The kitchen was small. There wasn't room for all six of them to sit down together. But it didn't matter, really. Dad wouldn't be home from his night job until morning. And the boys ate almost on the run. Now they came noisily into the kitchen to gobble up their food before returning to the street.

"Dennis," said Mom. She held her eleven-year-old by the back of his shirt. "You go wash yourself. You too," she added, darting a look at Dennis' younger brother, Christopher. "Come, Bonnie," she said more gently to the small girl beside Lucy. "Come, baby. Time to eat."

Bonnie slid into a chair and pulled her plate toward her. Mom put the casserole back in the oven. She didn't join her children at the table. There was room for only four.

"Take my place, Mom," said Lucy suddenly. Mom worked in a small factory and she seemed very tired tonight.

"No," said Mom wearily. "You go ahead. I'm going to stretch out for a little while before I eat. Right now I'm just too downhearted to think about food."

Bonnie, with her fork almost to her mouth, suddenly put it down. She called to her mother, about to leave the kitchen.

"Look, Mom. Look here." She put two fingers into her mouth and took hold of a front tooth. "Look, Mom. It's loose. It'll come out any day now."

"Don't I know it," said Mom. "It's been bothering me day and night. I've been planning on a bright and smiling picture of my littlest. But by the time I get the money saved up, she'll be gap-toothed."

The boys laughed and Mom threw them an angry

50

stare. "Go right ahead and laugh," she told them. "I got pictures of you at her age. Lucy too. But not one picture of my Bonnie and she's my littlest."

Mom went heavily from the room. The four at the table looked at each other with sudden soberness. It was not like Mom to talk to them in this way. Sure she got tired and grumpy. But she never said mean things like that. Mom must be more upset than they knew.

Lucy listened to be sure Mom had gone into her bedroom. Then she said very low, "I've been thinking about something." The other three fastened interested eyes on their big sister. The boys stopped chewing to listen.

"Next month is Mom's birthday."

"I know," said Dennis. "I want to get her something real nice. But what? Everything nice costs so much money. Where can I get some money?"

"And this birthday is very important to Mom," Lucy continued. "She calls it a milestone. She says she plans to live until she's eighty and this birthday puts her halfway there. Forty! Right in the middle. A milestone!"

Mom forty! It seemed a great age. They thought about it in silence as they cleaned up their plates.

Finally Christopher said, "Are you planning something for Mom?"

Lucy nodded. "In a way," she said. "I have an idea, that's all." She looked around the table. "You want to come in on it?"

Dennis' eyes grew cautious. "What do you have in mind?"

"I want to have a picture taken of all of us together. I want it right now before Bonnie's tooth comes out."

"Do you have the money for that?" asked Christopher, whispering.

Lucy shook her head. "That's the trouble. We've got to get the picture first and the money later. Bonnie will lose her tooth before we can get the money."

"Why not just a picture of Bonnie by herself? It might not cost so much," suggested Dennis.

"No," said Lucy. "This is the milestone picture. I want Mom to have us together just the way we looked when she got to be forty. A 'Group.' That's what they call a picture with lots of people in it."

"The Milestone Group," said Dennis slowly. "I can see it on the wall now. Mom would like that. You have a good idea there, Lucy."

"Then you'll come in on it?"

"What do you mean 'come in on it'?"

"You'll help get the money to pay for it?"

"How?"

"There must be some way you can help," Lucy said. "Stop hanging around the schoolyard after school and running up and down the streets on Saturday. Go look for something to do. You'll find something if you look hard enough. Christopher can look along with you."

"What are you going to do?" asked Christopher.

"Oh, I've several good leads," said Lucy.

"I want to do something too!" said Bonnie in a loud voice that surely reached the bedroom.

"Shoosh," hissed Lucy. "You're only six. You can help me here at home so I can get to my jobs faster. Helping me is the same as helping at a regular job. See?"

Bonnie nodded a bit uncertainly. But then she seemed satisfied.

Before leaving the table, the children agreed they would have the picture taken. Then they picked up their plates and stacked them in the sink. They would get around to washing them later.

Next day Lucy hurried home from school. She took the three flights of stairs without a stop. Bonnie, she knew, would be there waiting for her. Lucy hoped she

53

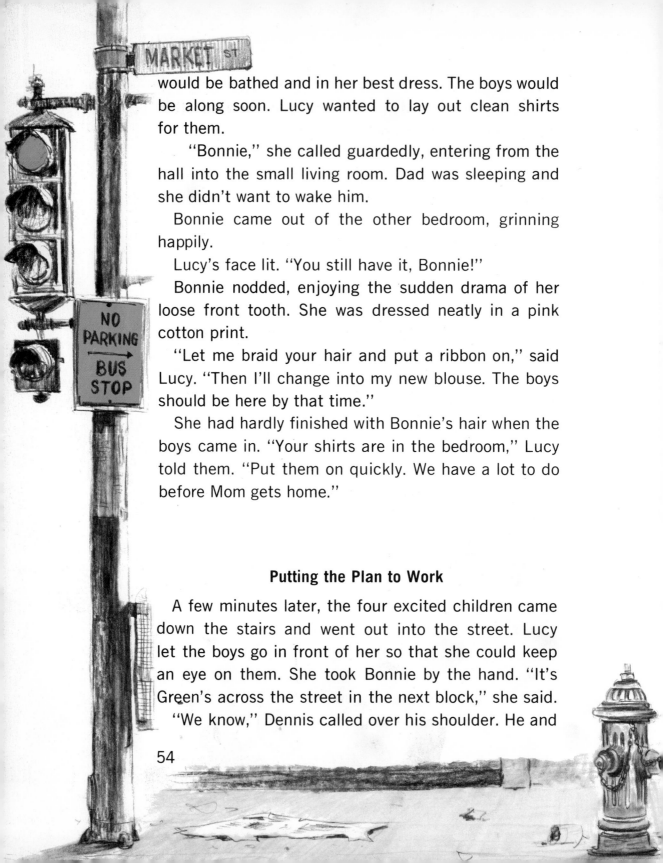

would be bathed and in her best dress. The boys would be along soon. Lucy wanted to lay out clean shirts for them.

"Bonnie," she called guardedly, entering from the hall into the small living room. Dad was sleeping and she didn't want to wake him.

Bonnie came out of the other bedroom, grinning happily.

Lucy's face lit. "You still have it, Bonnie!"

Bonnie nodded, enjoying the sudden drama of her loose front tooth. She was dressed neatly in a pink cotton print.

"Let me braid your hair and put a ribbon on," said Lucy. "Then I'll change into my new blouse. The boys should be here by that time."

She had hardly finished with Bonnie's hair when the boys came in. "Your shirts are in the bedroom," Lucy told them. "Put them on quickly. We have a lot to do before Mom gets home."

Putting the Plan to Work

A few minutes later, the four excited children came down the stairs and went out into the street. Lucy let the boys go in front of her so that she could keep an eye on them. She took Bonnie by the hand. "It's Green's across the street in the next block," she said.

"We know," Dennis called over his shoulder. He and

Christopher were off, dodging in and out among the people on the crowded sidewalk. Lucy hurried after them, pulling Bonnie along with her.

A buzzer sounded as they opened the door of Green's Studio. Mr. Green himself came out into the small showroom where they stood. Behind him they could see lamps on tall stands surrounding a single chair.

Mr. Green was round — round bald head, round cheerful face, round belly, round-toed shoes on his feet, and round glasses over his eyes, which were round and dark and wise.

"Something I can do for you?" he asked. He looked from one serious face to the other.

Lucy drew in a long breath. "Do you ever take pictures on credit?"

Mr. Green smiled at her. "Not usually," he said gently.

Lucy pushed Bonnie in front of her. "Show him," she said. Bonnie wiggled her front tooth for Mr. Green.

"Did you come here to have me take out the tooth?" he asked in some surprise.

"No!" said Lucy. "But we're here because of the loose tooth." In a rush of words she explained about Mom's milestone and their great desire to have a group picture to present to her on that important day.

"Your mama sent you?" inquired Mr. Green.

"Oh, no," said Lucy. "It would spoil everything if she knew."

"I see," said Mr. Green, slowly, thoughtfully.

"And if I take this picture, how will you pay?"

"We'll all go out and find something to do. Already we have two baby-sitting jobs for next week. We can also wash cars, or run errands to the grocery store—oh, anything," explained Lucy.

"But how do I know you will pay for the picture?" Mr. Green went on. "Sometimes people get a picture and forget about the money."

Lucy shook her head. "You don't understand. We won't take the picture away. We'll leave it right here. Then every time we get a quarter, even a dime, we'll bring it in to you."

"Then why not save up the money and *then* have the picture taken?" Mr. Green flung out his hands as if he had discovered the only answer.

"We already told you," said Lucy, her voice rising. "We've got to get this picture before Bonnie's tooth comes out. Don't you see?" She shook Bonnie's shoulder. "Show him again, Bonnie." And Bonnie did.

A light dawned on Mr. Green's face and he lifted his eyes to the ceiling. "Ah, yes. Now all is clear. I didn't get it at first." Again he looked from one to the other as if trying to make up his mind. All four returned his look, their brows wrinkled with worry.

At last he whirled about.

"Come," he said. "Come in," and he led them toward the tall lights and the waiting chair.

The next few days were worrisome for Lucy. If the others felt the same way, they didn't let on. Her worry

was their father. What would he say? Had they dared too much? What would he do when he found out that they had paid fifteen dollars for a picture?

"We won't tell him. It will be better that way," said Lucy.

"You can say that again," returned Dennis. "He would skin us if he knew we were spending that much money."

It wasn't easy that first week. Only three dollars and a quarter went into the little box under the counter in Mr. Green's studio. Three weeks to go, about. It seemed a very short time in which to earn eleven dollars and seventy-five cents.

But the three were eager to work and the news got around. Slowly the value of the coins in the studio box grew. On the day before Mom's birthday, they added up to fourteen dollars and seventy-five cents. Just a quarter to go. It might as well have been a hundred dollars! What could they do?

That night at supper, Bonnie's tooth came out.

"Look, Mom," she said, holding it out on her small palm. "My tooth!"

Mom gave a startled look at Bonnie's hand, then at her gap-toothed mouth. She burst into tears. "It happened!" she cried. "It happened just like I knew it would. My baby's tooth is gone and I never got a bright and smiling picture."

The children looked at one another. They were pleased that Mom was too upset to notice their secret smiles.

58

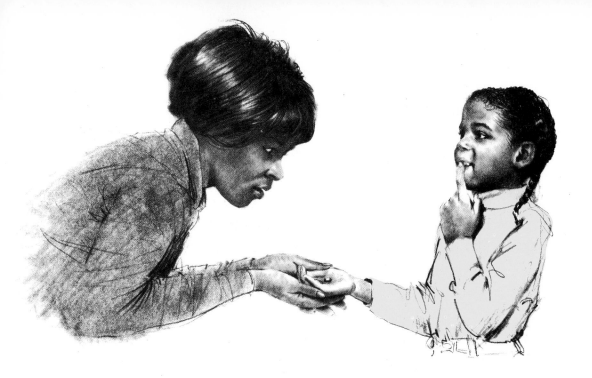

Then their faces sobered. Tomorrow was Mom's birthday. Since it was a Saturday, they would be free to find jobs. But they couldn't be sure they would get the needed quarter.

The next morning, Bonnie sprung her surprise. Dad had already eaten and gone to bed. Mom had picked up her string bag and gone out to do the weekly shopping.

"I got something to show you," she whispered as the four gathered together in the living room.

"What?" asked Christopher.

Again, as on the night before, Bonnie held her hand out straight. On her palm lay a shiny quarter!

"I put my tooth under the pillow last night and this morning the tooth fairy took it and left me a quarter."

"You're kidding?" asked Dennis.

Bonnie shook her head. "It happened to a girl at school, and now it's happened to me."

"How come the tooth fairy knew about *your* tooth?" asked Lucy. She had never found a quarter under her pillow.

Bonnie shrugged. "Maybe Dad told her."

The others looked at one another.

"Did you tell Dad about the tooth fairy?" asked Lucy.

Bonnie nodded. "When he started to bed, I followed him and I showed him my tooth. I told him I needed a quarter for Mom's birthday present. I said maybe the tooth fairy would leave it. And he said the tooth fairy wouldn't leave anything if I stood around. So I went away. When I came back, the tooth was gone and the quarter was under my pillow."

"Then you gave away our secret," said Lucy. "Did you tell about the Group?"

"No," said Bonnie. "When Dad asked me how much we spent on Mom's birthday, I told him. I said we all worked together. And he said what could a little kid like me do? And I said nothing until my tooth came out. But I could get a quarter with it, maybe. And so I did."

"And didn't Dad get upset because we spent so much money?" asked Dennis.

"No, he didn't," said Bonnie. "He just said we were good to remember Mom's birthday. And then he gave me a hug."

Lucy's face lit with joy. Now she knew Mom really

would be surprised. "Come on," she said, still remembering not to wake up Dad. "Let's hurry and get The Milestone Group."

Moving quietly, they made for the door.

—Doris Gates

61

What Do You Think?

1. Mom said that her fortieth birthday was important, a *milestone.* What other events in the story might also be called milestones? What are some milestones in your life?
2. Bonnie's loose tooth caused the problem, but it also saved the day. Explain how it did both.
3. If this were your story, how would you end it? Why do you suppose the author ended it the way she did?

Taking A Closer Look

1. You sometimes can read people's feelings by the way they act. How do you think each of the other children felt about Lucy's plan? How can you tell?
2. You never meet Dad directly in the story. From what the children say about him, what kind of person do you think he is?
3. Why do you think Mr. Green agreed to take the picture on credit?
4. Which part of Lucy's plan seemed the most difficult to carry out? Who do you think helped the most? Explain your answer.

Putting Ideas to Work

Write a paragraph about a time when you worked hard to do something special for somebody.

MY PEOPLE

The night is beautiful,
So the faces of my people.

The stars are beautiful,
So the eyes of my people.

Beautiful, also, is the sun.
Beautiful, also, are the souls of my people.

—Langston Hughes

63

Keiko[1] is visiting her Uncle Henry and Aunt Emi[2] in California. But Tama,[3] Keiko's cat, bothers Uncle Henry, and so Keiko asks Mike Michaelson to keep Tama in his home. Mike's mother works for Uncle Henry in his flower business, which had been ruined once by smog. When Aunt Emi becomes ill, the Michaelsons offer to take Keiko into their home.

Alarm in the Night

"Your Aunt Emi will get well much faster in the hospital, Keiko," Mrs. Michaelson said brightly. "Until she comes back, how would you like to stay with us? We'll put Mike in with his brother Ben. You can have Mike's room. How would that be?"

Keiko couldn't think of anything nicer. Mike Michaelson was her best friend and lived nearby. Uncle Henry seemed grateful too. He couldn't take care of Keiko alone, and he and Aunt Emi had promised Keiko's mother they would take good care of her while she

[1] Keiko (KAY-koh)   [2] Emi (AY-mee)   [3] Tama (TAH-mah)

64

visited them. And so that afternoon, Keiko packed her suitcase. Mike carried it home on the handle bars of his bike.

"We'll take good care of her," Mike's mother said to Uncle Henry.

Mike's house wasn't at all like Aunt Emi and Uncle Henry's. It was full of collections and all kinds of pets. In the midst of everything was Tama, Keiko's cat. Mike was keeping her for Keiko because her Uncle Henry didn't like cats. She was curled up happily on the couch, looking as though she had always lived there.

"We all love Tama," Mrs. Michaelson said warmly. "It's a shame your Uncle Henry is allergic to cats," she said. "How sad that is!"

Before Keiko knew what she was doing, she was sitting on the couch next to Mike's mother. She began telling her all her troubles. "Uncle Henry doesn't like me either," she said. "All he likes are the carnations he grows in his nursery."

Mike's mother put an arm around Keiko. "That's not so at all, Keiko," she said gently. "Your uncle just doesn't know how to show you. He really loves you very much. I know. You'll find out someday too."

Keiko wondered if she were right. If Uncle Henry really loved her, he certainly hadn't shown it. At least, not yet.

It was strange going to sleep in Mike's room that night. It was scary to see the shadows of his ship's model on the wall. And those model airplanes hanging from the ceiling seemed to be flying over her. But the one nice thing was that Tama was sleeping in the room.

"You can let her sleep in there," Mike had said. "But she can't have my dog's bed." And he went to get a box for Tama to sleep in.

Keiko let Tama come into bed with her for a little while. She was so glad to be with her again. She meant to put her back in the box later. But she fell asleep still holding Tama in her arms. It was Tama's sneezing that woke Keiko up during the night.

Keiko had opened the window before she'd gone to bed, and now she could feel the cool night air. No wonder Tama had caught cold. Keiko leaped out of bed to close the window. She sniffed the strange smell in the air outside. The night was still and windless. Keiko felt as though she could almost see the chemicals and gases. She was afraid they would burn Uncle Henry's carnations again. She knew his big Christmas order was to go out the next afternoon. Suppose it was smog. Suppose the flowers were ruined tonight. Then maybe there would be nothing worth shipping to Chicago tomorrow. Uncle Henry might lose not only his Christmas order, but also the orders for the rest of the year.

Keiko sat on her bed and wondered what to do. Tama sat beside her sneezing. Keiko looked at the clock. It was one o'clock. Mike's house was as still as a tomb. Suppose she woke everybody up and they thought she was being silly.

66

Keiko thought for another minute. Then she knew she had to tell Uncle Henry. She got up quickly and put on her bathrobe. Then she knocked on Mike's door. It would be easiest to tell him first.

"Mike!" she called softly. "Wake up."

But the house was still silent. This time Keiko shouted and banged on the door. "Mike, wake up!"

Ben popped his head out of the door. "What's wrong?" he asked.

"What is it? What's the matter, Keiko?" This time it was Mike's father. Then his mother called from the next room.

Soon, even Mike's dog came out the door. He squeaked as he yawned and stretched as he wagged his tail. He thought it was morning and time to have breakfast.

Keiko was able to wake up everybody except Mike. She quickly told his parents about the smell outside and Tama's sneezing. Then she told about the last time there was smog. If they'd only cut the flowers in time they might have saved most of the order.

Mike's father shrugged with a sleepy look. "I think we should let things go till morning," he said. "I don't think a few hours could make much difference."

But Mike's mother went to the window and opened it. "It does smell strange," she said. She remembered what had happened the last time too. She saw Tama wheezing and brushing at her nose with one paw.

"I know Henry would hate to lose even part of this shipment," she said. "Maybe I'd better call him."

By now, Mike was up too. "What's wrong?" he asked. "I'm hungry." And he fixed himself a bowl of corn flakes. His mother went to the telephone to call Uncle Henry.

Keiko would have liked a bowl of corn flakes herself. But she wanted to hear what Mike's mother said. Mrs. Michaelson told Uncle Henry how Tama had wakened them with her sneezing. She also told him about the strange smell outside.

"I thought, with the Christmas shipment so close, you might want to get them cut." She was silent a moment, listening and nodding. Then, when she hung up, she called out, "Get dressed everybody. Henry's decided not to take a chance. We're all going over to help him cut his flowers."

68

"Tonight?" Ben asked. "Right now?"

"Me too?" Mike asked, surprised. No one had ever asked him to help before. Usually, he was told to stay out of the way.

"Yes, you too, Mike," his mother answered. "We're all going right now. We're all up anyway, so I told Henry we would come. Put on your warm coat, Keiko," she said.

In fifteen minutes they were all out of the house and into the car. The big station wagon roared over to Uncle Henry's.

The greenhouses were cool and dark. The paths between them were like black ribbons of night. Keiko followed close after Mike, watching the beam of light made by his flashlight. At last, Keiko saw a dim light in one of the greenhouses. Uncle Henry was already at work there cutting the flowers. They found him working quickly, cutting them with a sharp pocket knife. He was leaving enough young shoots on each stalk for later blooms. A piece of newspaper was on the ground beside him. It was already piled high with the flowers he had cut.

"Tama woke me up," Keiko called out to him. "Tonight the smog made her sneeze and she woke me up and I smelled a funny smell. So I called Mike and his mother called you and we all came." Keiko couldn't seem to stop once she'd got started.

Uncle Henry nodded. "Well," he said, "so Tama smelled the smog. Well!" And then he was back at work again. He worked as though he couldn't waste another minute. "We'd better hurry," he said.

Mike's mother told everyone what to do. "Ben, you and Dad and I will help Henry cut the flowers. Mike can carry them to the packing house. If there is time, I'll start grading them."

"With four of us cutting, we should be able to cover most of the greenhouses in a few hours," Mike's father said. Quickly Uncle Henry began to show him how to cut properly.

"We need more newspapers too, Kei-chan,"[1] Uncle Henry said. He spoke as though she would know exactly what to do.

Keiko didn't know what in the world Uncle Henry was talking about. But Mike said he would show her. "Come on," he said. He ran toward the packing house.

Keiko felt the dampness all around. "Wait," she called. "Wait for me." She ran after him as fast as she could go. She was not going to be left behind in the dark shadows of the greenhouses.

Mike took her to a table piled high with newspapers. He showed her how to roll a few sheets together. Then he tucked in the ends to make neat, soft rolls. They would be put inside the big boxes to protect the flowers as they were packed. "See," he said. "It's simple."

Keiko nodded. It was simple. Keiko wanted to show Uncle Henry how fast she could work. She sat at the table and rolled newspapers until her arms hurt. Her

[1] Kei-chan (KAY-chan)

hands were dirty with printer's ink. She could barely keep her eyes open.

Mike helped her for a while. Then he ran back and forth between the packing house and the greenhouses with the cut flowers. He even stripped some of the low leaves from the stems. He had learned this from watching his mother and Keiko's aunt.

After a while, Mrs. Michaelson hurried back to begin work at the grading table. "Come help me, Keiko," she called.

Keiko was so surprised, she nearly fell off the stool. Mrs. Michaelson was asking her to do the work Aunt Emi herself would have done.

"The longer ones go here," she explained. "The shorter ones there, and the very shortest here. We put twenty-five in a bunch. Then Mike can put them into pails for us." Even while she talked, her hands flew as she sorted flowers.

Of course, Keiko couldn't begin to keep up with her. She picked up the flowers carefully. There must have been hundreds of them on the grading table now. There were Uncle Henry's prized White Sims and Red Sims. Others were pink and pale yellow and even white with red stripes. They smelled like spring and sunshine. They made Keiko's heart sing, they were so beautiful. And suddenly, Keiko knew why Uncle Henry took such good care of his plants. She knew then why he loved them as much as she loved Tama. She remembered what her father had said about his own dwarf pine.

"You must love the tree enough almost to become the tree yourself. Then you will know how to care for it. In return, it will grow and be beautiful for you."

Keiko had not understood at all then. But now she thought she understood a little. Maybe she was beginning to understand Uncle Henry a little too.

At last Uncle Henry and Mr. Michaelson had finished cutting the flowers. They quickly came back to the packing house. Uncle Henry looked pleased to see Keiko standing next to Mike's mother. She was working just as Aunt Emi would have done. She was working much harder than Mike or Ben. They were clowning together with rolled newspapers in the corner of the packing house. She felt proud to be working so hard at four in the morning.

Soon all the flowers were sorted and put into pails. Uncle Henry and Mike's father carried them into the big icebox. They would be safe there until they could be packed later into larger boxes. These boxes would keep them from freezing as they flew to Chicago.

"We'll get these flowers packed with your newspapers tomorrow morning," Uncle Henry said to Keiko. He looked tired. But he seemed happier than he had in a long time.

They all went inside then. Mike's mother made hot coffee and cocoa for everybody. Somehow, even the tiredness felt good.

"I don't know how to thank you," Uncle Henry said. He shook hands with Mr. and Mrs. Michaelson. "This is a bad case of smog. You've helped me save most of my Christmas shipment. We may have saved the orders for the rest of the year as well."

"It was Keiko who woke us up," Mrs. Michaelson said quickly.

"And it was Tama who woke *me* up," Keiko added. She wanted to be sure Tama would get proper credit.

"I'm very grateful," Uncle Henry said, "to all of you. To Tama too." He shook hands with Keiko and Mike and Ben.

Then they all said good night and climbed into the station wagon. Uncle Henry stood watching as they drove away. Keiko looked back as they turned the corner. He still stood there, all alone, waving in the half light. Though he looked very tired, Keiko knew he was pleased with her. That made her feel proud and happy too.

—*Yoshiko Uchida*

What Do You Think?

1. Reread what Keiko's father once said about his dwarf pine tree. How do you think his words help Keiko understand Uncle Henry a little better?
2. If Aunt Emi had been well, how might the story have been different?
3. How is air pollution dangerous for other things besides flowers? What are some ways of cleaning up the air?

Taking A Closer Look

1. Why did Keiko feel it would be easiest to tell Mike first about the strange smell outside?
2. What did each person in the story have to do to help save the carnations?
3. How could Keiko tell that Uncle Henry was pleased with her?
4. Should Uncle Henry allow Tama back in the house when Keiko moves back home? Make up good arguments for both "Yes" and "No" answers.

MEDIA LUNA

La luna va por el agua.
¡Cómo está el cielo tranquilo!
Va segando lentamente
el temblor viejo del río
mientras que una rana joven
la toma por espejito.

—*Federico García Lorca*

HALF MOON

The moon goes over the water.
How tranquil the sky is!
She goes scything slowly
the old shimmer from the river;
meanwhile a young frog
takes her for a little mirror.

—*Federico García Lorca*
Translated by W. S. Merwin

77

Boarding school can be fun, but sometimes a new student can have a hard time getting into the swing of things. In this story Robby Armstrong tells you in his own words about a new boy at his boarding school.

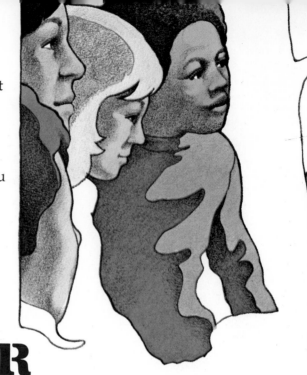

PITCHER

The New Boy

When boarding school opens in the fall, the smart thing to do is to get there early. Then you can grab the best bureau and the lower bed in your room. You just pile your stuff on them and they're yours for the year. Then spend the rest of the day fooling around with the other old boys, watching the scared new ones come in. I hope I didn't look lost and lonely the way they did when I was a new boy. But maybe I did.

Anyway, last fall we—that's me and Monk and Horse-face and Geezil[1] and a few other guys—were sitting on the stone wall in front of the dormitory watching the new boys come in. They walked past us, stiff and shy,

[1] Geezil (GEE-zǝl)

in clothes you could tell were new and uncomfortable. All of them were carrying suitcases. They wouldn't really look at us except out of the corners of their eyes. And they hurried past us into the building. We'd sit there and keep quiet while they walked by. But after they'd gone inside, we'd talk about them. We'd try to decide what kind of people they would turn out to be.

In the middle of the afternoon, a funny little character walked up the path. He wore great big glasses perched on a nose that looked kind of punched in. His ears stuck out like flags. Only he didn't hurry past us like the others. In front of us he put his suitcase down and smiled. It was a stiff smile, like the ones people had in pictures taken about forty years ago. But it was a smile. I guess he was trying to be friendly.

79

"Hello," he said.

"Hello," said Monk, without much interest.

The new boy smiled wider. "Hello," he said again. Then he waved his arm around. It was the longest and skinniest arm I've ever seen on a boy his age. "I guess this is the school." He bobbed his head and batted his eyes when he said it. You could tell that he really knew it was the school. He was only trying to be nice. But Monk's too sharp to let a simple remark like that get past him.

"The school?" Monk rubbed his chin. "What school?"

"Why, *the* school." When this new boy wrinkled his forehead, he looked more like a bewildered owl than before. "The school where you all go."

Monk scratched his head and turned to us. "Do you fellows go to school?"

"I haven't been to school today," said Horseface. That wasn't exactly a lie.

"And neither have I," said Geezil. "Do you go to school, son?"

The new boy laughed. It was a squeaky sound and showed he knew he was being kidded. "You fellows sure are funny," he said. "I think I'm going to like it here." With that he picked up his suitcase. "So long. See you later." At the foot of the steps he turned to wave his hand. But that was a mistake. I can see him now, smiling under his glasses. He was looking at us while his foot reached for the steps behind him. Then, he fell right up the stairs.

"Somebody's in for a bad time," Monk said.

"What?" I asked.

"Somebody has to room with him, you clown," he explained.

"That's right," I agreed. "Say, I wonder when my roommate is going to show up. It's beginning to get late."

Monk gave me his glassy stare that makes you think he's a moron. That's until you learn that he's as sharp as the next guy. "Maybe he has," he said.

"What?" I said again.

Monk nodded his head toward the door. "That last character rooms with *somebody* in there," he said. "You might be the lucky one."

"Oh!" I said, and I got up. A few seconds later I was standing in the doorway of my room. Monk was right.

The new boy had his coat and shirt off by now. He was over in front of the long mirror, trying to make a muscle with his left arm. His back was to me, so for a minute he didn't see me. I could see the smile on his face in the mirror. He stood there with one arm bent at

the elbow. It had the poorest excuse for a muscle in it that I've ever seen. Then he caught sight of me in the mirror. Even through the dust on the glass I could see him blush. But when he turned around, he was still smiling.

"Dynamic tension," he said.

Really, I didn't laugh. Right then I think I liked him for trying to carry it off with a laugh on himself. I think I was glad he was going to be my roommate. All the same I did a mean thing. I went to the window and stuck my head out. Then I signaled Monk and Horseface and Geezil to come up. They sure came running. I hardly had my head back in again before they were in the room.

"Why, hello again," said the new boy. "Come on in."

"Thanks," said Monk. By his tone of voice any fool could see that he was in already. He sat down on the bed. "What's your name, kid?"

"My name's Robert," said the new boy. He smiled all over.

Monk shook his head. "It won't do," he said. "That's Robby Armstrong's name." He pointed to me. "And he was here first." He turned to us. "Anyone got any ideas?"

"Handsome?" Horseface offered. The new boy winced, but smiled.

"Four-eyes," said Geezil. The new boy blinked, still smiling.

Monk snorted. "You clowns have no imagination."

"Of course you could do better," said Horseface.

"Sure," said Monk. "I named *you*, didn't I? Let's call him Pitcher."

Geezil nodded. "Turn your head, son," he said to Pitcher.

Pitcher showed us his profile. To this day I am still not used to his nose and his flappy ears.

"See what I mean?" asked Monk. "You know, little pitchers have big ears. Maybe someday he'll be a great baseball pitcher too. Or even a star on the football team. Who knows? Funny things happen."

"Right," said Geezil. "Well, what are we waiting for? Let's initiate him."

So we put Pitcher into the shower the way we do with all the new boys around here. Pitcher didn't mind it a bit. He smiled all the time, except when he slipped over the soap and fell flat on the floor. Then he laughed. He was such a good sport that I began to feel mean. I was glad when the guys got tired and left to look for some more new boys. I wanted to get Pitcher alone so I could talk with him. You see, already I was coming to like him!

When the first bell rang, I took him to the dining hall right away. That way I'd have ten minutes to show him the ropes. By that I mean where to get water and milk in case his table ran out. On the way we bumped into Coach. So I introduced Pitch.

"Coach, this is Pitcher," I said. They shook hands, both smiling.

"It's a good name, don't you think?" Pitcher asked. He put his hands over his ears.

"Yes. . . ." said Coach slowly. "And I'm glad you like it, because that helps." Then he asked, "Are you coming out for football tomorrow?"

Pitcher's eyebrows went up. "Me?"

"Certainly. Why not?"

"Well, I didn't know that I could. I mean, I'm not very big. . . ."

Coach put his hand on Pitcher's shoulder. "We have teams here for the smaller boys," he said. "We've noticed that they don't stay small very long. How about sitting at my table tonight? We'll talk about football."

84

"Gee, can I?" Pitch looked as pleased as a boy can be.

"Sure," I put in, maybe to show that I knew my way around. "On the first night you can sit anywhere. After that they assign you a table."

So we sat at Coach's table, Pitch on his right and me on his left. We talked football. Coach was telling Pitch how everybody in school is almost as interested in the Brat team (that's what they call us) as in the varsity. All the students come down to cheer the Brat games even louder than they cheer the big team.

Well, Pitch was able to live through the first night of school with all its troubles. The next afternoon we all went out for football. If Pitcher had been a big athlete he wouldn't have made such a bad start. But the trouble was, he was just the opposite. He was terrible, as we soon learned. He tried harder than anyone I ever saw. But he couldn't do anything right. He missed more tackles than all the rest of us put together. He'd dive at the ball carrier—dive like crazy. But the ball carrier would be long gone. When he ran interference for me—I'm quarterback—half the time he'd get caught in his own feet. He'd fall down just in the right place for me to fall over him.

I lost my cool a few times over things like that. After all, a guy wants to have his team win. You can't hate me for liking to make a few good plays myself now and then. But the other Brats were worse than I was toward him. Because, after all, I liked Pitcher. The others didn't, and they kept riding him. I don't need to tell you how they did it. You know how boys can be when they've found somebody to pick on.

Of course, I could tell from the way Pitcher acted in our room that his unpopularity was beginning to get under his skin. But it was nearly a month before I learned just how badly he felt. I'll say this for Pitch. He could keep his feelings to himself. It wasn't until I woke up one night and heard him crying that I had any idea of how much he'd been hurt inside. I listened to him for a while. I kept wondering what I could do to make it easier for him. Then he started to moan and talk out loud.

He gasped words out. Then I heard him beating his fist on his pillow. "I can't take it! I can't take it another day!" The way his voice sounded made my hair stand on end. Then he went on. "And I can't run away. I just can't quit and run away, that's all. What'll I do. . .?"

But I didn't hear any more. I stuck my fingers in my ears.

Coach Takes Over

The very next afternoon I went down to see Coach. I wanted to tell him the whole story. Coach listened. He didn't interrupt once. Toward the end he got up and stuck his hands in his pockets. Then he started looking for his pipe over behind where I was sitting. When I got through, he sat down quietly for a few minutes. He kept looking out the window and blowing

86

smoke rings the way he does when he's got something on his mind. After a while he laid down his pipe suddenly. He put his hands on his knees, and looked hard at me.

"Go get Pitcher," he said.

"Yes, sir," I said. I got out of there without asking any questions. Lots of times with Coach you don't ask any questions out loud. But you can be sure I was wondering plenty while I ran to the room.

When we got back, Coach had a football in his hands. He turned it over once or twice before he said anything.

"Pitcher," he said at last. "I sent Robby for you because I want you and him to learn a private play. A play that nobody else is going to hear about until we use it in your Brat game this Saturday."

"Yes, sir," said Pitcher. His voice sounded kind of eager, and sad too.

Coach turned to me. "You understand me, Robby? Nobody is to know this play but you and Pitch."

I nodded. The Coach was up to something.

"It's simple," Coach said. "So simple that it might do the trick. Especially against boys who haven't played much football. Robby, who plays right end against your team?"

"Monk does," I said.

"Perfect!" Coach smiled happily. "If we have to make a fool of somebody, it might as well be. . . ." All of a sudden he got serious. "Well, let's get down to business. Robby, you take the ball." He tossed it to me. "Now bend over and move to the right as if you were going on an end run. Get set exactly as you do in play eighteen. That's right. Now, Pitch, stand over here in the wingback spot. Right. Now Robby. Come over in this direction again on your end run. Give the ball to Pitcher as you go by him. He'll be starting in your direction."

"Yes, sir," I said.

As I remember, we practiced that play for half an hour. Finally we had our timing perfect. Pitch almost never dropped the ball when I put it in his hands. That is very good for Pitch. Coach stood there watching us and coaching us. He had me bend over farther and slip the ball to Pitch. Finally I hardly knew myself that I

had given it to him as he went past me. He had Pitch hold the ball behind his hip with one hand, until you couldn't see it from the front. I think he worked over us harder than he does with the big team. At last he seemed satisfied. He tossed me the ball again and sat down.

"Do any of the varsity backfield men live up in your dormitory?" he asked me.

"Yes, sir," I said. "Washburn lives on the first floor. And Star Collins lives on the second, right down the hall from us."

"Collins is the man," Coach said, sort of to himself. He looked at us. "I'm going to change my mind about no one knowing this play but you two. I want Star to help you practice. After all, both of you are rather inexperienced."

"Yes, sir," I said. That suited me fine, because Star is a good guy. Besides, he is a great backfield man.

"So take this ball to your room and keep things quiet," Coach told us. "Every night this week you two are to practice that play. Star will be watching you. I'll tell him myself what I want him to look for. Get that play perfect, understand?"

"Yes, sir," said Pitch. I nodded.

"Then Friday you'll come down here for a last work-out with me. If I can see that ball pass between you, or if Pitch drops it, I'll skin you both alive. Understand?"

"Yes, sir," I said. Pitch nodded. You can tell when Coach means what he says.

Well, we practiced with Star watching us. We practiced up in our room in front of our mirror. Before long even we couldn't see that ball slip out of my arms into Pitcher's. And we didn't say anything to anyone. Then on Friday we showed our stuff to Coach and he was satisfied. When we had done it for him several times without a slip, he made us sit down. Then he told us what to do in the game the next day.

You should have seen that game! Of course, the whole school was there, the way they always are for Brat games. And of course they were cheering and yelling the way they always do. The first half was full of good football too. I mean, as good as we can play. And it was plenty exciting. Most of the time our two teams rolled back and forth, up and down the field. But finally Monk, the captain of the Blue team, caught a pass and scored. But they didn't convert. So, when I slipped around right end later on and scored, we had them tied. We didn't convert either. So the half ended 6-6.

All this time the students in the bleachers were yelling and shouting and giving advice. Coach was sitting quietly on the bench. Pitcher was beside him, not saying a word. Once, during a time-out, I noticed that Pitch was biting his nails. Except for that he seemed all right. Even at the half he didn't say anything except, "Nice going, fellows. Let's beat them this half." Only no one noticed him. I'm afraid most of the fellows were hoping Coach would never send him into the game. They figured with him in the game we'd never beat

Monk's team. Maybe I felt the same way myself, even with that secret trick play. I began to wonder whether Pitch would hold on to the ball if we had a chance to try the trick in a real game. Then the second half started. Now I had to use all my wondering to figure what Monk's team would pull next.

Halfway through the last quarter the score was still tied. We took over the ball on our forty-yard line. I was trying to decide what plays to use when I saw Pitch come running out on the field. So did the rest of my team back there in the huddle. They all groaned.

"There goes the ball game," said Horseface.

"And how," said Geezil.

Then Pitch tripped over the grass or something and fell flat on his face before he was halfway to us. No one said anything more.

91

Even I was feeling worried until Monk called across to us. "Oh, you lucky fellows!" When I looked up and saw him laughing at me, I made up my mind to fix his wagon.

So, the way Coach had told me, I called play eighteen. That's a right-end run, with me carrying the ball and Pitch on the wing. It didn't work worth a darn, because I fell over Pitch on the line of scrimmage. But that was all right because it wasn't supposed to work. Back in the huddle I called the same play again. This time it went for two yards, because I was able to get out of Pitcher's way. In the huddle I yelled "Eighteen!" again, good and loud.

"Quiet, you dope, they'll hear you!" Horseface whispered to me.

"Well, let's run it anyway," I said. I didn't even smile. Horseface didn't know that the idea was to have Monk hear me call the play.

So we ran it, and how I got creamed! Even Monk was in on the tackle. He'd run behind the line of scrimmage all the way around from his end to get me. Which was what Coach had figured he would do.

"Play eighteen," I said in the huddle, good and loud.

"Have you gone crazy, Robby?" Horseface was part mad, part worried too. "Are you out of your mind or something?"

"Eighteen!" I said again, loud and clear.

"It's fourth down," said Geezil. "Coach will kill you if you don't kick on fourth down."

92

"Eighteen!" I yelled once more. "Me in the tailback, Pitch on the wing."

"Buddy, you asked for it," said Horseface. He walked up to the scrimmage line. He knew that Coach gets mighty sore if anyone but the quarterback tries to run the team. But I had an idea he was planning to kill me after we lost the game. I was kind of worried myself. But then the ball came back at me and I stopped worrying and got down to business.

It was as if we were in our room practicing in front of the mirror. I started off to the right and Pitch started toward me. We passed each other behind our right tackle. Even I didn't know when I slipped Pitch the ball. It went so smooth and easy. I was still doubled up, as if I had the ball, when Monk sailed into me from the side. He knocked me out of bounds. But I got up again as if I'd been made out of rubber. I wanted to see if our trick play was going to work. Brother, I saw!

Way out there across the field Pitch was galloping toward the goal line. He held the ball off behind his hip exactly the way Coach had taught him. Not a soul was near him. Even the safety on Monk's team had pulled way over to the right to get me. Coach's reverse play had worked.

It had worked so fine that even the crowd in the stands had not followed the play. You could tell because they didn't make a sound. They were just looking all over for the ball. And then they found it. Boy, you should have heard the yelling!

"Pitch has it!"

"Pitch has the ball!"

"Look at the boy run!"

"How did he get it?"

"Run, Pitch! Run with that ball, Pitch!"

I've heard noise on a ball field, but none like that. I've seen crowds stamp their feet and jump up and down and throw their hats in the air. Not the way they did that day when Pitcher went racing down the left sideline. He hugged the ball to his chest now, the way Coach had told him. And no one was near him. Everybody was screaming, "Pitch! Pitcher!" and pounding each other's back.

Mind you, I wasn't sitting on the ground with Monk in my lap all this time. As soon as I could, I'd pushed him away and taken off after Pitch. Not that there was any blocking to do. I just wanted to be around when he crossed the goal line. Even running as hard as I could, I heard the shouts for him. I could see his white teeth flashing the world's widest smile.

And then, of course, he tripped. On the two-yard line he caught one toe behind his ankle and went sprawling. So did the ball. It slipped out of his hands like wet soap. That didn't matter. It bounced over the goal line, and I was there to fall on it. That counts six points in any league.

When I sat up with the ball, Pitch was still lying flat on the ground.

"Hey, Pitch!" I yelled. I was worried. "Are you all right?"

Pitch sat up then and batted his eyes. He looked at the other players on the team running toward him. They were shouting and clapping and laughing. He listened to the crowd in the stands screaming his name while they jumped up and down. Then he smiled, the biggest smile I've ever seen on anyone his size.

"I'm all right," he said as he got up. He took a deep breath and smiled wider. Just before the team swamped him to beat him on the back, I heard him say, "I'm the happiest boy in all the world!"

—Stephen Cole

What Do You Think?

1. In what ways do you like or admire Pitcher?
2. Did you find a deeper meaning in this story? What do you think the author wanted you to think about?

Taking A Closer Look

1. What was Pitcher's problem and how was it solved?
2. Why did the other students pick on Pitcher during the first month of school?
3. How do you think Monk and the other students treated Pitcher during the rest of the school year? Explain your answer.
4. Try to explain what happens in the reverse play.
5. How does the author make you think the story was written by Robby Armstrong?

Putting Ideas to Work

Think of a person whom you respect. What qualities and abilities do you respect? Tell why.

Where Do Stories Come From?

Where do stories come from? Many writers get their ideas from the people and events they know and remember best. Some authors look to the past and try to imagine what might have happened at a certain time and place. Others eye the future and try to describe what is yet to come. Still others add a special touch to an old tale, creating a new one. And there are some storytellers who pick their thoughts right out of the air!

Lee Edward loved the way Mama Luka[1] told him time-ago tales of Jahdu.[2] But who is Jadhu, and how does Mama Luka know so much about him? Can you figure it out?

HOW JAHDU FOUND HIS POWER

Mama Luka liked to sit in her tight little room in a fine, good place called Harlem. She liked to sit with the window blinds drawn against the sunlight. And Mama Luka did, every day.

Mama Luka had black skin and a nose as curved as the beak of a parrot. She wore her hair in one long pigtail down her back. She called the pigtail her plait, and she could sit on it. She sat on it whenever she felt like telling tales.

Mama Luka took care of Lee Edward after his school was out for the day and until his mother came home from work. And Mama Luka sat all the while in her little room in the good place, telling Jahdu stories to Lee Edward. She told them slow and she told them easy. And Lee Edward listened. He sat on the floor with his eyes tight shut, which was the best way for him to imagine Jahdu.

[1]Luka (LOO-kah) [2]Jahdu (JAH-doo)

101

Lee Edward loved Mama Luka. She sometimes called him Little Brother just like his own mama did. And he loved his own mama and papa, too. Lee Edward loved Jahdu and Jahdu stories. And he loved the way Mama Luka told them like any child would.

"Now here we go, Little Brother," Mama Luka said one day.

"There are many a-thousand Jahdu stories," she told Lee Edward. "I know about two hundred of them. I've told you a roomful of Jahdu stories. So that leaves one more roomful of Jahdu stories to tell. Now, you pick out of the air in this room one more Jahdu story."

Lee Edward looked around the room. At last he pointed to an empty space just above Mama Luka's head.

"That one," Lee Edward said.

Mama Luka reached above her head. She cupped her hands around the place Lee Edward had pointed out in the air. And she brought her hands down slowly to her face. Mama Luka opened her mouth and swallowed what had been in her hands.

"Lee Edward, you picked a time-ago story out of the air," she said. "It has a strong taste to it, for it tells how Jahdu found out he had magic power."

"So tell it," Lee Edward said to Mama Luka.

"So I'm getting myself ready," said Mama Luka.

"Lee Edward," began Mama Luka, "the story you picked is about a time not long after Jahdu had been born. He had not much shape then and not much

size. And only his face was clear. Jahdu didn't know he had any magic at all.

"Lee Edward in that time-ago," said Mama Luka, "Jahdu wasn't as tall as you."

"What did his face look like?" asked Lee Edward. He hoped to catch Mama Luka before she had time to think. But Mama Luka wasn't to be caught this day or any other day. No, she wasn't.

"Little Brother, don't you try to trick me," said Mama Luka. "I know better than to talk about the face of Jahdu."

"Just give me a hint," said Lee Edward.

"Child, nobody who has seen the face of Jahdu will tell you what his face looks like. And I have seen it," said Mama Luka, "and I can't tell."

"Well then, get on with the story," said Lee Edward.

"Here it comes," said Mama Luka.

103

THIS IS THE JAHDU STORY WITH A STRONG TASTE THAT
MAMA LUKA TOLD TO LEE EDWARD.

Jahdu was running along. He was two feet tall. Yes,
he was. And he had been in the world one year.

Jahdu lived high atop the Mountain of Paths. He
made his home in the only black gum tupelo tree in
the pine forest covering the mountain. From his tree,
Jahdu could see all the paths to the valley below. He
could see which paths the animal children who lived
on the mountain walked along.

Jahdu believed the paths the animal children walked
along were good and safe. And only these good and safe
paths would Jahdu run along.

But Jahdu was only a year in the world. He did not
yet know everything. No, he didn't. One day Jahdu was
running along a path behind some animal children. All
at once the animal children stopped still.

104

A bandicoot rat fell to the ground. He grew stiff and he screamed and cried loudly for his mother.

A brown bear cub stood up on one hind leg. He hopped in circles, bumping into a fawn and stepping on a baby otter. The brown bear cub sang a wordless song. The young woodchuck, the raccoon girl, and the wolf child wandered away into the pine wood and were lost. Some of the other animal children sat down on the path, moaning to themselves and trembling all over.

It took Jahdu an hour to gather all of the animal children on the path again. Then he tied a rope around all of them and led them to another path he knew to be good and safe. There, he let them loose.

"I'd better go back to that first path," Jahdu said. "I'd better find out as fast as I can what caused those animal children to stop still and hop around and fall down and act silly."

Jahdu found the path on which the animal children had stopped still. As he went running down the path, something he couldn't see tried to catch him. But Jahdu was stronger than whatever it was that tried to stop him. He kept right on running along.

"Woogily!" whispered Jahdu to himself. "There are baneberries growing on both sides of this path. Everybody knows baneberries can make animal children sick. I'd better keep on this path to find out what it is that tries to catch me. I'd better find out why baneberries grow on both sides of a good and safe path."

Jahdu stayed on the path. Yes, he did. All at once Jahdu fell into a hole full of thorns.

"Ouch!" said Jahdu. "Thorns have points to hurt Jahdu!" Jahdu jumped out of the hole and bounced into a soft bed of sweet-smelling leaves.

"Woogily!" said Jahdu. "This funny path has good and bad about it. But it surely isn't safe for animal children to walk along."

Jahdu kept right on the good and bad path with baneberries on both sides of it, full of thorn holes and soft beds of sweet-smelling leaves. He ran and he ran until he came to a stream. He sat down in the middle of the stream to cool himself. Suddenly thirteen crawfish started pinching Jahdu. He leaped out of the water.

"Woogily!" said Jahdu. "That's a nice little stream so fresh and cold. But it has thirteen crawfish that can pinch the paws of little animals. I'd better hurry and find out where this funny path ends."

So Jahdu kept on hurrying along the good and bad path with baneberries on both sides, with thorn holes and soft beds of sweet-smelling leaves, and a stream across it with thirteen crawfish.

All at once Jahdu ran smack into a banyan tree at the end of the path. He bounced clear around the banyan tree. Yes, he did. He started running again and ran smack into the banyan tree once more.

"Woogily!" cried Jahdu. "How in the world did a banyan tree get into these pine woods on the Mountain of Paths? Running into banyan trees doesn't feel very good. Little animals will hurt themselves if they go walking into banyan trees!"

Up in the banyan tree was an animal who had a round, sweet face and a bell on its head. And up in the banyan tree was another animal who had a square, mean face and no bell anywhere. Both animals lay side by side peering down at Jahdu.

"I've never seen animals such as you," said Jahdu. "What in the world are you called?"

The animal with a bell on its head spoke first to Jahdu. "I'm called Sweetdream," it said in a soft, sweet voice.

"And I'm Nightmare," said the other animal in a harsh, mean voice. "You're Jahdu and we don't like you."

"Oh, for goodness sake!" said Jahdu. "Like me or not, I'm here to stay. And please tell me why there's a banyan tree at the end of a path on which little animals might walk."

"Because it's here," said Nightmare in a mean voice, "just as Sweetdream and I are here and the path is here, so there!"

"When the bell on my head tinkles," said Sweetdream, "Nightmare and I know little animals are walking along our path."

"Then we use our charms to get them," said Nightmare. "It's such fun watching our spells work on them."

"Just how do your spells work on the little animals?" asked Jahdu.

"Well," said Sweetdream, "my spell makes the animals stop still, then hop around and sing sweet songs, and do and say whatever sweet things are in their heads when my spell strikes them."

"And my spell makes them grow stiff," said Nightmare. "They fall to the ground and scream and cry. Or they moan and tremble all over and do whatever bad things are in their thoughts when my spell strikes them."

108

"Little animals ought to be able to walk along and do as they wish," said Jahdu. "I don't think it's right to use spells on them."

"I don't care what you think," said Sweetdream sweetly. "I do as I please."

"There's nothing you can do to stop *me*," said Nightmare, "so you better go on your way."

Jahdu was angry. He ran to the banyan tree and shook it as hard as he could.

"Come down from that banyan tree, you awful things!" Jahdu yelled. "Come down and I'll surely take care of you!"

Jahdu shook and shook the banyan tree until both animals sitting in it turned purple all over.

"Stop it!" said Sweetdream and Nightmare. "You're making us dizzy and sick!"

"Then come down," said Jahdu, "so Jahdu can take care of you."

"We can't come down," said Sweetdream. "We're attached to this banyan, we can't ever come down!"

Then Jahdu saw that the two animals were growing like figs on the banyan's branches.

"Woogily!" he said. "Now Jahdu's caught you for sure!"

Jahdu ran around and around the banyan tree as fast as he could. He was showing off for the two tree-grown animals. Yes, he was. And he ran so fast he shook the dust right out of himself.

Jahdu's dust rose up into the banyan tree. It settled

on Sweetdream and Nightmare and they fell fast asleep.

Jahdu stopped running.

"Woogily!" he said. "Did I do that? Did my dust put Sweetdream and Nightmare to sleep?"

Wherever the Jahdu dust fell, it put things to sleep. A spider walking along the banyan tree trunk got Jahdu dust on him and fell asleep. A bluebird flying low near the banyan tree got a whiff of the Jahdu dust and had to land in the tree. As the Jahdu dust settled on the bluebird, it fell asleep.

"Woogily!" said Jahdu. "I've got me some magic! I can put things to sleep! Maybe I have more magic. Let me see."

Jahdu tried wishing there was no good and bad path, no Sweetdream and Nightmare and no banyan tree. But

this didn't work. No, it didn't. For the path stayed. So did the banyan tree and the sleeping Sweetdream and Nightmare.

Jahdu had another idea. He started running around the banyan tree. Jahdu ran slower and slower and ever so slowly.

The Jahdu dust rose off the two animals up the banyan tree. It rose off the tree trunk and the spider, off the bluebird and off everything. Then the Jahdu dust fell back into Jahdu. All that had been asleep woke up. Sweetdream and Nightmare yawned and stared down at Jahdu.

"Woogily!" said Jahdu. "I can wake things up. I've got me another magic!"

"You shouldn't have put us to sleep," said Sweet-

dream. "We have to work in the daytime so we can watch the fun."

"You won't watch the fun anymore," said Jahdu, "for I'm going to make you work at night."

"You can't make us do anything we don't want to do," said Nightmare.

"If you don't do what I want you to do, I'll put you to sleep for a week," Jahdu told Nightmare.

"Oh, no," said Sweetdream. "Please don't put him to sleep for a week."

"A month," said Jahdu, feeling good all over.

"All right, you have us," said Nightmare. "Just don't get carried away."

Jahdu drew himself up two feet tall. Yes, he did. And he told Sweetdream and Nightmare what he was going to make them do.

"Nightmare will sleep from daylight to nightfall," said Jahdu. "He will work his spell only at night and only on sleeping animals. And if I ever catch him playing around with his spell when it's daylight, I'll put him to sleep for a year!"

Nightmare looked glum but he didn't say a word. He still felt sick from Jahdu's shaking the banyan tree.

"As for Sweetdream," said Jahdu, "she'll work her spell in the daytime only on those little animals who sleep by day. And then only once in a very long while. The rest of her work she will do at night and on sleeping animals, just the same as Nightmare."

Sweetdream smiled sweetly but said nothing.

112

"I'll never have any fun again watching my spell work," muttered Nightmare.

"That's the truth," said Jahdu. "I'm getting rid of that awful path, too. I'll put it to sleep for the rest of time!"

And so Jahdu did. He ran up and down the path as fast as he could go. Jahdu dust rose from Jahdu and fell all over the path. At once the path was fast asleep. The baneberries on both sides of the path dried up and slept, too. All kinds of forest plants started growing over the path.

Jahdu stood where once the path had begun. Now, young pine saplings started growing there. Jahdu shouted down the path at Sweetdream and Nightmare.

"Your path is gone," Jahdu shouted. "No little animals will come along here! Now you'll have to send your charms out on the night air. Your spells will never again be very strong. For the night air is so light it can carry only a little of your charms at a time!"

Jahdu went running along. Yes, he did. He could run very fast and he could run very slow. He could shake Jahdu dust out of himself and cause it to fall back into himself again. With his magic he could wake things up and put things to sleep.

THIS IS THE END OF THE JAHDU STORY WITH A STRONG TASTE THAT MAMA LUKA TOLD TO LEE EDWARD.

—*Virginia Hamilton*

What Do You Think?

1. When Lee Edward shut his eyes to hear the Jahdu stories, he might have imagined how Jahdu looked. How do you imagine Jahdu to look?

2. Do you think Mama Luka liked to tell Jahdu stories to Lee Edward? How do you know?

3. Mama Luka tells Lee Edward that this Jahdu story "has a strong taste to it." What is meant by this phrase?

Taking A Closer Look

1. Why do you think Lee Edward liked Mama Luka's stories about Jahdu so much?

2. What could Mama Luka have meant when she said the story was "a time-ago story"?

3. Why do you suppose Mama Luka would not describe Jahdu to Lee Edward?

4. One of Jahdu's favorite expressions is "Woogily!" What do you think "woogily" means? What word or words could you substitute for "woogily"?

5. "How Jahdu Found His Power" is a story-within-a-story. How is Mama Luka's story about Jahdu different from the story about Mama Luka and Lee Edward?

What I Would Like to Be

I think that I should like to be a tree.
Planted by some lonely stream to grow
and grow so green, so tall, so fresh
  and nice
to have some man, woman, or a child
stop beneath my green branches
to be comforted in the shade which my
  branches cast.
I think that I would like to be a tree
to brighten some yard or some lonely
  countryside
And then at some late summer day
to shed my leaves, to fall asleep
and awake at another season
to become so green, so tall and so
  nice
and to brighten someone's day.

—*Deidre Harris*

116

This true story comes from a book written by Laura Ingalls Wilder. In her book the author tells of exciting events that happened many years ago when she was moving West with her pioneer family. Why do you think Laura remembered this day from her childhood?

The Day They Stayed Alone

Summer was gone, winter was coming, and now it was time for Pa to make a trip to town. Here in Minnesota, town was so near that Pa would be gone only one day, and Ma was going with him.

She took Carrie, because Carrie was too little to be left far from Ma. But Mary and Laura were big girls. Mary was going on nine and Laura was going on eight, and they could stay at home and take care of everything while Pa and Ma were gone.

For going-to-town, Ma made a new dress for Carrie, from the pink calico that Laura had worn when she was little. There was enough of it to make Carrie a little pink sunbonnet. Carrie's hair had been in curl-papers all night. It hung in long, golden, round curls, and when Ma tied the pink sunbonnet strings under Carrie's chin, Carrie looked like a rose.

Ma wore her hoopskirts and her best dress, the beautiful challis with little strawberries on it, that she had worn to the sugaring-dance at Grandma's, long ago in the Big Woods.

"Now be good girls, Laura and Mary," was the last thing she said. She was on the wagon seat, with Carrie beside her. Their lunch was in the wagon. Pa took up the ox goad.

"We'll be back before sundown," he promised. "Hi-oop!" he said to Pete and Bright. The big ox and the little one leaned into their yoke and the wagon started.

"Good-bye, Pa! Good-bye, Ma! Good-bye, Carrie, good-bye!" Laura and Mary called after it.

Slowly the wagon went away. Pa walked beside the oxen. Ma and Carrie, the wagon, and Pa all grew smaller, till they were gone into the prairie.

The prairie seemed big and empty then, but there was nothing to be afraid of. There were no wolves and no Indians. Besides, Jack stayed close to Laura. Jack was a responsible dog. He knew that he must take care of everything when Pa was away.

That morning Mary and Laura played by the creek,

among the rushes. They did not go near the swimming-hole. They did not touch the straw-stack. At noon they ate the corn dodgers and molasses and drank the milk that Ma had left for them. They washed their tin cups and put them away.

Then Laura wanted to play on the big rock, but Mary wanted to stay in the dugout. She said that Laura must stay there, too.

"Ma can make me," Laura said, "but you can't."

"I can so," said Mary. "When Ma's not here, you have to do what I say because I'm older."

"You have to let me have my way because I'm littler," said Laura.

"That's Carrie, it isn't you," Mary told her. "If you don't do what I say, I'll tell Ma."

"I guess I can play where I want to!" said Laura.

Mary grabbed at her, but Laura was too quick. She darted out, and she would have run up the path, but Jack was in the way. He stood stiff, looking across the creek. Laura looked too, and she screeched, "Mary!"

The cattle were all around Pa's haystacks. They were eating the hay. They were tearing into the stacks with their horns, gouging out hay, eating it and trampling over it.

There would be nothing left to feed Pete and Bright and Spot in the wintertime.

Jack knew what to do. He ran growling down the steps to the foot-bridge. Pa was not there to save the hay-stacks; they must drive those cattle away.

120

"Oh, we can't! We can't!" Mary said, scared. But Laura ran behind Jack and Mary came after her. They went over the creek and past the spring. They came up on the prairie and now they saw the fierce, big cattle quite near. The long horns were gouging, the thick legs trampling and jostling, the wide mouths bawling.

Mary was too scared to move. Laura was too scared to stand still. She jerked Mary along. She saw a stick, and grabbed it up and ran yelling at the cattle. Jack ran at them, growling. A big red cow swiped at him with her horns, but he jumped behind her. She snorted and galloped. All the other cattle ran humping and jostling after her, and Jack and Laura and Mary ran after them.

But they could not chase those cattle away from the haystacks. The cattle ran around and around and in between the stacks, jostling and bawling, tearing off hay and trampling it. More and more hay slid off the stacks. Laura ran panting and yelling, waving her stick. The faster she ran, the faster the cattle went, black and brown and red, brindle and spotted cattle, big and with awful horns, and they would not stop wasting the hay. Some tried to climb over the toppling stacks.

Laura was hot and dizzy. Her hair unbraided and blew in her eyes. Her throat was rough from yelling, but she kept on yelling, running, and waving her stick. She was too scared to hit one of those big, horned cows. More and more hay kept coming down and faster and faster they trampled over it.

122

Suddenly Laura turned around and ran the other way. She faced the big red cow coming around a haystack.

The huge legs and shoulders and terrible horns were coming fast. Laura could not scream now. But she jumped at that cow and waved her stick. The cow tried to stop, but all the other cattle were coming behind her and she couldn't. She swerved and ran away across the ploughed ground, all the others galloping after her.

Jack and Laura and Mary chased them, farther and farther from the hay. Far into the high prairie grasses they chased those cattle.

Johnny Johnson rose out of the prairie, rubbing his eyes. He had been lying asleep in a warm hollow of grass.

"Johnny! Johnny!" Laura screeched. "Wake up and watch the cattle!"

"You'd better!" Mary told him.

Johnny Johnson looked at the cattle grazing in the deep grass, and he looked at Laura and Mary and Jack. He did not know what had happened and they could not tell him because the only words he knew were Norwegian.[1]

They went back through the high grass that dragged at their trembling legs. They were glad to drink at the spring. They were glad to be in the quiet dugout and sit down to rest.

[1]Norwegian (nor-WEE-jən)

All that long, quiet afternoon they stayed in the dugout. The cattle did not come back to the haystacks. Slowly the sun went down the western sky. Soon it would be time to meet the cattle at the big grey rock, and Laura and Mary wished that Pa and Ma would come home.

Again and again they went up the path to look for the wagon. At last they sat waiting with Jack on the grassy top of their house. The lower the sun went, the more attentive Jack's ears were. Often he and Laura stood up to look at the edge of the sky where the wagon had gone, though they could see it just as well when they were sitting down.

Finally Jack turned one ear that way, then the other. Then he looked up at Laura and a waggle went from his neck to his stubby tail. The wagon was coming!

They all stood and watched till it came out of the prairie. When Laura saw the oxen, and Ma and Carrie on the wagon seat, she jumped up and down, swinging her sunbonnet and shouting, "They're coming! They're coming!"

"They're coming awful fast," Mary said.

Laura was still. She heard the wagon rattling loudly. Pete and Bright were coming very fast. They were running. They were running away.

The wagon came bumpity-banging and bouncing. Laura saw Ma down in a corner of the wagon box, hanging onto it and hugging Carrie. Pa came bounding in long jumps beside Bright, shouting and hitting at Bright with the goad.

He was trying to turn Bright back from the creek bank.

He could not do it. The big oxen galloped nearer and nearer the steep edge. Bright was pushing Pa off it. They were all going over. The wagon, Ma and Carrie, were going to fall down the bank, all the way down to the creek.

Pa shouted a terrible shout. He struck Bright's head with all his might and Bright swerved. Laura ran screaming. Jack jumped at Bright's nose. Then the wagon, Ma, and Carrie flashed by. Bright crashed against the stable and suddenly everything was still.

Pa ran after the wagon and Laura ran behind him.

"Whoa, Bright! Whoa, Pete," Pa said. He held onto the wagon box and looked at Ma.

"We're all right, Charles," Ma said. Her face was grey and she was shaking all over.

Pete was trying to go on through the doorway into the stable, but he was yoked to Bright and Bright was headed against the stable wall. Pa lifted Ma and Carrie out of the wagon, and Ma said, "Don't cry, Carrie. See, we're all right."

Carrie's pink dress was torn down the front. She snuffled against Ma's neck and tried to stop crying as Ma told her.

"Oh, Caroline! I thought you were going over the bank," Pa said.

"I thought so, too, for a minute," Ma answered. "But I might have known you wouldn't let that happen."

"Pshaw!" said Pa. "It was good old Pete. He wasn't running away. Bright was, but Pete was only going along. He saw the stable and wanted his supper."

But Laura knew that Ma and Carrie would have fallen down into the creek with the wagon and oxen, if Pa had not run so fast and hit Bright so hard. She crowded against Ma's hoopskirt and hugged her tight and said, "Oh, Ma! Oh, Ma!" So did Mary.

"There, there," said Ma. "All's well that ends well. Now, girls, help bring in the packages while Pa puts up the oxen."

They carried all the little packages into the dugout. They met the cattle at the grey rock and put Spot into

126

the stable, and Laura helped milk her while Mary helped Ma get supper.

At supper, they told how the cattle had got into the haystacks and how they had driven them away. Pa said they had done exactly the right thing. He said, "We knew we could depend on you to take care of everything. Didn't we, Caroline?"

They had completely forgotten that Pa always brought them presents from town, until after supper he pushed back his bench and looked as if he expected something. Then Laura jumped on his knee, and Mary sat on the other, and Laura bounced and asked, "What did you bring us, Pa? What? What?"

"Guess," Pa said.

They could not guess. But Laura felt something crackle in his jumper pocket and she pounced on it. She pulled out a paper bag, beautifully striped with tiny red and green stripes. And in the bag were two sticks of candy, one for Mary and one for Laura!

They were maple-sugar-coloured, and they were flat on one side.

Mary licked hers. But Laura bit her stick, and the outside of it came off, crumbly. The inside was hard and clear and dark brown. And it had a rich, brown, tangy taste. Pa said it was hoarhound candy.

After the dishes were done, Laura and Mary each took her stick of candy and they sat on Pa's knees, outside the door in the cool dusk. Ma sat just inside the dugout, humming to Carrie in her arms.

The creek was talking to itself under the yellow willows. One by one the great stars swung low and seemed to quiver and flicker in the little wind.

Laura was snug in Pa's arm. His beard softly tickled her cheek and the delicious candy taste melted on her tongue.

After a while she said, "Pa."

"What, little half-pint?" Pa's voice asked against her hair.

"I think I like wolves better than cattle," she said.

"Cattle are more useful, Laura," Pa said.

She thought about that a while. Then she said, "Anyway, I like wolves better."

She was not contradicting; she was only saying what she thought.

"Well, Laura, we're going to have a good team of horses before long," Pa said. She knew when that would be. It would be when they had a wheat crop.

— *Laura Ingalls Wilder*

What Do You Think?

1. In what ways did Laura show courage in this story?
   In what ways did Mary, Ma, and Pa show courage?
2. Tell how you think Laura felt when she
   a. saw the big red cow running toward her.
   b. first saw the wagon coming over the prairie.
   c. saw the oxen run away with the wagon.
   d. sat snug on Pa's knee, with his beard tickling her cheek.
3. At the end of the story Pa says, "Well, Laura, we're going to have a good team of horses before long."
   Why do you think the Ingalls family did not have horses? How could horses make their lives easier?

Taking A Closer Look

1. The prairie seemed big and empty to Laura after Ma, Pa, and Carrie had left for town. Why do you think Laura felt this way then?
2. Why was it so important that Laura and Mary chase the cattle from the haystacks?
3. Why was the hoarhound candy that Pa brought from town such a treat for the girls?
4. How did the members of the Ingalls family show that they cared for one another? Give examples to support your opinion.

Putting Ideas to Work

Describe an emergency when you or someone you know had to think and act quickly. Tell what finally happened.

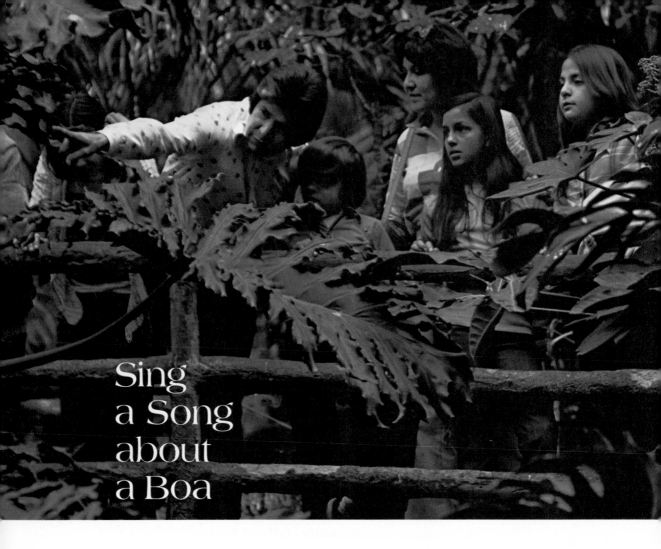

Sing
a Song
about
a Boa

Things you enjoy can be fun to write about. Ernesto Galarza visited a zoo and wrote poems about the animals he saw there. Read about the animals in his zoo and see what funny ideas they gave him.

Could you write a poem or two
About the animals in a zoo?

130

the boa

Sing a song
about a boa who was eight feet long.
His name was Bo-ab-dil.
But nearly everyone who knew him
    around the zoo
called him simply
Bill!

the elephant

If you had a trunk instead of a nose
you could swish it around like a garden hose.
If you had a trunk where your nose should be
you could pick up a log or even a tree.
If you had a trunk attached to your jaw
you could sip a soda without a straw.
If you want to know the reason you can't
it's because you are **not** an elephant.

131

the giraffe

I have a friend whose name was Titus.
Once he was sick with laryngitis.
By day he'd cough, by night he'd kaff,
just like any sick giraffe,
until he became a nervous wreck
from such a pain in such a neck.

132

the zebra

The zebra puzzle for today
is easy, if you're bright.
The two-tone stripes he wears, are they
white on black, or black on white?
The answer ought to make you laugh:
the two-tone stripes are half-and-half.

the flamingos

Flamingos are an elegant lot
with legs like stilts, which they are not.
They sleep on one as easy as pie
and hang the other one out to dry.

133

the vicuña[1]

The softest thing that you can touch
— like fuzz and fur and
fog and such —
is the vicuña. How do I know?
Because the vicuña says it's so.

the swan

Oh my, Oh me,
how beautifully
we glide across the pond.
Who would not want to be
a swan?

[1]vicuña (və-KOON-yə)

the alligator

When you observe an alligator grin
he may be saying: "Please come in."
Just tell him: "Thank you, Mr. Alligator.
I'll be around a little later."

— *Ernesto Galarza*

The next two stories are related. The first is an old
Greek tale told almost 2,000 years ago. If you've never
heard the story, you are in for a surprise. The second
story is a modern tale. Can you tell where the author of
"Andy and the Lion" got the idea for his story?

Androcles and the Lion

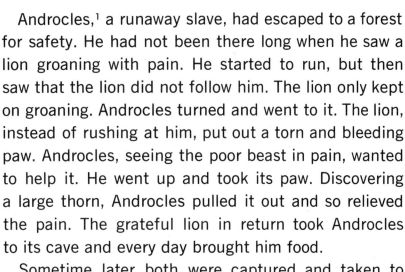

Androcles,[1] a runaway slave, had escaped to a forest for safety. He had not been there long when he saw a lion groaning with pain. He started to run, but then saw that the lion did not follow him. The lion only kept on groaning. Androcles turned and went to it. The lion, instead of rushing at him, put out a torn and bleeding paw. Androcles, seeing the poor beast in pain, wanted to help it. He went up and took its paw. Discovering a large thorn, Androcles pulled it out and so relieved the pain. The grateful lion in return took Androcles to its cave and every day brought him food.

Sometime later both were captured and taken to Rome. Androcles was sentenced to be killed by being thrown to a lion. The lion had not had food for several days. Androcles was led into the arena before the Emperor and his court. At the same time the lion was let go. It came running toward its prey. But when it came near Androcles, it did not attack him. Instead, it jumped up and fawned upon him like a friendly dog. The Emperor, much surprised, ordered that Androcles be brought before him to tell his story.

The Emperor freed both the slave and the lion. He thought such kindness and such gratitude were deserving of reward.

—An Old Fable

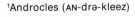

[1]Androcles (AN-drə-kleez)

Andy and the Lion

written and illustrated by James Daugherty

It was a bright day with just enough wind to float a flag. Andy started down to the library to get a book about lions. He took the book home and read and read. Andy read all through supper and he read all evening and just before bedtime his grandfather told him some tall stories about hunting lions in Africa. Every story ended with "and then I gave him both bar-r-r-e-l-l-s!" That night Andy dreamed all night long that he was in Africa hunting lions. When at last morning came Andy woke up. The sun was looking in at the window and Prince was tugging at the bed clothes. The lions had left but Andy kept thinking about them. Andy was still thinking lions after breakfast when his mother gave his hair a final brush and Andy started off to school.

Andy walked along swinging his books and whistling a tune. As he came to the turn in the road he noticed something sticking out from behind the big rock just at the bend. It looked very queer so Andy and Prince crept up cautiously to investigate. It moved! It was a lion! At this moment Andy thought he'd better be going and the lion thought so too. They ran and ran around the rock. Whichever way that Andy ran — there was the lion. Whichever way the lion ran — there was Andy. At last they both stopped for breath. The lion held out his paw to show Andy what was the matter. It was a big thorn stuck in his paw. But Andy had an idea. He told the lion to just be patient and they'd have that thorn out in no time. Fortunately Andy always carried his pliers in the back pocket of his overalls.

139

He took them out and got a tight grip. Then Andy braced one foot against the lion's paw and pulled with all his might until the thorn came out. The grateful lion licked Andy's face to show how pleased he was. But it was time to part. So they waved good-by. Andy went on to school and the lion went off about the business of being a lion.

In the spring the circus came to town. Of course Andy went. He wanted to see the famous lion act. Right in the middle of the act the biggest lion jumped out of the high steel cage and with a terrible roar dashed straight toward the people. They ran for their lives and in the scramble Andy found himself right in the lion's path. He thought his last moment had come. But then who should it be but Andy's own lion. They recognized each other and danced for joy. When the crowd came back ready to fight the lion and capture him, Andy stood in front of the lion and shouted to the angry people: "Do not hurt this lion. He's a friend of mine." Then the next day Andy led the lion and all the people in a grand parade down Main Street to City Hall. There the Mayor presented Andy with a medal for bravery. And the lion was very much pleased. And the next day Andy took the book back to the library.

—*James Daugherty*

What Do You Think?

1. Name as many features as you can that are the same in "Androcles and the Lion" and "Andy and the Lion." In what ways are the two stories different?

2. Is the lesson taught in Mr. Daugherty's story the same as the lesson in the Androcles story? Explain your answer by using examples from both stories.

Taking A Closer Look

1. What surprised you in these stories? Do you think the events in both stories could have really happened? Why or why not?

2. Which story do you think is funnier? Give reasons to support your answer.

3. Make up a modern-day fable that teaches a lesson. Your story can be funny or serious.

The Real Alice

Would you have guessed that a picnic and a girl named Alice were the beginnings of a famous story? Behind the make-believe character of Alice in *Alice's Adventures in Wonderland* was a real Alice.

On July 4, 1862, young Alice Pleasance Liddell and her two sisters went on a picnic with some of their parents' friends. One of these friends was Charles Lutwidge Dodgson, who later wrote under the pen name Lewis Carroll. At the picnic, Dodgson entertained the real Alice with stories about another adventuresome Alice. The lively Alice of the stories was very much like Alice Liddell herself, but what strange adventures she had!

Alice Liddell begged Dodgson to write down the Alice tales. Some months later, a hand-printed book called *Alice's Adventures Under Ground* arrived at Alice Liddell's home—and in the back was a picture of herself, the real Alice.

Later, additions to the story Charles Dodgson had begun that summer day were published for all to read in *Through the Looking-Glass*. The poem on the next page is from that book and tells about the picnic at which the first stories were told. Can you see Lewis Carroll's clue to the real Alice?

A boat, beneath a sunny sky
Lingering onward dreamily
In an evening of July —

Children three that nestle near,
Eager eye and willing ear,
Pleased a simple tale to hear —

Long has paled that sunny sky:
Echoes fade and memories die:
Autumn frosts have slain July.

Still she haunts me, phantomwise,
Alice moving under skies
Never seen by waking eyes.

Children yet, the tale to hear,
Eager eye and willing ear,
Lovingly shall nestle near.

In a Wonderland they lie,
Dreaming as the days go by,
Dreaming as the summers die:

Ever drifting down the stream —
Lingering in the golden gleam —
Life, what is it but a dream?

Not all of the story Charles Dodgson told Alice Liddell was in the final published book. After the printer set the following episode in type, Dodgson cut it out of the book. Why? Because the artist doing the pictures for *Through the Looking-Glass* claimed that a wasp in a wig was impossible to draw. Only in recent times has the Wasp been drawn successfully as in the picture above.

On the next pages are copies of some galley proof for *Through the Looking-Glass*. Galley proofs, called "slips" in those days, are long, numbered sheets of paper with all the text of a book printed on them. Authors make their final corrections on this proof before the book is arranged in pages. Here, just as the author marked them, are the "slips" for "The Wasp in a Wig."

Alice has just reached the edge of a brook.

144

The Wasp in a Wig

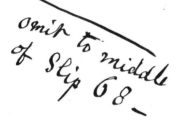

and she was just going to spring over, when she heard a deep sigh, which seemed to come from the wood behind her.

"There's somebody *very* unhappy there," she thought, ~~and she went a little way~~ *looking anxiously* back ~~again~~ to see what was the matter. Something like a very old man (only that his face was more like a wasp) was sitting on the ground, leaning against a tree, all huddled up together, and shivering as if he were very cold.

Omit to middle of Slip 68 —

64

"I don't *think* I can be of any use to him," was Alice's first thought, as she turned to spring over the brook :——"but I'll just ask him what's the matter," she added, checking herself on the very edge. "If I once jump over, everything will change, and then I can't help him."

So she went back to the Wasp——rather unwillingly, for she was *very* anxious to be a Queen.

"Oh, my old bones, my old bones!" he was grumbling (on) as Alice came up to him.

"It's rheumatism, I should think," Alice said to herself, and she stooped over him, and said very kindly "I hope you're not in much pain?"

The Wasp only shook his shoulders, and turned his head away. "Ah, deary me!" he said to himself.

"Can I do anything for you?" Alice went on. "Aren't you rather cold here?"

"How you go on!" the Wasp said in a peevish tone. "Worrity, worrity! There never was such a child!"

Alice felt rather offended at this answer, and was very nearly walking on and leaving him, but she thought to herself "Perhaps it's only pain that makes him so cross." So she tried once more.

"Won't you let me help you round to the other side? You'll be out of the cold wind there."

The Wasp took her arm, and let her help him round the tree, but when he got settled down again he only said, as before, "Worrity, worrity! Can't you leave a body alone?"

146

"Would you like me to read you a bit of this?" Alice went on, as she picked up a newspaper which had been lying at his feet.

"You may read it if you've a mind to," the Wasp said, rather sulkily. "Nobody's hindering you, that *I* know of."

So Alice sat down by him, and spread out the paper on her knees, and began. "*Latest News. The Exploring Party have made another tour in the Pantry, and have found five new lumps of white sugar, large and in fine condition. In coming back——*"

"Any brown sugar?" the Wasp interrupted.

65

Alice hastily ran her eye down the paper and said "No, It says nothing about brown."

"No brown sugar!" grumbled the Wasp. "A nice exploring party!"

"*In coming back,*" Alice went on reading, "*they found a lake of treacle. The banks of the lake were blue and white, and looked like china. While tasting the treacle, they had a sad accident: two of their party were engulphed——*"

"Were *what*?" the Wasp asked in a very cross voice.

"En-gulph-ed," Alice repeated, dividing the word into syllables.

"There's no such word in the language!" said the Wasp.

"It's in this newspaper though," Alice said a little timidly.

"Let it stop there!" said the Wasp, fretfully turning away his head.

Alice put down the newspaper. "I'm afraid you're not well," she said in a soothing tone. "Can't I do anything for you?"

"It's all along of the wig," the Wasp said in a much gentler voice.

"Along of the wig?" Alice repeated, quite pleased to find that he was recovering his temper.

"You'd be cross too, if you'd a wig like mine," the Wasp went on. "They jokes at one. And they worrits one. And then I gets cross. And I gets cold. And I gets under a tree. And I gets a yellow handkerchief. And I ties up my face——as at the present."

Alice looked pityingly at him. "Tying up the face is very good for the toothache," she said.

"And it's very good for the conceit," added the Wasp.

Alice didn't catch the word exactly. "Is that a kind of toothache?" she asked.

The Wasp considered a little. "Well, no,"

148

he said : " it's when you hold up your head——so——without bending your neck."

" Oh, you mean stiff-neck," said Alice.

The Wasp said " That's a new-fangled name. They called it conceit in my time."

" Conceit isn't a disease at all," Alice remarked.

66

" It is though," said the Wasp : "wait till you have it, and then you'll know. And when you catches it, just try tying a yellow handkerchief round your face. It'll cure you in no time ! "

He untied the handkerchief as he spoke, and Alice looked at his wig in great surprise. It was bright yellow like the handkerchief, and all tangled and tumbled about like a heap of sea-weed. " You could make your wig much neater," she said, "if only you had a comb."

" What, you're a Bee, are you ? " the Wasp said, looking at her with more interest. " And you've got a comb. Much honey ? "

" It isn't that kind," Alice hastily explained. " It's to comb hair with——your wig's so *very* rough, you know."

" I'll tell you how I came to wear it," the Wasp said. " When I was young, you know, my ringlets used to wave——"

149

A curious idea came into Alice's head. Almost every one she had met had repeated poetry to her, and she thought she would try if the Wasp couldn't do it too. "Would you mind saying it in rhyme?" she asked very politely.

"It aint what I'm used to," said the Wasp: "however I'll try; wait a bit." He was silent for a few moments, and then began again—

" When I was young, my ringlets waved
    And curled and crinkled on my head:
  And then they said 'You should be shaved,
    And wear a yellow wig instead.'

" But when I followed their advice,
    And they had noticed the effect,
  They said I did not look so nice
    As they had ventured to expect.

" They said it did not fit, and so
    It made me look extremely plain:
  But what was I to do, you know?
    My ringlets would not grow again.

" So now that I am old and gray,
    And all my hair is nearly gone,
  They take my wig from me and say
    'How can you put such rubbish on?'

"And still, whenever I appear,
  They hoot at me and call me 'Pig!'
  And that is why they do it, dear,
  Because I wear a yellow wig."

"I'm very sorry for you," Alice said heartily: "and I think if your wig fitted a little better, they wouldn't tease you quite so much."

"*Your* wig fits very well," the Wasp murmured, looking at her with an expression of admiration: "it's the shape of your head as does it. Your jaws aint well shaped, though—— I should think you couldn't bite well?"

Alice began with a little scream of laughing, which she turned into a cough as well as she could at last she managed to say gravely "I can bite anything I want,"

"Not with a mouth as small as that," the Wasp persisted. "If you was a-fighting, now ——could you get hold of the other one by the back of the neck?"

"I'm afraid not," said Alice.

"Well, that's because your jaws are too short," the Wasp went on: "but the top of your head is nice and round." He took off his own wig as he spoke, and stretched out one claw towards Alice, as if he wished to do the same for her, but she kept out of reach, and would not take the hint. So he went on with his criticisms.

"Then your eyes——they're too much in front, no doubt. One would have done as well as two, if you *must* have them so close——"

Alice did not like having so many personal remarks made on her, and as the Wasp had quite recovered his spirits, and was getting very talkative, she thought she might safely leave him. "I think I must be going on now," she said. "Good-bye."

"Good-bye, and thank-ye," said the Wasp, and Alice tripped down the hill again, quite pleased that she had gone back and given a few minutes to making the poor old creature comfortable.

What Do You Think?

1. In what ways was the Wasp strange? In what ways was he like people you might know?
2. Was the Wasp the kind of person you would like to have around? Why or why not?
3. Do you think Alice really helped the Wasp? Explain your answer.

Taking A Closer Look

1. What was Alice about to do when she decided to help the Wasp?
2. What did Alice do to help the Wasp forget his troubles?
3. How do you know that the Wasp was a complainer?
4. Why did the Wasp tell his story in the form of a poem?
5. What did the Wasp think was the main cause of his un-happiness?
6. In what ways does the Wasp find Alice "strangely shaped"?

The Real Ugly Duckling

More than a hundred years ago in Odense, Denmark, lived a boy named Hans Christian Andersen. Too poor to go to school, young Hans Christian spent his days in his imagination. He listened wide-eyed to the old tales of magic and adventure his grandmother told him. Then he acted them out in his toy theater. Not satisfied with only cardboard actors, he began to train himself. One day he would be a famous actor, he told everyone. To prove it, he would recite poetry, sing, and dance for anyone who would listen.

Unfortunately, all the practice in the world could not help Hans Christian. He was a homely child with a large nose and a long, sad face. Besides, he had no talent at all for acting. When he performed, he tripped over his clumsy legs and big feet. His audiences broke up with laughter. The boy's dream of becoming famous seemed foolish. Only his mother believed in him.

When Hans Christian grew older, he left Odense for Copenhagen. Here, he was certain, would be great chances to become an actor. There were, indeed, more opportunities, but not for Hans Christian. No one in Copenhagen appreciated his dancing or singing. Poor, hungry, and ragged, he became discouraged. Yet still he held to one idea: "First you suffer a great deal, then you become famous."

Then two things happened to change Hans Christian's fortune. First, he made an important decision. Since he couldn't be a successful actor or singer, he would become a great writer. Second, he caught the attention of a wealthy man who sent him to school. At sixteen, the tall, awkward Hans Christian sat with small children to learn. Again people laughed at him, but he held fast to his new dream.

After long years of schooling, Hans Christian began to write plays and books, and soon he turned to tales of magic and adventure. Some were his own tales. Others he borrowed from his grandmother's stories. One by one his fairy tales appeared, and finally they were all published in one book.

Finally Hans Christian had become famous. His tales were different from anything people had read before. Children and grownups alike loved them! Once people had laughed at him. Now even the kings of Europe admired him. He had suffered, but now he was famous.

Later, when Hans Christian Andersen wrote the story of his life, he said that it had been like a fairy tale. And indeed it had. The poor young dreamer had become the friend of kings.

THE UGLY DUCKLING

In his stories Hans Christian Andersen often included
lessons for his readers to think about. What do you
think he wants you to think about in this story? Where
do you think he got the idea for "The Ugly Duckling"?

The country was lovely then. It was summer. The cornfields were yellow. The oats were green. The hay had been put in bundles in the green fields. The stork went about on his long red legs and chattered Egyptian.[1] This was the language he had learned from his good mother. All around the fields were great forests. In the middle of these forests lay deep lakes. Yes, it was beautiful out in the country.

In the sunniest spot there stood an old house with deep water all around it. Great leaves grew from the walls of the house down to the water's edge. Some were so high that little children could stand up under them. Here, hidden among the leaves, a duck sat upon her nest. She was waiting to hatch her ducklings. No one had visited her for a long time. The other ducks would rather swim about in the water than sit and talk with her.

At last one eggshell after another broke open. From all the eggs little heads stuck out.

"Peep! Peep!" they said. And they all came tumbling out as fast as they could. They looked all around them among the green leaves. Their mother let them look as much as they wanted. For green is good for the eyes.

"How big the world is!" said all the young ones. They certainly had more room here than in the eggs.

[1] Egyptian (i-JIP-shən)

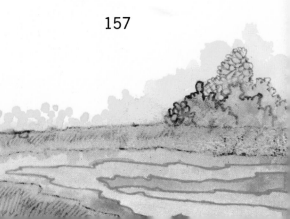

"Do you think this is all the world?" said the mother. "It stretches far across the other side of the garden. But I have never been that far yet. I hope you are all here now." And she stood up. "No, one of you is missing. The largest egg still lies there. I wish it would hatch soon. I am very tired of waiting." And she sat down again.

"Well, how goes it?" asked an old duck who had come to pay her a visit.

"Well, that one egg is taking a long time," said the mother duck. "It will not crack. Now, look at the others. They are the finest little ducks I have ever seen!"

"Let me see the egg that will not hatch," said the old visitor. "You may be sure it is a turkey's egg. I was once cheated in that way. My young ones were afraid of the water. I hate to tell you, but I couldn't get them to go in. I quacked and quacked, but it was no use. Let me see that egg. Yes, it is a turkey's egg. Let it lie there while you teach the other children to swim."

"I think I will sit on it a little longer," said the duck. "I've sat so long now that I can sit a few days more."

At last the great egg broke. "Peep! Peep!" said the duckling as it came out. It was very large and very ugly. The duck looked at it.

"What a large duckling," said she. "None of the others look like that. Can it really be a turkey chick? Well, we shall soon find out. It must go into the water, even if I have to push it."

158

The next day was bright and beautiful. The sun shone on all the green leaves. The mother duck went down to the water with all her family. Splash! She jumped in. "Quack! Quack!" she said, and one duckling after another plunged in. The water closed over their heads. Then, in a moment, they came up and swam like their mother. The big ugly gray one swam with them.

"No, that is no turkey," said the mother duck. "See how well it uses its legs. And see how straight it holds itself. It is my own chick! On the whole, it's quite pretty if one looks at it properly. Quack! Quack! Come with me. I'll lead you out into the great world and present you in the duck yard. But keep close to me

so that no one will step on you. And watch out for the cat!"

And so they came into the duck yard. A terrible row was going on there. Two families were quarreling over an eel's head. And in the end the cat got it.

"See how it goes in the world," said the mother duck. She licked her bill, for she too wanted the eel's head. "Now, use your legs. Shake yourselves and don't turn in your toes. A proper duck turns its toes out, just like father and mother—so! Now bend your necks and say, 'Quack!'"

And they did. But the other ducks looked at them angrily. They said, "Look there. Now we're to have these ducklings hanging on. There are enough of us already! And—ugh—how ugly that duckling yonder looks. We won't stand that!" And one duck flew up at the ugly duckling and bit it in the neck.

"Let it alone," said the mother. "It is not harming anyone."

"Yes, but it's too large and strange," said the duck who had bitten it. "It should be put down."

"Those are pretty children," said an old duck with a rag around her leg. The rag meant that she was very special. "They are all pretty but the big one. I wish the mother could hatch it over again."

"That cannot be done, my lady," replied the mother duck. "The big duckling isn't pretty, but it has a good disposition. Besides, it swims as well as any other. Yes, I may even say it swims better. I think

160

it will grow up pretty, and perhaps even become smaller in time." Then she patted the ugly duckling's neck and smoothed its feathers. "Besides, it is a drake," she said. "His appearance is not so important. I think he will be very strong. He will make his way in the world."

"The other ducklings are pretty enough," said the old duck. "Make yourselves at home. And if you find an eel's head, you may bring it to me."

Now they all felt at home, all except the ugly duckling. Everyone looked down on him. He was made fun of, as much by the ducks as by the chickens. "He is too big," they all said.

Then a turkey nearby blew himself up like a ship in full sail. He came running straight at the ugly

duckling. He gobbled and gobbled and grew quite red in the face. The poor duckling did not know which way to turn. He felt sad because he looked so ugly. He was the joke of the whole duck yard.

So it went on the first day. And afterwards things grew worse and worse. The poor duckling was attacked by everyone. Even his brothers and sisters were quite angry with him. They said, "If only the cat would catch you, you ugly creature." And the mother said, "If only you were far away." The ducks bit him. The chickens pecked at him.

Then he ran off and flew over the fence. The little birds in the bushes flew up in fear.

"They hate me because I am so ugly," thought the duckling. And he shut his eyes and ran farther on. Soon he reached the great marsh where the wild ducks lived. Here he lay a long while, weary and sad.

Toward evening he left the marsh. Wandering on, he came to a poor old cottage. It looked as though it was ready to fall. A storm was coming up and the wind whistled around the duckling. The poor thing could hardly stand against it. The wind blew harder and harder. Then the duckling noticed that one of the hinges of the door was loose. There was a small opening where the door was hanging. He saw he could slip through the crack into the room. And that is what he did.

A woman lived here with her cat and her hen. The cat could arch his back and purr. When anyone patted him the wrong way, his fur gave off sparks. The hen had tiny short legs. But she laid good eggs. The woman loved the hen as if she were her own child.

In the morning the cat and the hen noticed the strange duckling. The cat began to purr and the hen to cluck.

"What is this?" said the woman looking all around. But she could not see well. She thought the duckling was a fat duck that was lost. "What an unusual prize!" she said. "Now I shall have duck's eggs. I hope it is not a drake."

She let the duckling stay on trial for three weeks. But no eggs came. The cat was still master of the house and the hen was the lady. They always said, "We and the world." They thought they were half the world, and by far the better half. The duckling had different ideas, but the hen would not hear of them.

"Can you lay eggs?" she asked.

"No."

"Then will you hold your tongue?"

And the cat said, "Can you arch your back and purr and give off sparks?"

"No."

"Then you will please say nothing when people with sense are speaking."

And the duckling sat in a corner and was very sad. Then one day the fresh air and the sunshine streamed in. The duckling wanted to float on the water. He felt he should speak of his longing to the hen.

"What are you thinking of?" cried the hen. "You have nothing to do. That is why you have these fancy ideas. Lay eggs or purr and these foolish thoughts will go away."

"But it is such a pleasure to float on the water," said the duckling. "It feels so good to let it close over your head when you dive to the bottom."

"Yes, that must be a great pleasure," said the hen. "I think you have gone crazy. Ask the cat about it. He's the cleverest animal I know. Ask him if he likes to float on the water or to dive down. I won't speak about myself!"

"You don't understand me," said the duckling.

"We don't understand you? Then who is to understand you? You surely don't pretend to be cleverer than the cat. I won't say anything of myself. Don't make a fool of yourself. And be thankful for all the kindness you have received. You have a warm room, don't you? And you have us wiser ones to learn something from, don't you? But you are always chattering. It is not pleas-

ant to have you around. Believe me, I speak for your own good. I tell you these things so that you may know I'm your friend. Just learn to lay eggs, or to purr, or to give off sparks!"

"I think I will go out into the wide world," said the duckling.

"Yes, do go," replied the hen.

And so the duckling went away. He floated on the water and dived. Still no one paid attention to him because he was so ugly.

Now came the autumn. The leaves in the forest turned yellow and brown. The wind caught them so that they danced about. Up in the air it was very cold. The clouds hung low, heavy with snow and hail. The poor little duckling did not have an easy time of it.

One evening—the sun was just setting—a whole flock of great, handsome birds came out of the bushes. They were very white, with long necks. They were swans. They gave out a peculiar cry and spread their great broad wings. They flew away from that cold place to warmer lands and open seas. They flew so high that the duckling felt quite strange as he watched them. He turned round and round in the water like a wheel. He let out such a strange, loud cry that he frightened himself.

Soon he could see the handsome birds no longer. He dived down to the very bottom of the pond. When he came up again, he was quite beside himself. Oh, he could not forget those beautiful, happy birds. He did not know their name or where they were flying. But he loved them more than he had ever loved anyone. He did not envy them at all. How could he think of wishing for such loveliness as they had? He would have been glad if only the ducks would have put up with him—the poor ugly creature!

The winter grew cold, very cold. It would be too sad to tell all the trouble the duckling had to go through during the hard winter.

But at long last spring arrived. The duckling lay among the marsh reeds in the sun. The weather began to get warm again and the larks began to sing.

All at once the duckling could flap his wings. They beat the air more strongly than ever before. Then suddenly they took him away. Before he knew where he was, he found himself in a great garden. Trees bent their long branches down to the shores of a lake. Oh, here it was so beautiful, the joy of spring! Suddenly, from the thicket came three lovely white swans. They shook their wings and swam lightly over the water. The duckling knew the wonderful birds at once. He was filled with a sudden strange feeling of sadness.

"I will fly to them, to the royal birds. They will beat me because I, who am so ugly, dare to come near them. But it is better to be killed by *them* than to be snapped at by ducks, pecked at by chickens, or suffer hunger in winter!"

He flew out into the water and swam toward the beautiful swans. They looked at him. They came sailing down upon him, their wings spread wide.

"Kill me!" he cried. He bent his head down upon the water, expecting nothing but death. But what did he see in the clear water? It was himself. But he was no longer a clumsy, gray bird, ugly to look at. He was a—swan!

It does not matter if one is born in a duck yard. It only matters if one has come out of a swan's egg.

The ugly duckling forgot all the trouble he had been through. Now he realized his happiness. The great swans swam round him and stroked him with their bills.

Into the garden came little children who threw bread and corn into the water. The youngest cried, "There is a new one!" And the other children shouted with joy. "Yes, a new one has come." They clapped their hands and danced about. They threw bread and cake into the water for all the swans. And they all said, "The new

swan is the most beautiful of all. He is so young and handsome!" And the old swans all bowed their heads before him.

He felt quite shy now and hid his head under his wing. He did not know what to think. He was so happy and yet not at all proud. He thought how he had been attacked and hated. And now he heard them all saying that he was the most beautiful of all birds. Even the trees bent their branches straight down into the water before him. The sun shone warm on his back. He shook his wings and lifted his long neck. Happily he cried out, "I never dreamed of so much happiness when I was the Ugly Duckling."

—Hans Christian Andersen

What Do You Think?

1. Why were Hans Christian Andersen and the ugly duckling unhappy at first? How did they both find happiness?

2. Where do you think Hans Christian Andersen got his idea for "The Ugly Duckling"? Who was the real ugly duckling?

3. Why didn't the ugly duckling have confidence in himself at first? How did he find confidence?

Taking A Closer Look

1. Tell how the ducks and chickens in the duck yard treated the ugly duckling. Why did they treat him in this way?

2. To help us understand how humans behave, Andersen makes the animals talk and act like people. Name five different animals in the story and tell in what ways each animal talks and acts like a person.

3. In your opinion, what was the happiest part of this tale? What was the saddest part? Explain your answers.

4. "What you are inside is more important than how you look or where you come from." Why do you think this saying is true of the ugly duckling? Think of an example to show what this saying means to you.

Crispus faces a real problem when Sheba, his pet dog, runs off. If your dog were lost in colonial Boston, and you were worried about the dogcatchers, what would you do?

NOT OVER TEN INCHES HIGH

170

That morning, long before the first cock crowed, Crispus was up and on his way to find Sheba. Perhaps if he retraced his steps to all the places they liked best, he might find his little dog.

With fast, long strides Crispus made his way to the docks and down the length of Long Wharf, where they had often spent whole days. There were the boats hugging their moorings and the rows of barrels filled with molasses and rum. And in the counting-houses, heavy-jowled merchants wrapped in great fur coats sat on high stools poring over mountains of figures.

Every few yards, Crispus stopped and called. But no brown and white dog came running. And he grew sadder and sadder. What if she's run away for good? What if she's been caught by a dogcatcher? I'll have no one — and she'll have no one. Crispus blew a bit of warm breath on his cold hands to keep from crying, dug his hands deep into his breeches pockets, and headed for the market. An icy wind whistled round the two-story houses, and the trade signs squeaked shrilly as they swung back and forth on rusted chains.

His head tucked deep into the neck of his jacket, Crispus had just turned into King Street when his ears picked up the bawling screams of cattle and the sharp yelps of hungry dogs. There, in the middle of the street outside the butcher's shop, a small herd of cattle brought in for slaughter milled about in a bellowing, stomping, kicking panic as a pack of street dogs circled them, barking, and nipping at their hocks.

171

The butcher stood in the doorway red-faced and yelling orders to his apprentices, who waded in after the dogs with clubs swinging. Onlookers hung out windows and thronged the street shouting encouragement — some to the dogs, and some to the butcher's boys.

It was not long before a whole brigade of constables, with their whistles tooting and their nightsticks raised, arrived to join the crowd. Cattle stampeded down nearby side streets. Dogs romped past the robust butcher into the shop, then dashed out again, with large hunks of meat locked tight between their jaws.

"After them! After them!" shouted the butcher. And the chase began.

Crispus watched in fascination as little by little the cattle were rounded up and the dogs caught. Then his eyes grew wide with horror. For coming down the street toward him was Sheba, her long tail wagging gaily.

"Sheba!" cried Crispus, but it was too late. A constable had spotted the little dog and had collared her.

172

"Hey, mister," called Crispus breathlessly. "That's my dog. I'll look after her."

"Not anymore you won't," said the officer gruffly. "She's over ten inches high, she is. And the law wants her."

Crispus tagged along beside him, pleading to have his dog released. "You can't take her," he said tearfully. "She's mine."

"Over ten inches high. Do you hear?" snapped the constable. "There's a city ordinance against it."

When they reached the far end of King Street and had crossed the Commons, Sheba was tossed into a high wire cage which served as the city pound. "There she stays," said the officer in a voice full of anger, "until she's properly disposed of." The constable marched off swinging his short stick, his pot belly bulging against his uniform.

Crispus ran after him and tugged at the officer's long coattails. "Please, please," he said, "can't I have my dog?"

"Take it up with the judge," said the officer out of the side of his mouth.

Crispus stood at the cage and choked with sobbing. Sheba tried again and again to scale her way over the wire but fell back each time.

"I'll do just that. I'll go and see the judge," said Crispus suddenly. "Yes, I will." He brushed away the tears with the sleeve of his jacket, then ran across the mall to the courthouse.

As Crispus entered, the bailiff put up a restraining hand, but hearing the boy sob as though his heart were breaking, he let him go by. In minutes Crispus was standing before the judge.

"Please, your honor," he began, "it's about my dog, Sheba."

"What dog?" snapped the judge, austere in his long black robe. "This court has no time for tomfoolery. Bailiff," he called, "show the boy out."

The bailiff moved close to Crispus and was about to set a hand on him when Crispus drew away.

"You can't take my dog away," gulped Crispus. "She's my dog, and you can't take her away." He broke into a torrent of tears.

"Just a moment, bailiff," called the judge. "Let the boy come before me. And now," he said more softly to Crispus, "what is your story?"

Crispus dried his tears and tried to speak calmly. "Sheba and me, we go everywhere. We do everything together. Please, judge, don't take my Sheba."

The judge straightened up. "Well now," he said, "this case needs looking into." He reached for his snuff box, withdrew a pinch and filled his right nostril. He sneezed once, twice, and then a third time. Next he filled the other nostril and sneezed some more. Then he fixed his spectacles to the tip of his nose and smoothed his great woolly wig. "This needs some careful studying," he said. "Ahem, ahem." He slowly looked over the court-room. "Who is the arresting officer?" he asked.

In a little while the constable pushed his way forward and stood before the judge.

"What is the charge?" asked the judge, stroking his chin and regarding the constable with interest.

"Over ten inches high," declared the officer. "And caught while disturbing some cattle."

"Sheba didn't bother the cattle. She was minding her own business. She just happened to be passing by, that's all," broke in Crispus.

"In any case, your honor," continued the constable stiffly, "there is a city ordinance against dogs over ten inches high being loose on the street or otherwise."

"So there is, so there is," the judge quietly whispered under his breath. He took another pinch of snuff and toyed with the edge of his great wooly wig. "Bailiff," he said, "fetch the dog."

Sheba was quickly brought into the courtroom. Crispus went to his knees and threw his arms around the dog's neck. "They can't take you away," he wept.

"Now, young man, get to your feet," said the judge sternly, "and approach the bench. Are you aware that this dog is over ten inches high?"

"No, your honor," said Crispus haltingly. "Last time I measured her she wasn't more than nine."

"But dogs grow, son," said the judge, "and you know that in our city there is an ordinance to protect butchers against just such incidents as this."

"Yes," said Crispus, trying hard to focus his tear-filled eyes.

"However," continued the judge, "perhaps something can be done."

He cleared his throat and rested his elbows on the bench. "Bailiff," he called. "You will please have a barber clip the dog and then return her. You will also bring a measure back with you." The judge then turned toward the arresting officer. "You," he said, "will be good enough to stand by and wait. I shall have further need of you."

In less than half an hour the bailiff was back with a clean-shaven Sheba and a measure.

"And now, constable," said the judge, with a merry twinkle in his eye and a touch of lightness in his voice. "You yourself will have the pleasure of taking the height of the dog."

The constable stepped forward while Crispus and the others looked on in silence. He applied the measure and scratched his head, very much puzzled. Again he applied the measure and looked even more puzzled. Crispus was beginning to understand.

"Well, well," called the judge, with the passing of time, "what has the constable found?"

The constable dropped both hands to his sides and looked sheepish. "Not over ten inches high," he remarked painfully.

"Not over ten inches high," repeated the bailiff showing delight.

"Not over ten inches high," chuckled the judge. He helped himself to another pinch of snuff. Then he rested his elbows on the bench and looked straight at Crispus. "The case is dismissed."

Crispus picked up Sheba and hugged her to him. "Not over ten inches high—not over ten inches high!" he cried joyfully. "They're not going to take you away from me." He started in the direction of the door, then stopped and turned to the judge. And his deep brown eyes were filled with thanks.

In another moment the bailiff was beside Crispus holding open the courtroom door. "She's a right pretty dog you have there," he said.

Crispus looked up at him, a wide smile slowly breaking across his face. "Sheba and me, we both thank you, sir," he said and stepped into the hall.

"Another thing," said the bailiff pleasantly. "If I were you, I'd forget about her height. Her kind never does grow any bigger."

"Did you hear that?" said Crispus, and he squeezed Sheba to him. The little dog wriggled all over and licked his face till he had to put her down. Then she thumped the ground with her tail and led the way out of the courthouse. Crispus sang as loud as he was able:

> A loaf of bread, a double bed,
> And scuttles full of coals;
> A spotted hog, my little dog,
> And shoes with worn-down soles . . .

"Come, Sheba. Up, girl!" he cried, clapping his hands. And up she sprang into his arms. "Oh, Sheba, you're my best and only friend. Friends forever," he crooned into her droopy ear. "And you're a fine watchdog, too," he whispered.

—*Harry Levy*

180

What Do You Think?

1. Why did Crispus care so much about Sheba's being taken away? Tell about a time when you lost a pet or had something precious taken away from you. How did you feel?
2. Do you think the ordinance about dogs not being over ten inches high was a good law? Would such a law be a good one today? Explain your answer.
3. In what ways is the Boston of colonial times different from your own town or city today? Are they the same in any way?

Taking A Closer Look

1. How might Crispus have described Sheba?
2. Under two columns headed *Sounds* and *Sights* list some of the things Crispus saw and heard on Long Wharf and in the market place.
3. In a sentence or two, describe the duties of the constable, the judge, and the bailiff.
4. Read the underlined words in the sentences below. What do they tell you about how each person felt about Sheba's height?
   a. "Not over ten inches high," the constable remarked painfully.
   b. "Not over ten inches high," repeated the bailiff.
   c. "Not over ten inches high," chuckled the judge.

Here are four stories written by young people about your age. The stories are as different from one another as are the authors themselves. As you read these stories, can you guess where the young writers may have gotten their ideas?

Quiet Fishing

My float was silent and still, and its yellow and white markings gleamed in my ever fading eyes. The gentle fall of distant water could be heard as it pounded the stream. My mind went with the water, up and down, in and out, moving forward as it went. You let your mind run away, as if swept away by the stream.

—*Michael Freeman*
England

182

Gaining My First Goal

Up, up, up and oh help. Why didn't it go in like it should have? It should go up and in so very perfectly, and it's got to. Up, up, ah, it's going, going, gone. Blast it. I know I'm standing wrongly and yes, um Barbara always says, "The sun's in my eyes." Well, "The sun's in my eyes." But it can't be, I'm inside.

I know, maybe I'm better at long shots. When Barbara takes them she stands nine feet away, and I'm four years younger and one foot smaller, so, four plus one is *six* and nine take away six equals *two*. Therefore I stand two feet away.

Hey this looks better, just right. Oh, not again it can't miss. But it's not, it's going to go in.

Oh help, aren't I just so good.

—Pamela McHenry
New Zealand

183

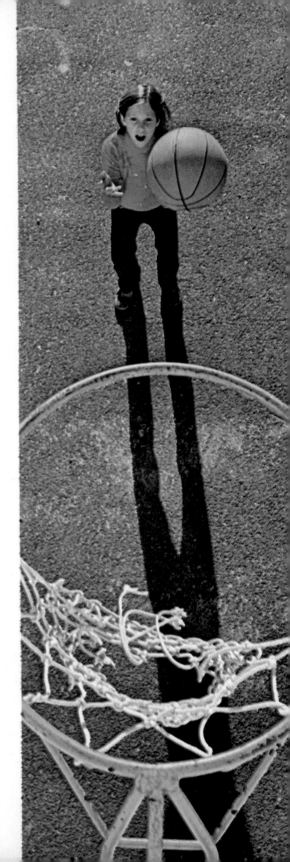

The football players run faster and faster when suddenly whirling colors appear on the field. The football players are dancing now. They begin running again but they are running in slow motion. The football is thrown and in mid air it turns into a whirling colorful grapefruit. Suddenly a siren-like sound comes from the spinning grapefruit. The pitch of the sound gets higher and it becomes piercing. It still gets higher until it is a deafening, screeching shrill. Then it stops! The grapefruit hits the ground but does not bounce up from the ground the slightest amount. But there are no football players rushing for this still grapefruit. The field is lone and empty. The only thing on the field is this one grapefruit. It begins shrinking and getting smaller and smaller. If one listens carefully one can hear a faint song which has no source.

—*John Auerbach,*
United States

Why They Changed Their Minds

At the first of the year my so-called friends called me "Too Tall Irma." That really made me angry because I couldn't help it. The story changed when we played baseball and they all wanted me on their team. I could run, I could catch, and I could really hit the ball.

—*Irma Hernandez*
United States

185

Everywhere Tales

In all parts of the world there have been storytellers
who could hold their listeners spellbound with tales of
wonder and adventure. Often these tales spoke of
natural events people feared or could not understand.
Sometimes stories of mighty heroes and heroines were
created to give courage and comfort to people. And
once in a while a good tale was told just for fun. The
old tales of this unit were told and retold for hundreds
of years before they were written down.

This folk tale takes place on an island in the South Pacific. The people of the island have a problem. You decide whether the solution is a good one or not.

The Battle That Tilted the Sea

Once, two boys of Opoa[1] went fishing in a holy place. Because they did this, the island of Raiatea[2] was destroyed by a flood. Several hundreds of years later the waters withdrew, and people lived there again.

The chief of the island at this time was a man named Covered-with-Scars. He had a son called Hiro,[3] who was ten years old.

[1] Opoa (ah-POH-ə)   [2] Raiatea (rah-yah-TAY-ah)   [3] Hiro (HEER-oh)

Hiro was a very wise and clever boy. He knew many things that most boys don't bother to learn about. For instance, he knew where the bush turkeys buried eggs on the sandy beaches. He knew where the best bread-fruit grew. He knew the best pools in which to catch fish. And he knew all about the great sea monsters that guarded the openings in the coral reefs around the islands. Hiro knew so much that his father often asked his advice about important matters.

One day Covered-with-Scars said to Hiro, "My son, I am very troubled."

"What about, Father?" asked Hiro.

"Too many sharks are getting past the guardian of our reef into the lagoon," said Hiro's father. "Ten of my people have been eaten by them in the past week alone. If this keeps up, we won't have anybody left alive on the island. What do you suppose is the matter?"

Hiro thought for a minute. Then he said, "The giant octopus that guards our reef must have gone to sleep again, Father. That's my opinion."

Covered-with-Scars nodded. "That's what I think too," he said.

"Shall I go and wake him up?" asked Hiro.

"It won't do any good, I'm afraid," said Hiro's father. "He'll stay awake for a few days and then fall asleep again. Then the sharks will come into the lagoon as they please. No, Hiro. We need a better answer to our shark problem than that lazy old octopus."

"He may be lazy," Hiro said, "but he's a fine shark fighter. When he's awake, no shark can get past him, Father. He's not like the giant turtle that guards the Tahaa[1] reef. And he's not like the giant eel that stands in the passage to Bora Bora.[2] They stay awake all the time, it's true. But they can't fight sharks as well as our lazy octopus."

"Be that as it may," said Covered-with-Scars. "Something must be done to protect our people from the sharks. Have you any ideas, Hiro?"

"Give me a little time," said Hiro. "Perhaps I can think of something."

"Take all the time you need, my son," said Hiro's father. "But be sure you think up a clever plan. It must be a better plan than waking up that sleepy old octopus."

So Hiro went off and thought a long time. How, he wondered, could he protect the people of the island from the sharks? He finally thought of a possible way to do it. But he wasn't sure it would work, and he said nothing to his father about his plan.

Instead, he swam far out in the lagoon the next morning, all by himself. He floated around out there until he

[1] Tahaa (ta-HAH-ah)   [2] Bora Bora (BOR-ə BOR-ə)

190

saw a big shark swimming by. It had come in through the reef opening past the sleeping octopus. The shark saw Hiro at the same time. He came swimming up to take Hiro in one bite for his breakfast. But just as he opened his mouth wide to snap off Hiro's leg, Hiro cried out. "Wait, shark! Do not eat me! I have a message for your master, the King of the Sharks!"

"That doesn't sound very likely," said the shark. He shut his mouth so his sharp teeth wouldn't show.

"All I want," said Hiro, "is a chance to talk to your king."

"Get on my back and I'll take you to him," said the shark. "And if you've lied to me about having a message for him, I'll eat you up then."

So Hiro mounted the shark's rough back and held on to his big fin tightly. He was carried swiftly through the reef opening into the great ocean. There—deep, deep down under the waves—was the King of the Sharks. He lay on the sea bottom, covered with barnacles, sand, and seaweed.

"This boy on my back says he has a message for you, Master," said the other shark.

The King of the Sharks moved his huge body slightly. Barnacles and seaweed began to slip off his skin. "What is your message, boy?" asked the King of the Sharks.

"I thought you'd want to know something," answered Hiro. "The giant turtle who guards the reef opening at Tahaa tells everybody you're getting old and weak. He says you can no longer defeat even the weakest reef guardian of the islands. The turtle of Tahaa challenges you to a battle, Your Majesty."

At once the King of the Sharks became very angry. He swished his huge tail, shook the barnacles off his belly, and gnashed his many rows of teeth together like thunder. He roared angrily, "We'll see about that foolish turtle!" And he set off with the speed of lightning to the reef opening at Tahaa. Hiro, on the other shark, followed him to see the excitement. They found the giant turtle there, guarding the opening.

When the huge turtle saw the King of the Sharks coming, he called out, "Halt, Shark! You cannot go past me, even though you are the King of the Sharks himself! I am the guardian here. You shall not pass!"

"See if you can stop me, you foolish turtle!" roared the Shark King. He swam at the turtle. And almost before Hiro knew what was happening, the Shark King opened his enormous jaws very wide. He swallowed the turtle down, shell and all. "Old and weak, am I?" laughed the King of the Sharks. "What do you think now?" He turned around and saw Hiro. Then he said, "There, boy. That ought to teach him to test his betters, don't you think?"

Slyly Hiro said, "He wasn't the only reef guardian that thinks you're old and weak, Your Majesty. The giant eel who guards the reef opening at Bora Bora thinks so too. He wants to battle you also."

"He does, does he?" And the King of the Sharks set out instantly for Bora Bora. He was burning with anger once more. "I'll show him that the King of the Sharks is still the most powerful creature in the world!" Hiro and the shark that carried him followed again. They were eager to see who would win this battle.

The Shark King soon came in sight of the Bora Bora reef. At once the giant eel who guarded the opening rose up to his full height. Standing upon his tail, with his sharp teeth bared, he said, "Hold on, Shark! I am the guardian here. You shall not go past me into the lagoon. It doesn't matter to me that you are the King of the Sharks!"

"Get out of my way," shouted the Shark King, "If you don't, I'll treat you as I treated the turtle of Tahaa!"

"How is that?" asked the eel.

"Like this," replied the Shark King. He opened his mighty jaws. Then he swallowed down the giant eel as if it were a tiny sardine.

"Now, boy," said the Shark King to Hiro. "Do you believe I am the most powerful creature in the sea?"

"I certainly do, Your Majesty," said Hiro. "But that giant octopus who guards the reef at Raiatea doesn't agree with me. He's a lazy old fellow, and seldom on the job. But he thinks he can whip you in battle any time you care to try him."

"There's no better time than now!" cried the King of the Sharks. He snapped his teeth together and made such a loud noise that it hurt Hiro's ears. "Come on. We shall teach your octopus at Raiatea a lesson he'll never forget!" And he swam rapidly off to Raiatea. Hiro followed, still holding on to his shark's back.

When they came near the reef opening at Raiatea, Hiro shouted, "Wait, Your Majesty! You want to fight him fair, I'm sure. And perhaps he's asleep. So why not be sure he's awake and ready to fight his best? Call out to him that you are coming!"

At once, the Shark King called out in a voice that could be heard for a hundred miles. "Octopus of Raiatea! I, the King of the Sharks, am coming to fight you! Wake up, you lazy fighter. Prepare to meet your death!" The Shark King was all blown up with pride after defeating the turtle and the eel so easily.

Well, the octopus of Raiatea woke up. He yawned and stretched and answered in a sleepy voice. "I was having a lovely nap. But now you've spoiled everything by waking me up. So come on and fight me, if you must. But I'd much rather go back to sleep. I am the guardian here. You will not get past me, Shark!"

Then, to prepare for the battle, the octopus reached four of his long strong legs down beneath the sea. He wrapped them around a large rock in the sea bottom to anchor himself. He stretched his other four legs across the opening in the coral reef. Then he waited for the Shark King's charge.

It came at once. Like an angry, swift shadow, the Shark King swam at the octopus. Jaws snapping, he rammed against the four legs of the octopus that were barring the entrance. Instantly, those huge legs wrapped themselves around the Shark King's body like bands of iron. Then the octopus let go his hold on the rock under the sea. He brought his other four legs up and wrapped them around the Shark's thrashing body. Only the Shark's jaws were free of the octopus' legs. The Shark twisted his mighty head this way and that, trying to bite off those crushing legs. But he couldn't quite reach them with his teeth.

The octopus slowly began to draw his legs tighter and tighter around the King of the Sharks. The legs were squeezing, squeezing, squeezing the great fish until he gasped and groaned. Madly the Shark threw himself about, trying to escape the octopus. But those strong legs only squeezed tighter and tighter.

The terrible battle between these two sea monsters went on and on for six hours. Each fought with every muscle and nerve and trick to defeat the other. Their fight caused a mighty turmoil in the sea from the surface of the waves clear down to the deepest deeps. The battle was so fierce that it caused the whole ocean floor to tilt. Huge tidal waves formed and went crashing into the land all over the world.

At last the Shark King whispered, "That's enough. I give in! You're squeezing me to death. I know I have been defeated. Now let me go. I was only joking about killing you anyhow. So let me go, what do you say?"

"Oh, no!" said the octopus, squeezing harder than ever. "I shall kill you, King of the Sharks, for spoiling my nice nap!"

197

"Please let me go, good octopus," begged the Shark.

The octopus paid no attention. He went on squeezing. Then, when the Shark King was nearly dead, Hiro left his place on the small shark's back and went over to the octopus. "I am one of your people of Raiatea, dear guardian," he said. "While you have slept, many sharks have gone past you through the reef. They have eaten a lot of people from the island. So why not spare the life of this King of the Sharks now? Then you'll be able to sleep as much as you like from now on. And you can keep your people safe from sharks as well."

"How is that?" asked the octopus. "I admit I am very sleepy much of the time. And I don't keep a very good watch on the opening. But I don't quite see how sparing this monster's life will help things in any way."

Hiro said, "Make him promise you that he will never trouble any man, woman, or child of Raiatea ever again. Make him promise that all his shark people will leave us alone forever. Tell him to leave us alone whether we are swimming, fishing, bathing, or sailing. If he promises that, we won't need a reef guardian any more. You can sleep for the rest of your life, if you care to."

The octopus loosened his legs from around the King of the Sharks. Now the fish could talk. "You heard what this boy said just now, didn't you?" the octopus asked the Shark King. "Will you promise all that if I spare your life?"

"Yes! Yes! Gladly!" cried the Shark King, drawing a deep breath. "I and my people will never trouble the

198

people of this island again. I swear it. Only spare my life!"

So the octopus unwrapped his legs and let the King of the Sharks go free. And Hiro, knowing that now he was safe, climbed on the Shark King's back. He asked to be taken home to his father's house. He wanted to spread the word of the Shark King's promise. The giant octopus, relieved of his duties as reef guardian, yawned widely and went back to sleep.

That is why the people of Raiatea have no fear of sharks to this day.

—Retold by James Holding

What Do You Think?

1. Why, according to this story, do the sharks of the deep sea stay out of the lagoon?
2. Hiro tricked the Shark King into doing just what he wanted. What do you think Hiro may have known about the Shark King that made him think his trick would work?
3. Think of another title for this story and tell why you think your title is a good one.

Taking A Closer Look

1. How does this "why" story explain tidal waves?
2. How do you know that this story couldn't really happen?
3. Why do you think Hiro didn't fight the Shark King himself?
4. Why didn't Hiro let the octopus kill the Shark King?
5. Can you think of other folk tales in which a small hero outwits a large enemy?

"The Sun Callers"
and Other Tales of How and Why

Do you ever wonder how the sun rose, or how the
Milky Way came to be, or why the sun is brighter than
the moon? From earliest times such wonders of nature
have amazed and puzzled people in all parts of the
world. Often stories have been told to help "explain"
how and why things are the way they are.

The Sun Callers

A tale told by the Hopi Indians

At a certain place north of Oraibi,[1] Coyote was living there, and a little beyond that the rooster was living. Now, it was in the dark of the night, and Coyote was going around looking for something to eat. There in the darkness he met the rooster, who was sitting on a high rock. He greeted the rooster, saying, "Ha'u," and the rooster greeted Coyote the same way.

Coyote said, "What are you doing there? Why are you not at home this time of the night?"

The rooster said, "I have work to do. I have to make the sun rise."

Coyote said, "You take yourself too seriously. Anyone can make the sun rise."

The rooster answered, "No, indeed, it is only I who can do it."

Coyote said, "On the contrary, I am the one who has the power to make the sun come up."

[1] Oraibi (oh-RIGH-bee)

"Let us have a test," the rooster said. "Whoever makes the sun appear, he shall be acknowledged as the Sun Caller."

"That is good," Coyote said. "I will try first."

He sat back on his haunches, pointed his nose toward the sky, and howled to summon the sun. He went on doing this until he was breathless, but the sky remained as black as ever.

"Enough," the rooster said, "Now I will try." He stretched his neck, flapped his wings, and crowed. Once, twice, several times he crowed, but still the night was black.

Coyote said, "Now it is my turn," and again he howled until he was breathless, but around them there was still nothing but darkness.

The rooster said, "You are wasting your time. I will show you how it is done." He stretched his neck, flapped his wings, and crowed. Again and again he called the sun, but nothing happened.

"Now pay attention," Coyote said. "This is the way to do it." He put his nose up and howled with great feeling, telling the sun it was time to appear. But everything was still the same, and there was only darkness all around them.

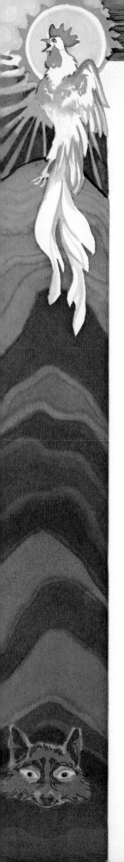

They went on this way, taking turns all through the night. And one time after the rooster crowed, things were a little lighter. "You see," the rooster said, "I am beginning to do it."

Then Coyote tried again, and things were a little lighter still. Coyote said, "It is quite clear that I did better than you."

But the sun had not appeared, and the rooster tried once more. He filled his lungs with air, stretched his neck, flapped his wings, and crowed mightily. And as he did so, the red edge of the sun appeared over the horizon.

"My friend," the rooster said, "you can judge for yourself. As anyone can see, it was I who brought the sun up from down below."

Coyote said, "Yes, I acknowledge it. You have powerful medicine. You are the Sun Caller."

Coyote went away. But he kept thinking, "I almost did it. Once when I called, the night grew a little lighter. Perhaps with practice I can do it." And even to this time, every so often in the night you can hear Coyote trying again to make the sun rise. But the rooster, he is the one that really does it. And because his work goes on and on without ever ending, he has grown hoarse. You can hear it for yourself.

—*Retold by Harold Courlander*
American Southwest

How the Milky Way Came to Be

Up there, in the sky, there are billions of stars. No one knows how many, because no one can count them. And to think that among them is a bright road which is made of wood ashes,—nothing else!

Long ago, the sky was pitch black at night, but people learned in time to make fires to light up the darkness.

One night, a young girl, who sat warming herself by a wood fire, played with the ashes. She took the ashes in her hands and threw them up to see how pretty they were when they floated in the air. And as they floated away, she put more wood on the fire and stirred it with a stick. Bright sparks flew everywhere and wafted high, high into the night. They hung in the air and made a bright road across the sky, looking like silver and diamonds.

And there the road is to this day. Some people call it the Milky Way. Some call it the Stars' Road. But no matter what you call it, it is the path made by a young girl many, many years ago, who threw the bright sparks of her fire high up into the sky to make a road in the darkness.

—*Retold by Charlotte and Wolf Leslau*
South Africa

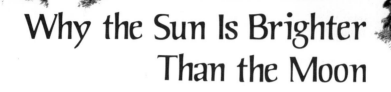

Why the Sun Is Brighter Than the Moon

A tale told by the Lilloet[1] Indians

Once the sun was pale, as pale as the moon.

The sun saw a boy fishing. The boy wore a garment of feathers, and the feathers were bright. The sun said to himself, "If I had such a garment, I would be more splendid than the moon."

The sun came down to the boy. "Give me your feather robe," he said. "And I will give you my goatskin blanket for it."

The boy looked at the plain goatskin blanket. He looked at the feather cloak. "My grandmother made this for me," he said. "I cannot give it to you."

"But you can say that the sun gave this blanket to you. Is there anyone else who has a blanket from the sun?"

"My grandmother was long in making this robe," the boy said. "And longer in getting the feathers for it."

"Your grandmother can look into the sky every day and see her feather robe if you give it to me."

[1] *Lilloet* (LIL-ə-wət)

206

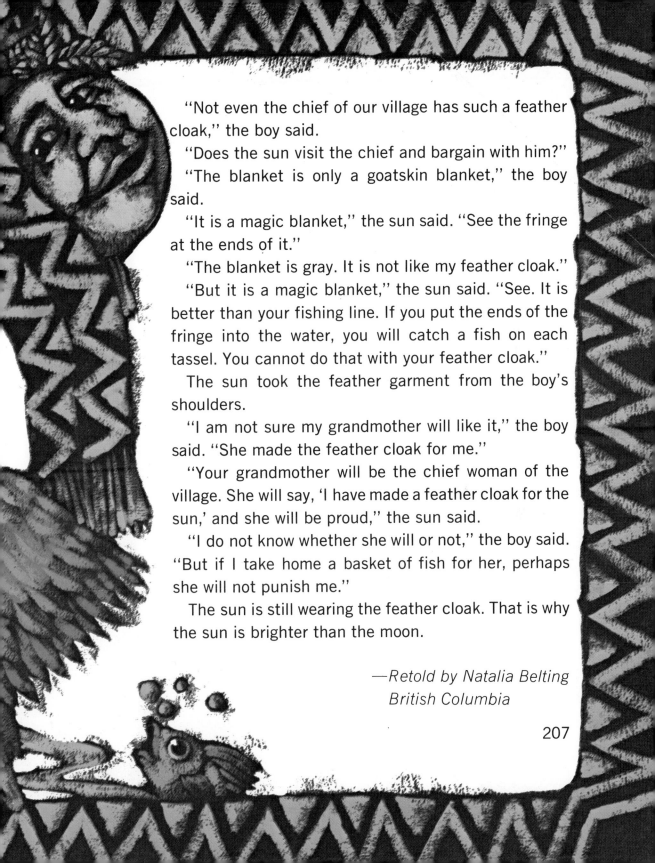

"Not even the chief of our village has such a feather cloak," the boy said.

"Does the sun visit the chief and bargain with him?"

"The blanket is only a goatskin blanket," the boy said.

"It is a magic blanket," the sun said. "See the fringe at the ends of it."

"The blanket is gray. It is not like my feather cloak."

"But it is a magic blanket," the sun said. "See. It is better than your fishing line. If you put the ends of the fringe into the water, you will catch a fish on each tassel. You cannot do that with your feather cloak."

The sun took the feather garment from the boy's shoulders.

"I am not sure my grandmother will like it," the boy said. "She made the feather cloak for me."

"Your grandmother will be the chief woman of the village. She will say, 'I have made a feather cloak for the sun,' and she will be proud," the sun said.

"I do not know whether she will or not," the boy said. "But if I take home a basket of fish for her, perhaps she will not punish me."

The sun is still wearing the feather cloak. That is why the sun is brighter than the moon.

—Retold by Natalia Belting
British Columbia

How the Birds
Came to Have Their Many Colors

A tale told by the Tahltan[1]

In the days when all the birds lived together in one village, there was war between Raven and Grizzly Bear.

Raven called the birds. "Tomorrow we will fight Grizzly Bear. Today I will give a feast. Today we will dance the war dance."

Then Raven got out the pots of war paint and painted the birds. He painted stripes on the birds, and lines that were straight and lines that were sharp and jagged and lines that made circles. He painted the birds with black and green and purple and yellow and red. He painted Mallard Duck and Baldpate Duck and Teal. Raven painted Nutcracker and Cedar Waxwing. He painted Warbler and he painted Robin's breast red and made him war chief.

[1] *Tahltan* (TAHL-tən)

208

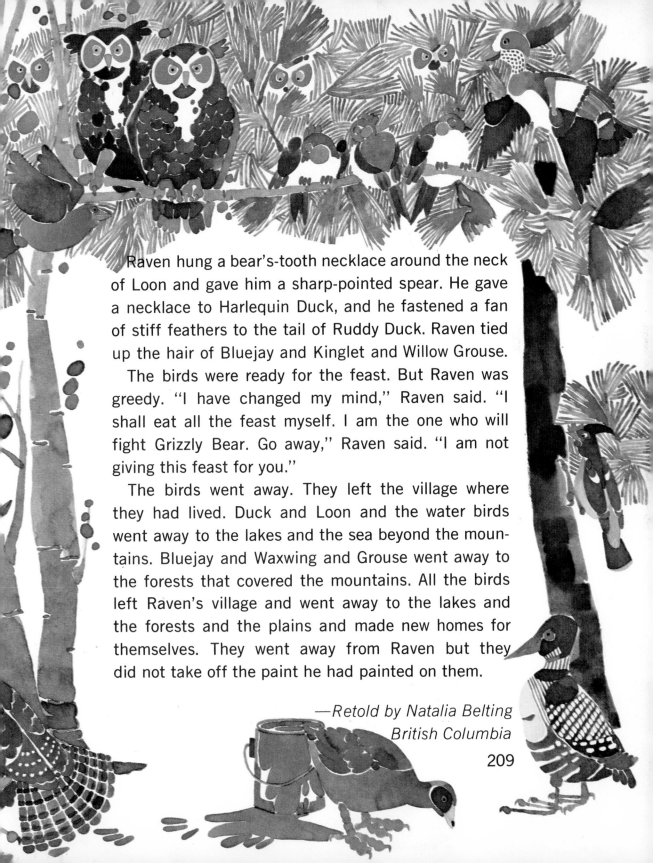

Raven hung a bear's-tooth necklace around the neck of Loon and gave him a sharp-pointed spear. He gave a necklace to Harlequin Duck, and he fastened a fan of stiff feathers to the tail of Ruddy Duck. Raven tied up the hair of Bluejay and Kinglet and Willow Grouse.

The birds were ready for the feast. But Raven was greedy. "I have changed my mind," Raven said. "I shall eat all the feast myself. I am the one who will fight Grizzly Bear. Go away," Raven said. "I am not giving this feast for you."

The birds went away. They left the village where they had lived. Duck and Loon and the water birds went away to the lakes and the sea beyond the mountains. Bluejay and Waxwing and Grouse went away to the forests that covered the mountains. All the birds left Raven's village and went away to the lakes and the forests and the plains and made new homes for themselves. They went away from Raven but they did not take off the paint he had painted on them.

—Retold by Natalia Belting
British Columbia

209

Nature Cannot Be Changed

One day, a rabbit and a monkey were talking together. However, while talking, each of them constantly gave in to his own bad habit. The monkey, of
course, kept scratching himself with his paw. The
rabbit, fearing to be attacked by an enemy, kept turning his head about in all directions. The two animals
were not able to keep still.

"It's really amazing," said the rabbit to the monkey,
"that you cannot stop scratching yourself even for a
moment."

"It's not more amazing than to see you always turning your head for no good reason," answered the
monkey.

"Oh, I could easily stop doing that," said the rabbit,
"if I only wanted to."

"Very well! Let's see if you can. Let's both try, you
and I, to keep still. The one who moves first will lose
the bet."

210

The rabbit agreed. And so they both watched to see if the other moved.

Soon it became impossible for both of them. The monkey itched all over. Never in his life had he itched so badly. The rabbit, on the other hand, was sure that some enemy was going to jump on him from behind.

Finally, when the rabbit could stand it no longer, he said, "Our bet did not mean that we could not tell each other stories to pass the time. Or did it?" "It did not," answered the monkey, foreseeing some trick on the part of the rabbit. The monkey was planning to use the same trick himself. "All right then, I'll start," said the rabbit. "Imagine, one day when I was in an open field, I was in terrible danger. . . ." "Strangely enough the same thing happened to me one day," interrupted the monkey. "Oh really?" continued the rabbit. "I saw dogs jumping through the field in all directions. They came from the left, from the right, from the front, from behind. I turned my head this way, that way. . . . You see? Like this. . . ." To make his point, the rabbit turned his head in all the directions he had mentioned in his story.

211

Of course the monkey too had a story to tell. "That day," he said, "I was bothered by a group of children who kept throwing stones at me. They threw one here, and another there. . . ." With each place he mentioned in the story, he gave himself a good thump with his paw to stop the itching.

The rabbit, who knew why the monkey was doing that, burst out laughing. Then he said to his friend, "Let us be frank. As much as we would like to, we cannot change our natures. This proves it. Neither of us has won the bet, nor lost it."

—Retold by Charlotte and Wolf Leslau
Sierra Leone

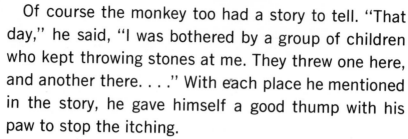

What Do You Think?

1. Which of these tales did you enjoy the most? Tell why.
2. Do you agree that nature cannot be changed? For example, could you change your own nature in any way if you wanted to? Tell why or why not.
3. What event of nature is the most amazing or puzzling to you? Create your own tale to "explain" this event of nature.

Taking A Closer Look

1. What questions does the tale "The Sun Callers" try to answer?
2. What is the Milky Way? Try to imagine another explanation of how the Milky Way came to be.
3. When the boy came back to his grandmother with a goatskin blanket instead of her feather cloak, how do you think she acted? What might have happened?
4. Why do you suppose the birds didn't change back to the way they looked before Raven gave them their many colors?
5. Did the monkey and the rabbit really want to change their ways? How can you tell?

213

The Inuit, people of the arctic plain, were sick and hungry. They depended on Sedna to save them. But Sedna, spirit of the sea, had troubles of her own.

SEDNA

Winter's darkness cast
her shadow over the arctic plain.
The Inuit were hungry and sick.
They longed to fill their stomachs
with the tender meat
of the seal and walrus.

214

Day after day the hunters
waited for Sedna,
the powerful sea spirit,
to release her animals.

   The Inuit called to the Angakok
to work his special magic.
"Please help our people.
Ask the sea spirit to
send forth her gifts."

   When the Angakok
chanted his magic song,
the earth trembled
and the sea churned.

   As he listened to the troubled sea,
Sedna rose from the waves.
She paid no attention to the pleas of the Angakok.
Instead she told a story
to the man of magic.

   "When I was young and beautiful,
I was wooed by many men.
But I loved only one.
His song was so enchanting
that I agreed to become his wife.

"Much later I discovered
that he was a cunning spirit,
a sea bird who had changed him
into a man. To take on human shape
he had shed his feathers
and removed his beak.

"We lived among the petrels, and their
constant chatter was like the cries of
a thousand winds. Oh, how frightened
and confused I became.
I longed for the peace of my village.

"One day I left the cliff nest
and returned to my people.
I begged them to save me.

"But the bird spirit was too powerful.
He made the dogs howl and caused
huge waves to swallow the huts.
Many people and animals died.

"'You must return Sedna to me,'
the bird spirit warned. But my
father did not listen. We climbed
into an oomyak to escape. 'Return Sedna,'
demanded the petrel, once again.

217

"My father shivered when he looked up
and saw the sky grow black.
Helpless against the fierce bird spirit,
he threw me into the icy waters.
I struggled to breathe
and clung to the boat.

"To save himself my father struck
at my hands.

"My fingers broke into little pieces
and fell into the sea.

"As I watched, I saw my fingers become
shiny seals, fat walruses, and great
whales. And so I became mother of
all sea beasts. Now I live beneath
the sea. I am a powerful spirit,"
she sighed, "but I am clumsy.
I cannot plait my hair."

The Angakok was moved
by Sedna's sad story.
He knew what he must do.

Quickly he plunged
past the ice floes
and followed Sedna
to the bottom of the sea.

He found Sedna in a dark hut.
The entrance was guarded by a giant dog.
Sedna was covered with seaweed,
and little animals crawled in her hair.
In a bitter tone she demanded:
"Plait my hair and rid me
of these animals."

The Angakok replied:
"Yes, I will do so.
But you must promise to send
your gifts of food to our people.
Drive the seal and walrus
toward us so that we may live!"

Sedna agreed.
She guided the seals up
through the breathing holes,
letting the hunters trap them.
The women prepared the seals
and cut off large chunks of meat
for the hungry people.
Joy came to the Inuit.
They gave thanks
before the great feast.

The sea was calm once more,
for the powerful mother
of all sea beasts was pleased.
She was grateful to the Angakok
for arranging her hair
and satisfied that the people
had shown respect for her bounty.

The Inuit know that
whenever there is
hunger and sickness
it is because the spirits
of the dead are unhappy.
The living must never forget them.

—Adapted by Beverly Brodsky McDermott

What Do You Think?

1. Do you think Sedna really helped the Inuit? Why or why not?
2. The story of Sedna is written like poetry. Is this a good way to tell this story? Explain your answer.

Taking A Closer Look

1. Why did the Inuit need Sedna's help?
2. Who had Sedna married?
3. Why did Sedna's father decide to return her to the bird spirit?
4. Where did seals, walruses, and whales come from?
5. Why was Sedna unhappy as the spirit of the sea?
6. How did the Angakok help Sedna?
7. What did Sedna do in return for the Angakok's help?

WHY the SEA is SALT

This old Norwegian folk tale, rewritten as a play,
explains a mystery that puzzled people long ago.
According to this play, why is the sea salt?

CHARACTERS:

STORYTELLER
RICH BROTHER
POOR BROTHER
OLD BEGGAR
POOR BROTHER'S WIFE
1ST VISITOR
2ND VISITOR
3RD VISITOR
4TH VISITOR
5TH VISITOR

6TH VISITOR
SEA CAPTAIN
MEMBERS OF HIS CREW

*(The curtain is down. Story-
teller strolls to center stage
from left carrying a guitar.
At center stage Storyteller
makes a deep bow to the audience over the guitar, which is
held in place.)*

STORYTELLER:

There were two brothers as
you shall hear,
And one was rich and one
was poor.
The poor one stands at the
rich one's door,
A-begging of food and nothing more.

(Storyteller returns to the left side of the stage and sits cross-legged on the floor as the curtain rises . . . .)

SCENE I

TIME: *Long ago*

PLACE: *A wood with the terrace of a house just visible at right of stage. (The Rich Brother and the Poor Brother are talking. The Rich Brother, richly dressed, stands on his terrace, his back to his front door. The Poor Brother is in rags and stands facing his brother, but in such a way that the audience can see his face, which wears a pleading expression.)*

RICH BROTHER: This is the fourth time you've come begging, and I say I have had enough. Begone and don't bother me again!

POOR BROTHER: But, Brother, I beseech you. My wife and I are without a morsel to eat. Help me this *one* time and I will bother you no more.

RICH BROTHER: *(Hesitates, scowls, then throws up his hands.)* Very well then. But this is the last time. *(He enters the house and reappears with two loaves of bread and a side of bacon.)* Here, take this and begone. *(He goes quickly back into the house.)*

(Poor Brother turns from the terrace and walks down the path through the wood. From stage left, an old beggar

enters and meets him on the path.)

OLD BEGGAR: In the name of charity, give a poor old starving man a morsel to eat.

POOR BROTHER: I have just been a-begging myself and yet I am not so poor that I can't help someone who is worse off than I. At least I have food and you have none. Here, take this. *(He hands over the two loaves and is about to cut the side of bacon in half when the beggar stops him.)*

OLD BEGGAR: Oh enough, enough! Do not cut the bacon. Keep it for now and your generosity will be rewarded.

POOR BROTHER: And how will that be? Surely you are hardly in a position to reward me.

OLD BEGGAR: I will tell you something. *(He draws close to Poor Brother as if to share a secret.)* Not far from here is the entrance to the underground home of the dwarfs. Go there with the bacon. They love bacon and I happen to know they have none, so they will want yours. But don't give it to them until they agree to give you in return a little hand mill, which they keep hidden behind the door. When you have it, meet me here and I will tell you how to use it.

POOR BROTHER: Thank you, good man. Now tell me how to find the entrance to the dwarfs' home.

OLD BEGGAR: *(Turning to point down stage left, while Poor Brother bends to follow the direction in which he is pointing.)* You follow that path until you come to a large stone and then . . .

CURTAIN FALLS

226

(Storyteller strolls to center stage as before.)

STORYTELLER: So the Poor Brother found the home of the dwarfs where they live down among the roots of these very trees. *(Gesturing.)* They wanted the bacon, just as the old man said they would, and they offered many fine things in exchange for it. But the Poor Brother wouldn't trade unless they gave him the mill. So at last they did.

(Storyteller returns to the left side of the stage and sits cross-legged on the floor as the curtain rises. . . .)

SCENE II

TIME: *A little later*

PLACE: *The path in the wood. (Poor Brother hurries toward the Old Beggar, who has been waiting for him. Poor Brother is carrying the mill.)*

OLD BEGGAR: Good, good! I see you have it.

POOR BROTHER: *(Grinning happily.)* That I have, and I am eager to know how it works, for surely this is a magic mill.

OLD BEGGAR: It is a magic mill. You have only to ask it for whatever you want and it will grind out your wish. It will keep on grinding until you say, "Good little mill, I thank you for enough." *(He shakes his finger under Poor Brother's nose.)* Now don't forget those words. "Good little mill, I thank you for enough."

POOR BROTHER: You can be sure I won't. And thank you, kind sir. This is my lucky day! *(He turns and hurries along the way he has come as the . . .)*

CURTAIN FALLS

(Storyteller strolls to center stage as before.)

STORYTELLER: Now the Poor Brother ran home to his wife. He could hardly wait to show her the wonderful mill. Besides, he himself was eager to see what it could do, for don't forget, he was very, very hungry. *(Storyteller returns to the left side of the stage and sits cross-legged on the floor as the curtain rises. . . .)*

SCENE III

TIME: *A little later*

PLACE: *Inside the Poor Brother's cottage. There is a window without any curtain over it, a bare table with a drawer in it, and some rough, straight chairs. There is a door at right. All has an air of poverty and want. (Poor Brother's wife is sitting in front of an empty, cold fireplace.)*

POOR BROTHER: *(Rushing in.)* Look, Wife. Just see what I have here. This is our lucky day!

WIFE: *(Looking around, but not leaving the chair.)* I see nothing but a little hand mill. What has taken you so long? I am cold and I am hungry. Where is the food you went to get?

POOR BROTHER: *(Placing the mill on the table.)* It is all here. This is a magic mill. It will grind whatever you want. Speak, Wife, what would you like to eat?

WIFE: *(Getting slowly out of her chair and approaching the table.)* Sausages. I'd like some sausages and some good white bread.

POOR BROTHER: *(Leaning over the mill.)* Grind sausages and white bread!

(There is a grinding noise. There should be a drawer in the table which the Poor Brother now opens. The drawer should be facing away

from the audience. From the drawer the Poor Brother draws a long string of sausages, pretending it comes from the mill. Next he lifts out some loaves of white bread.)

POOR BROTHER: Look at this, Wife. *(He holds up the string of sausages as the grinding noise continues.)* And just look at this. *(He shows her the loaves of white bread.)* Didn't I say this was our lucky day?

WIFE: *(Overjoyed.)* Husband, husband, you are right! This is our lucky day! What a fine husband you are.

POOR BROTHER: *(Loudly over the grinding noise.)* **Good little mill, thank you for enough.** *(The grinding noise stops.)*

(Poor Brother and Wife look at one another with joy, then they join hands and dance around the table as the . . .)

CURTAIN FALLS

(Storyteller strolls to center stage as before.)

STORYTELLER: Now that they knew how to get all the food they wanted, the Poor Brother and his wife planned a feast for all the poor people of the town.

230

When the Rich Brother heard about this, he hurried over to the Poor Brother's house to find out where he had gotten the money to pay for so much food.

(Storyteller returns to the left side of the stage and sits cross-legged on the floor as the curtain rises. . . .)

SCENE IV

TIME: *A little later*

PLACE: *Inside the Poor Brother's cottage as before. Now there is a white cloth on the table. (Three couples besides Poor Brother and his wife are standing around the table helping themselves to the feast spread there.)*

1ST VISITOR: *(Popping berries in his mouth.)* What wonderful strawberries!

2ND VISITOR: *(Smacking his lips.)* Taste this roast beef.

3RD VISITOR: *(Smelling and then eating the cheese.)* I never ate such delicious cheese.

4TH VISITOR: *(Wiping her mouth.)* Nor I such wonderful cake.

5TH VISITOR: *(Reaching across the table greedily.)* I must have one of those jelly tarts.

6TH VISITOR: *(Grabbing up the plate.)* No you don't. There are just enough for me.

WIFE: *(Hurrying over.)* Let her have them. The mill will grind as many more as we want.

1ST VISITOR: Will it grind *anything* you want? Even money?

5TH VISITOR: Of course, silly. Didn't you hear them say it is a magic mill?

1ST VISITOR: *(Taking Poor Brother by the arm.)* Ask it to grind money, enough money for us all.

POOR BROTHER: A fine idea. *(He starts toward the shelf where the mill is sitting, when there comes a loud knock on the door.)*

WIFE: *(Opening door.)* Why, Brother! What brings you to our humble house? Come in, come in. You are welcome!

RICH BROTHER: *(Entering and approaching the table, too astonished to answer her greeting. Visitors step back as he draws near.)* What is this? What is this? How did you come by all this wonderful food? I gave you only bacon and bread.

POOR BROTHER: *(Approaching with the mill in his hands.)* By means of this, Brother. This is a magic mill. It will grind anything we wish.

RICH BROTHER: *(Reaching for the mill.)* Then I must have it. You must let me borrow it. I promise to bring it back. Yes, yes. I must have it! *(He seizes the mill and starts out the door.)* I promise to bring it back. *(He runs out.)*

POOR BROTHER: *(Running out after him.)* Stop, stop! There is something you must know. Come back! *(He stops in doorway and shakes his head.)* He must think I want to take the mill from him. See how fast he is running.

WIFE: Let him go. We can get the mill later if he does not bring it back.

POOR BROTHER: *(Turning to her.)* You don't understand. He doesn't know how to make the mill stop.

(Everyone stares from one to another, shaking their heads, as the . . .)

CURTAIN FALLS

(Storyteller strolls to center stage as before.)

STORYTELLER: *(Striking some chords and chanting.)*

The Rich Brother took the mill on the run
For he thought that now he'd have some fun.
But he couldn't make it stop with pleading or swearing,
So he's up to his neck in soup and herring.

(Storyteller returns to the left side of the stage and sits cross-legged on the floor as the curtain rises. . . .)

SCENE V

TIME: *A few minutes later*

PLACE: *Inside Poor Brother's cottage as before. (Villagers have gone and Poor Brother and Wife are seated at the table licking their fingers and looking well-fed, when the door bursts open and Rich Brother rushes in. He is wet and bedraggled and highly excited.)*

RICH BROTHER: Come, come quickly! It's the mill; it's your *miserable* mill. How I wish I had never heard of it! You played a trick on me, that's what you did. Now, come and untrick me!

POOR BROTHER: *(Rising from his chair.)* What happened? What did you ask the mill to grind?

RICH BROTHER: Soup, you fool. Seeing all the good food here made me hungry. So as soon as I got home, I asked the mill to grind soup and serve up herring. Now my house is awash in soup, my garden is flooded, and there are herring all over the house.

WIFE: *(Starts laughing as Rich Brother talks, then throws her apron over her face and rocks back and forth in a fit of merriment.)*
(Rich Brother and Poor Brother run out of the house as the. . .)

CURTAIN FALLS

(Storyteller strolls to center stage as before.)

STORYTELLER: The next one to hear about the magic mill was a sea captain who traveled back and forth across the ocean bringing shiploads of salt to his countrymen. He thought it would be a good thing to borrow the mill and have it grind salt. Then he wouldn't have to go a-sailing for a good long time.
(Storyteller returns to the left side of the stage and sits cross-legged on the floor as the curtain rises. . . .)

SCENE VI

TIME: *Some weeks later*
PLACE: *Inside Poor Brother's*

cottage. But what a change! There is a white, fluffy curtain at the window. There is a picture above the hearth and a fire glowing within it. (In a comfortable rocker sits the Wife wearing a fine gown and a lace cap on her head. Her back is to Poor Brother and the Sea Captain who are sitting on a sofa, legs crossed and at ease.)

SEA CAPTAIN: As I was saying, if you would let me borrow the mill, I could fill my ship with salt here and sail home instead of having to go to a very distant port each trip.

POOR BROTHER: You would be sure to bring the mill back to me.

SEA CAPTAIN: Of course I would. I'm an honest man.

POOR BROTHER: Very well, then. You may borrow the mill. *(He goes across the room to where the mill sits on its shelf.)* Here you are,

only there is one thing you must remember . . .

SEA CAPTAIN: *(Grabbing the mill out of Poor Brother's hands and not waiting for him to finish his sentence.)* Don't you worry, I'll remember to bring it back. I'll remember. *(He rushes out of the room as if he were afraid Poor Brother might change his mind as the . . .)*

CURTAIN FALLS

(Storyteller strolls to center stage as before.)

STORYTELLER: But the Sea Captain wasn't an honest man. No sooner did he have the mill aboard his ship than he ordered his crew to weigh anchor and set sail for home. And as soon as the ship was under way, he ordered the mill to grind salt. It began to grind and soon all the sacks were full and then the hold began to fill. But the Sea Captain couldn't make the mill stop grinding.

(*Storyteller returns to the left side of the stage and sits cross-legged on the floor as the curtain rises. . . .*)

SCENE VII

TIME: *A few minutes later*
PLACE: *The deck of a sailing ship. (Sailors appear at right as the Sea Captain comes running onto center stage from left.)*

SEA CAPTAIN: Man the boats! Man the boats! The ship is filling with salt. It will sink; it *is* sinking. We shall all be drowned! (*They all go running off right as the . . .*)

CURTAIN FALLS

(*Storyteller strolls to center stage as before.*)

STORYTELLER:
The ship *did* sink to the
bottom of the sea,
And the mill kept grinding
as busy as could be.
It has kept on grinding with
never a halt,
And that is the reason why
the sea is salt.
(*Storyteller plays a few chords on the guitar, then bows deeply and exits.*)

the
End

—*Norwegian Folk Tale Retold*

What Do You Think?

1. Which characters in the play were greedy? In what ways were they punished for being greedy?
2. How does the play explain why the sea is salt? Try to find a scientific answer to this question.
3. Who is your favorite character in this play? Why do you like this character?

Taking A Closer Look

1. Do you think Rich Brother and Poor Brother were selfish? Do you think either of them was generous? Why?
2. The play doesn't tell, but why do you think Rich Brother was rich and Poor Brother was poor?
3. There is a saying, "A fool and his money are soon parted." Put the word *mill* in place of the word *money* in this saying. Now tell how the play proves this new saying to be true.
4. An actor should use his face and voice to show how a character feels. Say each line below and show with your face and voice how the character felt.
   a. Rich Brother: "Begone and don't bother me again!"
   b. Poor Brother: "Help me this one time and I will bother you no more."
   c. Wife: "This is our lucky day!"
   d. Sea Captain: "The ship is filling with salt. It will sink; it *is* sinking. We shall all be drowned!"

Tales of Wit and Wisdom

The wise person and the witty person have always been popular characters in folk tales. As you read the three tales that follow—from Viet Nam, Africa, and China—decide which character you admire the most, and why.

THI KINH

Thi Kinh[1] was very beautiful. Her black hair was long and fragrant, and her big, dark eyes sparkled like living stars when she spoke or laughed. Young men for miles around had begged for her hand in marriage, but Thi Kinh refused them all, preferring to marry a poor and simple man from her own village.

Thi Kinh worked in the rice fields by day and attended to her household chores at night. It was a hard life, but Thi Kinh didn't mind the endless toil. Because she loved her home and her husband with all her heart she was content.

One afternoon Thi Kinh was sitting outdoors shelling shrimp for the evening meal, while her husband napped in a hammock.

Thi Kinh gazed fondly at her husband. And then she noticed that one of the hairs in his beard was growing in the wrong direction. She went into the hut and got a

[1] Thi Kinh (TIGH kin)

239

sharp knife. Then Thi Kinh tiptoed over to where her husband lay and bent over him, intending to shave off the hair while he slept.

Just then Thi Kinh's husband stirred in his sleep. The knife slipped and scratched his cheek, and he awoke with a start. When he saw Thi Kinh standing over him and holding a knife, he leaped to his feet in alarm.

"You were trying to murder me!" he screamed at the astonished Thi Kinh. "Murderess! Leave my house at once!"

Thi Kinh was so surprised by her husband's angry words that she was unable to speak. But several neighbors heard the commotion and came running to see what was the matter.

"Thi Kinh tried to kill me!" her husband told them. "Look at the knife! There's blood on it!"

Shamed by her husband's awful accusation, Thi Kinh bowed her head and began to weep. Her silence and her tears seemed to prove that what her husband was saying was indeed the truth, and Thi Kinh was told to leave the village and never to return.

Homeless and friendless, Thi Kinh trudged through the countryside. She did not know where she ought to go or what she ought to do. When she could walk no longer, she lay down beneath a tree and wept until she fell asleep.

The next day Thi Kinh came upon an old pagoda which had become a monastery. Thi Kinh stood very still and watched the brown-robed monks go about their business of meditation and prayer. The peace and the beauty of life in the monastery soothed Thi Kinh's aching heart, and she decided to disguise herself as a man and seek refuge within the monastery's walls.

She cut off her long hair, rubbed her smooth face with dirt, and rearranged her clothes. Then she went to the gates of the monastery and begged for admittance. Not realizing that she was a woman, the Superior of the monastery welcomed her and bade her stay as long as she wished.

Life was slow and peaceful within the monastery. As the days passed, Thi Kinh began to forget the trouble and heartbreak that had brought her to the monastery. She kept to herself and never spoke. None of the other monks suspected that she was a woman.

Several years later a baby was left upon the steps of the pagoda. The baby's mother was so poor that she could no longer afford to care for the child, so she had wrapped it in a ragged blanket and abandoned it to the charity of the monks.

When the motherless infant opened its eyes and saw the cluster of brown-robed monks peering down at it, it began to cry. Thi Kinh alone understood that the baby was frightened of the monks and wanted its mother. She knelt and cradled the child in her arms, crooning to it until it stopped crying and nestled against her shoulder.

The other monks stared at her in horror for now they realized that she was a woman.

241

The Superior of the monastery was very angry at having been tricked by Thi Kinh. He ordered her to take the baby and leave the monastery within the hour. Thi Kinh had no choice but to obey.

Although Thi Kinh was so unhappy that she no longer cared what became of her, she knew that the baby depended upon her for its food and shelter. And she did all that she could. She trudged from village to village, working in the fields, gathering firewood, and sometimes begging from door to door so as to get enough food for the child.

The long weeks of hunger, worry, grief, and wandering took their toll. Thi Kinh's beauty faded. Her lustrous black hair became gray. Her smooth cheeks and forehead were lined. Her once-sparkling eyes grew dull. She was thin and ragged.

At last her roaming brought her to the outskirts of the village where she had lived with her husband years ago. She was so changed that no one recognized her as she walked slowly down the street, holding a begging-bowl in one hand and the baby in the other.

A man came forward and dropped several coins into the bowl.

"You remind me of someone I loved," he said sadly, when Thi Kinh thanked him for his generosity. "I give you this in her name."

Thi Kinh stared at him. She knew the man at once. It was her husband!

"I had a wife named Thi Kinh," he continued. "I drove her away with my false accusations, and I have regretted it ever since. Oh, what I wouldn't give to see her again!"

Tears filled Thi Kinh's eyes, and her hands shook so that she could hardly hold the bowl. In a halting voice she told her husband who she was and all that had happened since she'd left the village.

When she had finished, her husband took the begging-bowl from her hands and smashed it to the ground.

"You will never have to beg again," he told her.

For at last Thi Kinh had come home.

Many years later Thi Kinh's story reached the ears of the King. He was so impressed by her courage and her goodness that he bestowed upon her the title of Quan-Am Tong-Tu,[1] which means The Compassionate Protector of Children.

And so she is remembered to this day.

—Retold by Gail B. Graham

[1] Quan-Am Tong-Tu (KWAHN-ahm TAWNG-too)

The Children of Rain

Rain was a beautiful woman who lived long ago where the sky grows rosy before the sunrise. She wore a rainbow about her waist.

Rain married a man and they had three daughters. When the eldest was grown up, she decided to visit the people on earth.

Rain said, "When you go to the earth you will find good people and bad people. Beware of the bad ones."

The daughter went to the earth, fell in love, and married there. So from that time on she lived among the people of the earth.

In time her mother in the sky had a fourth child, a boy named Son-eib. The eldest sister on earth did not know about this son.

Years passed. The two younger girls missed their sister. One day they said to their mother, "We would like to visit our sister on earth."

Son-eib wanted to go, too. But Rain was afraid to let all her children go. "You might get lost," she said.

Wolf was then living in the sky. He heard what the mother said and he approached her. "I will go with your daughters and your son and show them the way," he said. "I know the earth people."

So Wolf and the children all set out together.

But Wolf had evil plans. As they traveled along, Son-eib could feel that something was wrong. He was worried. When Wolf and his sisters were not looking, he caught a pretty red bird and hid it under his belt.

They walked for a long time, many days and many nights. Finally they came to a large village where good and bad people lived. A woman approached. She looked Son-eib up and down. "This boy's eyebrows are so like my mother's," she said. "How can this be?"

Wolf was annoyed. "Don't pay any attention to him," he said. "He is not a human being, he's just a thing. We don't even give him food."

Son-eib was very angry when he heard this, but he said nothing. When the villagers brought food for the travelers, Son-eib did not eat.

Towards evening the same woman came again and said, "This boy has my mother's eyebrows. Let him sleep in my house."

Wolf was angry, and he shouted, "You don't know what you are talking about! He is just a thing. He must sleep in a hut by himself."

There were bad people in the village who listened to Wolf. They shut Son-eib up in a hut outside the village and fastened the door on the outside.

At last it was dark. The woman and all the other good people of the village were asleep. Wolf and the bad people crept up to the hut where Son-eib was sleeping and set it on fire. Tall flames rose to the sky. Son-eib perished in the flames. But a beautiful red bird rose up from the flames and flew through the clouds.

The bird flew to where Rain lived and sat in a tree beside her. "Son-eib's sister did not know him," the bird sang. "Son-eib is dead. He perished in the fire."

Rain called to her husband, "Come and hear what the bird has to tell!"

He came and listened. "What shall we do?" he asked.

Rain was angry. "Why ask *me* what to do? Your name is Fire! I am only Rain." And they walked away from each other.

A little later a small cloud came floating through the sky. It moved towards the village where Son-eib had died in the fire. Around the cloud was a rainbow. It grew bigger and bigger.

The people in the village were very much afraid when they saw this. They ran towards their huts. But there was no use in hiding. Out of the rainbow fire flashed down to earth. This was a special fire from the sky and it killed only Wolf and the bad people.

The rainbow then stretched wide over the earth, and a mighty voice was heard coming from the sky. "Do not kill the children of the sky!"

Ever since that time, the Bushmen say, people have been afraid of the rainbow. When they see it in the sky, they take two pieces of wood, strike them together, and shout: "Go away! Do not burn me! Go away!"

—Retold by Elizabeth S. Helfman

The Young Head
of the Cheng Family

In the Cheng family, there were a father, three sons, and two young daughters-in-law. Plum Blossom and Peony were brides of the elder brothers, and they had but recently been brought into the household. Both girls came from a village a few miles beyond the Cheng farm, and they both grew homesick frequently. Since they had no mother-in-law living, they had to ask their father-in-law for permission to visit their parents. This became quite a bother to the old man.

The next time they begged to visit their mothers, he said, "You may go, but only on one condition. When you return, you must bring me things I want. You, Plum Blossom, must bring me some fire wrapped in paper. And you, Peony, bring me some wind on a paper. If you fail to get these things for me, you are never to come back here."

Old Cheng thought that the girls would not accept these conditions for their visit. But they were so eager to get away, they would have promised him anything.

It was a long, hot walk to their native village. After a while, they sat down to rest by the roadside. When they began to think of their promises to their father-in-law, some of their happiness drained away. Before long, both girls were weeping noisily.

As they sat there rocking and crying, a young girl rode out of a field on the back of a big water buffalo. "Are you in trouble?" she asked.

"*Ai-yee, ai-yee!*" wailed the girls, and they told her of the promises they had made to their father-in-law.

Instead of grieving with them, the girl, whose name was Precious Jade, laughed. "Dry your tears!" she said. "Come home with me. I will show you how to bring your father-in-law exactly what he wants. And then you can go and have a happy visit with your mothers."

When they reached her family's house, Precious Jade gave Plum Blossom a paper lantern. "When you light the candle inside this lantern, your father-in-law will have his fire wrapped in paper," she said. To Peony, she gave a paper fan. "Wave the fan. There is some wind on paper!" she exclaimed.

The two young wives thanked Precious Jade again and again. Then they fairly flew to the homes of their mothers. There, they had a glorious visit with their little sisters and brothers, and they returned to their father-in-law happily.

"What!" he shouted. "You have dared to come back without the things I commanded you to bring me?"

"Oh, no, Most Honorable Father-in-Law!" exclaimed the young wives. "Here are the things you wanted."

The old man was astonished when he saw the lantern and the fan. He wondered how his flighty young daughters-in-law could suddenly have become so clever. He did not have to wonder long, because the girls soon told him about Precious Jade.

"What a remarkable young person!" he thought, stroking his wispy gray beard. "I should like to have her in the family."

At once, Old Cheng engaged the services of a go-between. Before long, a marriage was arranged, and Cheng's youngest son married Precious Jade.

When the wedding festivities were over, Old Cheng made Precious Jade the female head of the household. She was to take charge of everything.

Before the young sons returned to their work in the fields, they went to Precious Jade for instructions, as their father had ordered. She told them never to go to or from the fields empty-handed. When they went to the fields, they were to carry tools or seed or fertilizers. When they returned, they were to bring bundles of sticks for firewood. Her instructions were sensible, and the men followed them faithfully. So the sons kept the farm in fine condition. They gathered so much fuel that it was not necessary to buy even one stick of firewood that whole winter.

In the spring, Precious Jade told the men to gather up all the stones in the field and to heap them in the courtyard near the house.

One day, Yu Kai,[1] a man who went about the countryside to buy precious stones, passed the great pile of stones in the Chengs' yard. He had no more than glanced at the heap when he saw a large piece of precious green jade. In order to get a bargain, Yu Kai pretended that he wanted the stones to build a bridge. He offered to buy the whole heap for a trifling sum. But Precious Jade became suspicious of the stranger. Instead of agreeing to his price, she asked an unreasonably large sum for the pile. She refused to consider anything less. To her surprise, the stranger agreed to the high price she had set. He told Precious Jade he would return in two days to remove the stones and bring her the money.

[1] Yu Kai (YOH KIGH)

254

When the stranger left, Precious Jade looked thoughtfully at the pile of stones. They appeared to be quite ordinary, and yet she realized that there must be something of great value in them. Could it be that there was a gem in that heap of rocks?

The next day, Precious Jade sent her father-in-law to invite Yu Kai to a feast. She advised the men of her household to serve the best wine to their guest. Before dinner, she asked her father-in-law to bring the conversation around to precious stones, and to ask their guest just how one could recognize a gem among ordinary rocks.

Everything was done as she instructed. And their guest proved himself to be very fond of good wine. After the feast the ladies left the room, and the men continued drinking and talking. Precious Jade hid behind a screen. When their guest had gotten pleasantly tipsy, his tongue loosened. In no time at all, the girl learned what she needed to know.

As soon as it was light Precious Jade hastened to the rock pile. She found the piece of jade and removed it from the heap.

When Yu Kai came to collect his pile of rocks, he saw that the value had departed from his purchase. He went to see Precious Jade again. This time, she bargained so shrewdly that she was able to get from him not only the original high price for the rock pile, but an additional sum for the jade stone.

Before this, the Cheng family had been well-off. Now they were wealthy. They built a splendid ancestral hall, and over the entrance Precious Jade had inscribed the words *No Sorrow*.

亦 有 憂 愁

One day, a mandarin passed that way and noticed the remarkable inscription. He ordered his sedan chair set down before the Cheng door, and he sent for the head of the family.

256

When Precious Jade appeared, he was astonished. "Yours is a most unusual family," he declared. "Never before have I seen one without sorrow. Nor have I ever seen a family with such a young head. You are much too bold. Therefore, I will make you pay a fine. You must weave for me a piece of cloth as long as this road."

Precious Jade put her hands together and bowed respectfully before the great man. "I will begin weaving the moment Your Excellency tells me exactly how long this road is," she told him.

The mandarin gave her a long hard look. "I will also fine you as much oil as there is water in the Eastern Sea," he told her.

Again Precious Jade bowed respectfully. "Excellency, if you will measure the sea and tell me exactly how much water it contains, I will begin at once to press the oil from my beans."

"Indeed!" gasped the mandarin. "Since you are so clever, perhaps you will tell me what I am thinking. If you do, I will give you no more fines. In my hand is my pet quail. Tell me, do I mean to hold on to it or to set it free?"

"Your Excellency," Precious Jade said calmly, "I am an ordinary girl, and you are a mandarin, a great magistrate. If, sir, you know no more of these matters than I do, you have no right to fine me at all. Observe that I stand with one foot on one side of the threshold and the other foot on the other side. Tell me, do I mean to go into the house or to come out of it? If you cannot

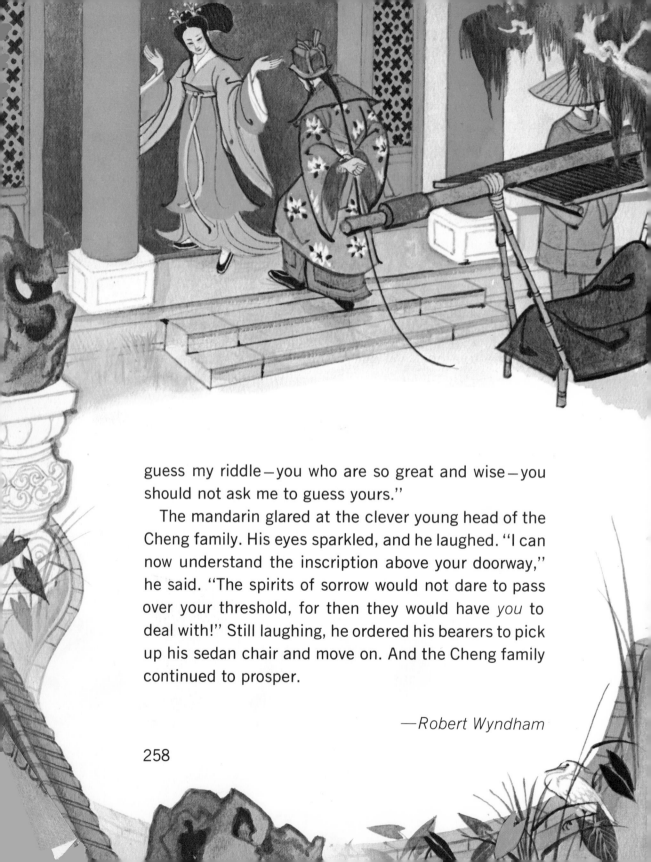

guess my riddle—you who are so great and wise—you should not ask me to guess yours."

The mandarin glared at the clever young head of the Cheng family. His eyes sparkled, and he laughed. "I can now understand the inscription above your doorway," he said. "The spirits of sorrow would not dare to pass over your threshold, for then they would have *you* to deal with!" Still laughing, he ordered his bearers to pick up his sedan chair and move on. And the Cheng family continued to prosper.

—Robert Wyndham

258

What Do You Think?

1. Which character in this group of stories do you think is the wisest? Give reasons for your choice.

2. Do you think any of the characters were *not* very wise or witty? What might you have done in that character's place?

3. If Thi Kinh and Precious Jade could have changed places, how might their stories have been different?

Taking A Closer Look

1. Why do you believe Thi Kinh deserved the title "The Compassionate Protector of Children"? What other title might the King have given her?

2. Rain warns her children to watch for good and bad people on earth. Which character in the story do you think was the most "good"? the most "bad"? Explain your answer.

3. Why do you think Precious Jade chose the inscription "No Sorrow"?

4. Find some of the riddles in "The Young Head of the Cheng Family." Can you think of some other puzzling requests the father-in-law or the mandarin could have made?

5. Which one of these stories could also be thought of as a "how" or a "why" tale? Explain your choice.

How does a rich person become a rich person? Is it by work, or by chance? Saadi[1] and Saad[2] cannot agree on an answer. And so they decide to put the question to a test.

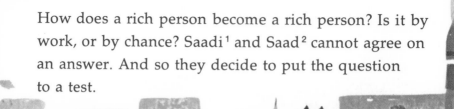

The Maker of Ropes

In the wonderful city of Baghdad,[3] the city of peace, there lived two friends named Saadi and Saad. Saadi was very rich. He always said that no one could be really happy unless he was rich. But his friend Saad laughed at this, saying, "I am not rich. Yet no one in Baghdad is happier than I am!"

One day they were walking together down the long line of shops in the bazaar. They were having a great argument. Saadi said, "Anyone can become rich by working hard, if there is enough money to get started. But a person must have money and must work."

"That is the best way, and the most certain way," said Saad. "But it is not the only way. Some people get rich by chance."

[1] Saadi (SAH-dee)　　[2] Saad (SAD)　　[3] Baghdad (BAG-dad)

260

They went on arguing, until Saadi said, "Let us put it to the test."

They stopped outside a very small shop. A rope-maker, who looked very poor, was hard at work inside.

"What is your name, my friend?" asked Saadi.

"My lord," answered the man, "my name is Hassan."[1] He bowed politely to his important visitors.

"And you make ropes, I see. Are they good ropes?"

"Indeed they are," answered Hassan quickly. "There are none better in Baghdad. Fishermen and captains of ships come to my shop to buy them."

"Then, why are you so poor?"

"I have no money, my lord," said Hassan very sadly. "I work hard all day long, but I earn very little. I have only enough to buy rice for my wife Ayesha[2] and our four children, charcoal for the stove, and oil for the lamp. I can never save enough to buy all the hemp I need. Without hemp I cannot make my business grow."

"This is just the person we want," said Saadi to Saad. Then he gave a purse to Hassan, saying, "Here are two hundred gold dinars. I give them to you in the name of Allah.[3] I hope your business will now prosper."

Hassan was so surprised that he could not speak. He fell on his knees and kissed the hem of Saadi's long silk robe. Then the two friends said goodbye and left him holding his riches.

His first thought was, "Where can I put all this money to keep it safe?" There was no safe place for it in his

[1]Hassan (ha-SAN)   [2]Ayesha (AH-ee-shə)   [3]Allah (AL-ə)

little shop. At last he put ten gold dinars in his pocket. He took off his turban and hid the purse under the long folds of cloth.

Then he went out. With six dinars he bought some hemp. Then he bought grapes, oranges, and a large piece of meat. His family had had nothing but rice to eat for many a day. Then a terrible thing happened. As he was walking along the street a hungry vulture swooped down from the sky. It tried to grab the meat from Hassan. He struggled so hard that his turban fell off. At once the vulture leaped down on it and carried it away.

He screamed at the bird, and everyone in the street joined in. But it took no notice. Bird and turban were soon out of sight in the sky.

Poor Hassan! He had to buy a new turban, which left him with very little money. Then he went home sadly to Ayesha to tell her the story. She ranted and raved, but he took it more quietly. "It is the will of Allah," he said very sadly. "I must not complain. I must get on with my work."

A few months later Saad and Saadi paid Hassan another visit. They were surprised to find him working as before. He told them what had happened.

"What!" cried Saadi angrily. "Do you expect us to believe that? Who ever heard of a vulture carrying off a turban? What have you done with the money?"

"By Allah, it is true, my lord," said Hassan sadly. "You can ask along the street. Many people saw it happen."

"There are many strange stories of vultures," said Saad. Saadi, a kindly man, soon forgot that he was angry.

Taking out his purse, he counted two hundred gold dinars onto Hassan's bench. "There," he said. "Let us try again and hope for better fortune." He would not wait for Hassan's thanks. Taking Saad's arm he went quickly away.

Hassan stared at the gold, hardly able to believe his eyes. "How can I keep it safe?" he asked himself. "I will take it home and find a safe hiding place."

So he tied the coins in a large piece of rag. With great care he carried them home. Ayesha and all the children were out. He looked around carefully. There were no hiding places. He had only a table and stools and cooking pots, and straw beds on the floor. The only possible place was an old pot full of bran which had stood in a dark corner for months. He hid the gold deep in the bran and went back to his work.

Soon after his family came home, a peddler went from house to house selling washing balls. Ayesha wanted to buy some, but she had no money at all. She looked wildly around the house for something which could be spared. Then she said to the peddler, "How many washing balls would you give me for this pot of bran?"

"Four," he answered.

"Oh," she said. "This is a very good bran and a very good, strong pot. Could you not give me six?"

"Five," he answered.

He carried away the pot, while Ayesha set to work to cook rice for the family supper.

Very soon Hassan came home. He went straight to the dark corner where the pot had stood. It was gone!

"Ayesha," he cried in horror, "where is the pot of bran?"

"Oh, that old thing!" she answered. "I gave it to a peddler for five washing balls which I wanted badly."

"Who is he?" shouted her husband. "Where does he live? How can I find him?"

"I don't know," she answered, stirring the rice. "I've never seen him before."

Hassan pulled at his hair and his beard, and beat his breast. Then he told Ayesha about the two hundred gold dinars. She immediately got angry. "You fool! You should have told me," she wailed. "You should have told me they were there!" And all the children burst out crying.

"They are gone," groaned Hassan. "There is no hope. It is the will of Allah that we should be poor." And next morning he went off sadly to his work.

Six months later Saad and Saadi once again passed that way. They stopped at Hassan's shop. He was so

264

frightened that he made believe he did not see them. Then Saadi spoke to him.

"Well," asked Saadi, "how is it with you, Hassan? Have you begun to grow rich?"

Hassan fell on his knees and in tears told them about the pot of bran.

"Stand up, man!" cried Saadi angrily. "How dare you tell me such lies? What have you done with the money?"

"In the name of Allah, it is true!" sobbed Hassan, beating his breast.

"I believe you," said Saad. "Many accidents more strange than that have happened."

He set to work to calm his friend. Then Saadi said, "Well, I have done. Now, Saad, perhaps you can show me how this unhappy man can get rich by accident. Money does not help him."

Saad took out of his pocket a piece of lead. He gave it to Hassan, saying, "I found this in the street just now. How much is it worth?"

"Nothing," answered Hassan.

"Then keep it carefully until you have a use for it. Perhaps it will bring you good fortune."

Hassan put it into his pocket and the two friends went away.

Late that night there came a loud knocking at the door. When Ayesha opened it she saw a woman whom she and Hassan knew. The visitor said, "My husband has lost the piece of lead which holds down his net. If he can't go fishing tonight, our family shall have nothing to eat tomorrow. The shops are all shut. I have asked all our other neighbors, but no one has one. You are our last hope. Can you lend us a piece of lead?"

"Very gladly," answered Hassan. He searched about in the dark until he found it and gave it to her.

"Thank you a thousand times," she cried. "My husband will give you all the fish he catches in the first throw of his net tonight." And she went away happy.

Next morning she came back, carrying a very fine large fish. "This was the only one he caught in his first throw," she said. "But it is the largest he has ever caught. It is yours for your kindness."

Thanking her warmly, Ayesha took the fish and cut it up for cooking. Inside it she found what she thought was a large smooth piece of glass. She gave this to her children to play with and went on with her work.

The children, who had no toys, played with the piece of glass all day. After dark they found that it gave out a beautiful light. Soon they began to quarrel over it. They made such a noise that Hassan stopped them to find out what it was all about. He told his wife to put out the oil lamp. To his surprise, the glass shone so brightly that it lit the hut.

"See how lucky we are!" cried Hassan. "This piece of glass will save us from having to buy any more oil for the lamp."

The children were so excited that they made a great noise. At last their father sent them to bed.

266

Now in the hut next door there lived a jeweler. He was too miserly to live in a good house, even though he was rich. Next morning his wife Rachel came to complain about the great noise the children had made the night before.

"I am very sorry," said Ayesha. "It won't happen again. I hope you will forgive us. They got so excited over this piece of glass which I found in a fish. It's pretty, isn't it?"

"Yes, it is," said Rachel. "And do you know I've got a piece very like it. They would make a nice pair. Would you like to sell it to me?"

But the children, who had heard all this, did not want to lose their toy. They began to cry, begging their mother not to sell it. So to quiet them she said, "No, thank you, Rachel." The jeweler's wife went away.

She went straight to her husband's shop in the bazaar to tell him about the piece of glass. Then she went back to Ayesha. She called her out of the hut so that they could talk without the children hearing.

"Ayesha," said she, "will you sell me that piece of glass for twenty gold dinars?"

At that moment Hassan came home for dinner. Ayesha asked what he thought of Rachel's offer.

Hassan was silent. He was turning over in his mind what Saad had said about the piece of lead bringing him good fortune. Seeing him look so doubtful, Rachel said to him quickly, too quickly, "Would you take fifty dinars?"

"No," he answered, for he was growing very suspicious. "I want a great deal more than that."

"A hundred dinars," said Rachel.

Now he felt sure. "No," he said. "For such a fine diamond as this I want a hundred thousand dinars. Nothing else."

"Oh, that's an impossible price," she cried. "No stone could be worth it. Come, neighbor, take twenty thousand while you can. You will be a rich man."

"A hundred thousand is my price," said he, "and that is because you are a neighbor. If I take it to a jeweler in the bazaar I shall ask more — and get it."

268

"Fifty thousand dinars," she said.

"No," he answered.

She sighed. "I cannot offer you more for this stone," she said. And away she went.

It was not long before the jeweler himself appeared. "Good neighbor," he said, "will you show me this diamond of yours?"

He examined it lovingly. At last he said, "Rachel offered you fifty thousand gold dinars. I will give you twenty thousand more."

"No," said Hassan. "My price is one hundred thousand."

The jeweler argued and argued, but it was no good. Hassan would not change his mind. Finally the jeweler agreed. That night he gave Hassan ten leather bags. Each contained ten thousand gold dinars.

Ayesha fell into Hassan's arms, weeping for joy. The children all laughed and cried too, though they only half understood. "Let us give thanks to Allah," said Hassan. "I was wrong. He does not want us to stay poor."

Hassan would have gone on his knees before Saad and Saadi. He wanted to thank them, but he had no idea where they lived. He gave a large gift of gold dinars to the fisherman. Then he set to work to build up his business. He went to see all the best ropemakers in Baghdad to buy all the rope they could make. He promised to pay them quickly, and this pleased them very much. He built a large warehouse to store the rope, with a shop where people could buy it. He also added fine rooms for his family to live in. Very soon everyone in Baghdad knew him for his honesty and his riches. Now he and Ayesha and their children had fine clothes and enough to eat.

Some time after this Saad and Saadi called at his little shop in the bazaar to see how he was getting on. They found the shop empty. But some people told them where to find him. At once they set out for his new home and warehouse.

Hassan saw them coming. He ran to meet them and would have bent down to kiss their robes. They would not let him. Instead, they both embraced him. After he had thanked them most warmly, he led them into his fine house. Hassan seated them in the place of honor. He sent for sweetmeats, and for sherbet, and for drinks that were scented with rose water. Then Hassan told them his story.

"This is a fine tale," said Saadi. "But I do not believe it any more than your tales of the vulture flying off with your turban, or your wife's giving away the pot of bran. I am sure that it was the four hundred dinars I gave you which have made you rich. But never mind. All that matters is that you have succeeded. I am very glad."

"Nonsense!" cried Saad, with a laugh. "I am sure that all three stories are true. It was my piece of lead which brought him good fortune."

"My lords," said Hassan, "it is now growing late. If you would honor my poor house by staying the night, I

270

should like to take you tomorrow on a day's outing to my house in the country."

They both accepted gladly. Hassan gave them a splendid feast, with music, singing, and dancing. He was eager to show how grateful he was to them both.

Next morning early, while the air was still cool, they went down to the great river Tigris.[1] There a pleasure boat was waiting for them. Thanks to six strong rowers they quickly reached Hassan's country house beside the river.

Hassan showed them the house. Then he led them into the grove of orange and lemon trees in his garden. The trees were heavy with fruit and flowers. Little streams ran musically. The cool air was sweet with the smell of flowers and filled with the song of many birds.

In the coolest part of the garden, they found Hassan's two little boys playing. A servant looked after them. They had just seen a very large nest in one of the tallest trees. So they asked the servant to climb up and get it for them.

He found to his surprise that the nest was in a turban. When he gave it to the boys, they ran with it to their father.

[1] Tigris (TIGH-gris)

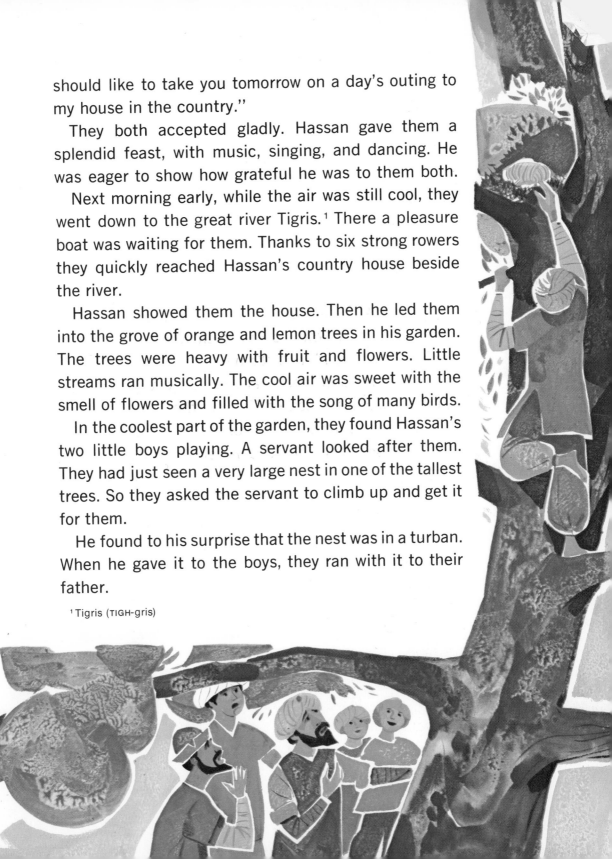

Hassan knew it at once. He showed it to his two guests. "My lords," he said. "Do you think this turban has been long in that tree?"

"It looks as though it has been there for many months," answered Saadi. "And the nest inside it is an old one."

"Let us sit down," said Hassan. He led them to a stone seat. There he took out the nest, while they watched. He unwound the cloth of the turban until a large purse fell out of it. It was the same large purse which Saadi had given him on his first visit.

Hassan emptied the purse on the bench. Then he asked Saadi to count the coins. There were a hundred and ninety gold dinars.

"This," said Hassan, "is the turban which the vulture flew away with."

"There can be no question about it," said Saadi. "You have shown us, friend Hassan, that your first tale was true. I believe now that the other tales were true also. I hope you will forgive me for not having believed you."

"I will gladly," answered Hassan. "For I owe all my good fortune to you and Saad."

Saadi turned to Saad and said with a smile, "This has shown that I was wrong and you were right. A person may sometimes get rich by a lucky chance."

—*John Hampden*

What Do You Think?

1. Would you pick Saad or Saadi for a friend? Give reasons for your choice.
2. Which saying do you agree with more: "Some people get rich by chance" or "Anyone can become rich by working hard"? Explain your answer.
3. Do you believe Hassan's good fortune changed his nature? Explain your answer.

Taking A Closer Look

1. Find parts of the story that show it takes place in another country.
2. Name some ways fishermen and captains of ships could use the ropes Hassan made.
3. Which of the three stories Hassan told Saadi and Saad would you find the hardest to believe? Why?
4. How did the piece of lead help Hassan to become rich?
5. Compare the way the members of Hassan's family lived at the beginning of the story with the way they lived at the end. In what ways do you think the new wealth made the most difference to Hassan's family?

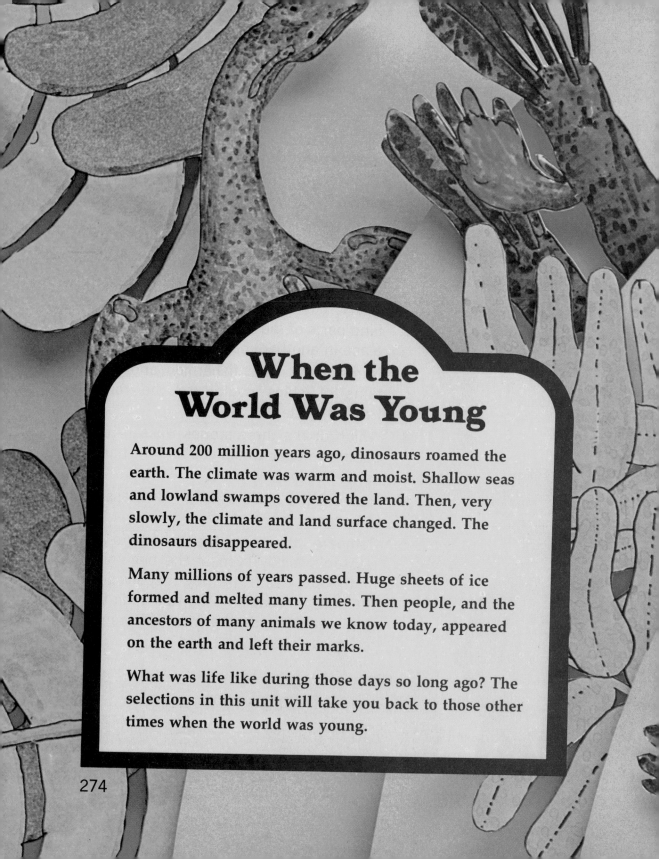

When the World Was Young

Around 200 million years ago, dinosaurs roamed the earth. The climate was warm and moist. Shallow seas and lowland swamps covered the land. Then, very slowly, the climate and land surface changed. The dinosaurs disappeared.

Many millions of years passed. Huge sheets of ice formed and melted many times. Then people, and the ancestors of many animals we know today, appeared on the earth and left their marks.

What was life like during those days so long ago? The selections in this unit will take you back to those other times when the world was young.

The dinosaurs ruled the earth for a longer period of time than any other creatures. Some dinosaurs were the most powerful animals ever to live on this planet. Then why do we not see dinosaurs today? Why did they disappear from the earth? Perhaps in this story you will find some clues to an answer.

The Battle of the Dinosaurs

Triceratops[1]

"Three-Horned Face" really describes this great ugly beast. It was the last of the horned dinosaurs, and a powerful fighter.

Triceratops was sometimes nearly 30 feet long. Its legs were heavy and strong, with the hind legs longer than the front ones. It stood about eight feet high at the hips. But its head was the thing to fear most. With it the dinosaur could drive a punishing wound into its enemies.

Three-Horns' head was almost one third the length of its body. A frill fanned out over neck and shoulders like a curved shield of bone. Jutting out from this shield were long pointed horns. They grew straight out from

[1]*Triceratops* (trigh-SEHR-ə-tops)

above the eyes. A smaller, thicker horn grew above the nose. Below that was a beak, like a parrot's, but much larger.

Though Three-Horns ate plants, it was far from a gentle animal. Nature had given Three-Horns wonderful weapons. And it was quick to use them. Some of its fossil bones show many scars. You can see that this was an animal who lived to fight another day.

Triceratops must have had a frightening charge, rather like the rhinoceros of today. Its neck muscles were powerful, its body and legs massive. When Three-Horns matched its swordlike horns against the dagger teeth of *Tyrannosaurus,*[1] there must have been a battle that shook the earth!

[1]*Tyrannosaurus* (ti-ran-ə-SAWR-uhss)

277

Tyrannosaurus Rex

"King of the Tyrant Lizards" is the name given to the greatest and strongest meat-eating animal that has ever walked the land. Lions and tigers are as gentle as pussycats when compared to this monster.

When you see *Tyrannosaurus,* you understand why the other dinosaurs had developed strange armor. Some had grown queer snorkels that would allow them to hide out in the deepest water. This giant, striding across the earth on two powerful legs, meant death to all others. *Tyrannosaurus* feared no one.

The Tyrant King was 47 feet long. It was 19 feet high when it walked among its subjects. The giant's hind legs were massive and clawed. *Tyrannosaurus* had a heavy tail with which it kept balance. Its little arms had become so tiny that they just hung uselessly. The two small claws on each "hand" were too weak to help the beast hold food and too short to reach its mouth.

278

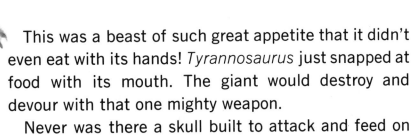

This was a beast of such great appetite that it didn't even eat with its hands! *Tyrannosaurus* just snapped at food with its mouth. The giant would destroy and devour with that one mighty weapon.

Never was there a skull built to attack and feed on other giants like *Tyrannosaurus*'! In the first place, that skull itself was over four feet long! The powerful jaws were hinged so they could open wide. And the jaws were armed with curved teeth that had sharp edges. They were like the blade of a saw. Some of these teeth were six inches long.

Tyrannosaurus could bite through the thickest hide and crush the most powerful bones. It hunted the smaller meat-eaters and the giant plant-eaters, even the armored ones. There were few dinosaurs who could escape those terrible jaws. Let us imagine what one of these prehistoric battles might have been like.

Fight to the Finish

The long summer of the dinosaurs is drawing to a close. Volcanoes rumble and there is smoke in the distance. These are warning signs of changes soon to take place on the earth. But the strange beasts who rule the earth know only that there are green plants to be eaten, and living enemies to escape from.

They clump through ferns and flowering plants. They move slowly, chewing on juicy leaves, enjoying the warm air. The world is a fine place for dinosaurs. And then there is a sudden stir. A few of the smaller, swifter, two-legged dinosaurs hurry past. They are running from something still unseen. A dinosaur with a duck bill pounds by on her heavy hind legs. She leans well forward as she tries to reach the nearby lake quickly.

Triceratops lifts her head slowly, and stops chewing. She, too, decides to move, clumsily, slowly. Only *Ankylosaurus*[1] stays where he is. Safe under his curved armor, he lies low, hoping the danger will pass.

And then the cause of all this stir appears. *Tyrannosaurus* comes crashing through a grove of young oak trees, towering as tall as some of them. His great jaws are open and ready as he strides heavily across the green ground.

His little eyes catch sight of *Ankylosaurus*. He bounds over toward him, his jaws opening wider. The

[1]*Ankylosaurus* (ANG-ki-loh-sor-əs)

280

Tyrant King's tiny arms are useless. So he lowers his great head and prepares to attack with his teeth.

The huge sharp teeth strike the armored back of *Ankylosaurus*. But they make no mark on this fortress of bone. Instead, *Ankylosaurus* swings his heavy club of a tail. There is a sharp crack as it connects with the Tyrant's jaw. A tooth breaks, and the great animal backs off. He grunts in pain and anger. *Ankylosaurus* is evidently not good to eat!

The little red eyes look for other game. They glow as they see *Triceratops* moving behind a bush. Three giant strides of *Tyrannosaurus'* huge legs and he is almost upon Three-Horns. But Three-Horns knows better than to try to run away. Her strong point is not speed.

Triceratops turns to face her towering enemy. There stands *Tyrannosaurus*, more than twice as tall as *Triceratops*. He has dined on many of Three-Horns' kind. Yet even the Tyrant King can be defeated sometimes by a desperate fighter.

Triceratops thrusts her heavy head forward. Her huge collar stands up like a shield above her neck and shoulders. But the rest of her is all too easy to attack. The Tyrant King swings his great jaws open. He starts to drop down for the attack. But *Triceratops* stands firm on her heavy legs and thrusts forward.

The long, pointed horns find a soft spot in the giant's underside. The earth shakes as the two great bodies clash. *Tyrannosaurus* stabs at Three-Horns'

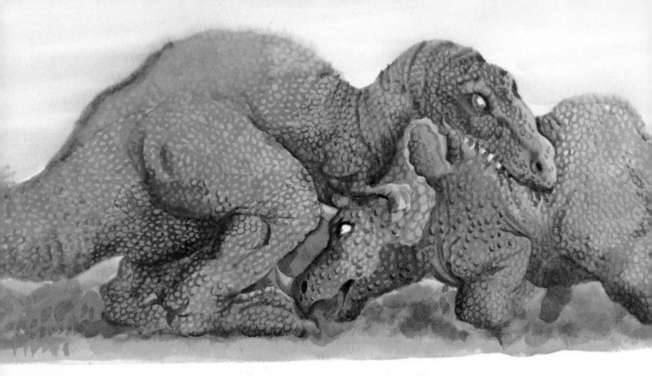

back with his teeth. But he does not get a firm hold. Three-Horns lumbers backward and gets ready to charge again.

There is a hush over the land as the two dinosaurs fight it out. The tall palm trees shudder as the earth shakes beneath them. But everything else is still. The plants are trampled flat by the heavy feet and tails of these beasts. And they are stained bright red where the beasts have spilled their blood.

The Tyrant King is badly wounded and his breath comes in gasps. But he cannot turn and run for his life. He is a slave to his hunger. Instinct tells him he must get meat in his jaws.

Once again, *Tyrannosaurus* snaps at the back of *Triceratops*. Once again, the long teeth cut to the bone. But *Triceratops* makes one last painful charge. The

282

three horns go deep. The terrible giant shudders and thrashes as he falls to the ground. *Tyrannosaurus* has fought his last fight.

This is a rare victory for *Triceratops*. Usually *Tyrannosaurus* gets what he goes after. But this day a lucky *Triceratops* limps away from the battle. She will carry the scars of her victory for the rest of her life. And millions of years later, her fossil bones in a museum will tell her story to us.

As the plant-eaters began to die out, *Tyrannosaurus* had fewer animals on whom to feed. And finally, even the mighty king died out too. His size and strength and terrible jaws were of no use to him in a changing world where he could find no food. In the end, the king was no greater than his subjects.

—*Darlene Geis*

What Do You Think?

1. Name four reasons why the author would call dinosaurs "strange beasts."
2. If you did not already know the outcome of this battle, which dinosaur would you have picked as the winner in the "fight to the finish"? Give reasons for your choice.
3. How can the fossil bones of *Triceratops* in a museum tell you anything about this dinosaur?

Taking A Closer Look

1. How do the animals fit their names: *Tyrannosaurus Rex* ("Tyrant King") and *Triceratops* ("Three-Horned Face")?
   From their descriptions in the story, make up some other good names for them.
2. List four facts that describe the earth when the age of the dinosaurs was drawing to a close.
3. Scientists do not have all the facts about the disappearance of the dinosaurs. Using clues from this story and from other books you have read, name some possible reasons for their disappearance.
4. Why didn't the Tyrant King run for his life after being wounded so badly?
5. Reread the last sentence in the story. What do you think it means?

Putting Ideas to Work

You have read how dinosaurs protected themselves with their horns or tails. Imagine some other ways dinosaurs might have protected themselves from being eaten. Write a paragraph about one of them.

The Brontosaurus

The Brontosaurus[1]
Had a brain
No bigger than
A crisp;

The Dodo
Had a stammer
And the Mammoth
Had a lisp;

The Auk
Was just too Aukward—
Now they're none of them
Alive.

Each one,
(Like Man),
Had shown himself
Unfitted to survive.

This story
Points a moral:
Now it's
We
Who wear the pants;

The extinction
Of these species
Holds a lesson
For us
ANTS.

—*Michael Flanders*

285

[1] Brontosaurus (BRAHN-tə-sor-əs)

Was there really an "Ice Age"? Was there really a time when many parts of the land surface of the world were covered by fields of thick ice? And were there people and animals living in those days? How can we possibly know anything about a time so long ago?

THE ICE AGE

THE SECRETS OF THE WINTRY PAST

Slowly—inch by inch, foot by foot—the ice crept forward. From the far north great sheets of ice spread out, swallowing the land. From the high mountains rivers of ice reached down and filled the valleys.

All things gave way before the ice.

Ice ground up rock. It carved the sides of mountains. It dug great hollows in the earth. It scooped up dirt, gravel, stones, and boulders. Whole forests fell, trees snapping like toothpicks before the flow of ice.

287

There was snow, driven by howling winds. There was rain that fell and froze. The ice grew thousands of feet thick. And growing, it pushed farther south. Year after year it flowed on, covering meadows, lakes, and hills.

The ice was felt far away, for winds sweeping across it carried the cold of winter to the land ahead. All living things fled before the cold — or died.

And this went on for thousands of years.

Sometimes the ice would melt at the edges and shrink back. Then the forward flow would start again. Creeping, grinding, carving, scraping, the ice of ever-winter would swallow the land.

Finally the great tongues of ice, the great sheets of ice, drew back for good, leaving behind their floods of melt-water.

In time, life came back to the land, for the ice was gone. It had drawn back to the far north, back to the mountain heights.

The land, of course, was changed. There were new lakes and rivers born of melting ice. Ice had carved out hills and valleys. There was land scraped bare of soil. There was land made rich by soil the ice had dropped.

On this ice-free land, plants grew and spread. Animals came to live on it. And people followed the animals.

Thousands of years passed. People made the land theirs. They grazed herds, planted crops, and built cities where once sheets of ice had glittered in the sun. And no one guessed the wintry secrets of the past.

THE SECRETS ARE UNLOCKED

The earth holds many secrets of its past. For thousands of years the Ice Age, the time of ever-winter, was one of those secrets. Only two hundred years ago people still did not dream that thick sheets of ice had once covered a third of the earth's land.

In the places where people lived, there was no year-round ice. In winter snow might fall and water freeze. But the spring sun melted the snow and ice and called the land to life, making it green with plants. This same thing happened year after year.

In some parts of the world there were glaciers, big masses of ice that did not melt away in summer. But glaciers were found only in the far, cold places—in polar lands and in the high mountains. There the glaciers were, and there they stayed.

The only people who had ever known about the ice were those who lived during the Ice Age. Some saw the ice. Some fled the floods when the glaciers began to shrink and melt. But these were early people who could not write, and they left no record of the ice or floods. What they had seen and known became forgotten. People who lived later did not learn of it.

And so it happened that two hundred years ago the Ice Age was still a secret. No one knew that it had taken place. Yet the story of the Ice Age had been written. It had been written, not by people, but by the ice itself. Where the ice had been, it left its marks upon the land. By learning to read these marks, scientists discovered the Ice Age.

There were, for example, many puzzling boulders. These boulders were puzzling because they did not match any kind of rock in the place where they were found. It was clear that something must have carried them miles from the place where they had formed.

Scientists had wondered about these boulders for years. Most scientists thought that a great and sudden flood must have carried and dropped the boulders. Then, in the early 1800's, a new idea was put forward. Perhaps, some scientists said, glaciers had carried the boulders. Perhaps these glaciers once reached down from the mountains, scooping up rocks and carrying them along. When the glaciers melted and shrank, they dropped the rocks and left them behind.

Was this new idea true? To find out, daring Swiss scientists climbed the Alps. They camped on glaciers and studied them. And they made several discoveries. One was that glaciers move. In time, ice from the upper end of a glacier flows to the lower end, where it melts. Moving, the ice leaves its marks on rocky, mountain walls. It polishes some rock smooth. It makes deep scratches in other rocks.

The marks of modern glaciers were found in the Alps. The same kinds of marks were found in many

other places where there are no glaciers today. That was how scientists started to read the secret of the Ice Age, as written in the earth. That was how they learned of a time when sheets of ice and rivers of ice flowed over lands that are now green and free of ice.

Since that time of discovery, scientists have learned much more. They now know that the earth has had several ice ages. The older ones took place hundreds of millions of years ago. Their marks are very faint, but they can still be read. The last ice age is the one we call the Ice Age.

No one yet knows when the Ice Age began, but some scientists think it started some ten or twenty million years ago. It did not come suddenly upon the earth as a huge snowstorm. Instead, it began as a slow cooling of the air. As time passed, the air grew cooler and cooler, and the oceans also cooled. In faraway places, more snow fell in winter than the summer sun could melt. Year after year the snows fell and piled up. The weight of new snows packed the old snow into ice. The ice grew thicker and thicker.

With their great weight of ice and snow, the glaciers began to flow. Rivers of ice crept down from the mountains. Sheets of ice spread out over polar lands. Only an ocean could stop the ice, for glaciers are land ice and do not form over water. Where glaciers met an ocean, their tongues broke off and floated away as icebergs. But on land the glaciers flowed on and on, over mountains, hills, and plains. New snows fell on this ice and made it even thicker. The ice flowed on, covering large parts of Asia, Europe, and North America. In North America the ice reached as far south as where St. Louis is today.

Then something happened, and the glaciers stopped growing. They melted and shrank back, back to the far places of the earth. After a time they began to grow again. Once more ice covered once-green lands. And this happened four times during the Ice Age. Four times the great glaciers reached down. Four times they melted and shrank back. The last started to draw back about 19,000 years ago. By 6,000 years ago most of the land was once more free of ice. The land was beginning to look very much as it does today.

In the past 150 years scientists have learned much about the Ice Age, but there are some secrets they have not yet discovered. What caused the cooling and made the glaciers grow? What stopped them from growing and made them shrink? Why did they grow and shrink four times? Has the Ice Age ended, or will the glaciers grow a fifth time? Many scientists have ideas about these questions, but no one can answer them for sure.

Over the years scientists have also asked many questions about life in the Ice Age. They have wondered about the animals that lived during the Ice Age. Why did some kinds die out, while others did not? Why did some kinds live through the Ice Age but die out at its end? And what about early people? Did they keep away from the ice? Or did they find a way to live near the wall of ice and hunt the cold-loving animals? Some of the answers to these questions have been found, as you will see in the next part of the story. But you will also discover that many mysteries still remain about "Life in the Ice Age."

LIFE IN THE ICE AGE

There was a time when elephants crashed through the forests of North America, when camels lived upon the land along with horses, deer, and mammoths. Huge herds of bison, or buffalo, roamed the plains. Saber-toothed tigers sprang from hiding at passing horses or deer. Giant, shaggy-coated ground sloths uprooted trees and ate their leaves. The land was

alive with wolves, lions, wild pigs, bears, and dozens of other kinds of animals.

Then the ice came. By the end of the Ice Age, three-fourths of all these animals had disappeared from North America. Some are still found in other lands, but some are long gone from the earth.

The Ice Age made itself felt in many ways.

To begin with, there was the ice, creeping forward, covering the land, and making whole forests fall. Where the ice lay thick upon the land for thousands of years, there could be no life at all.

Then there was the cold that moved ahead of the ice, carried by winds that swept the glaciers. Because of the cold, plants of the north kept spreading south, while southern plants spread farther south. At times when the ice melted and drew back, the plants spread slowly north again.

The shifting of plant life was important because plants are the basic form of food on earth. Many animals eat plants. Other animals eat the animals that eat plants. And people eat both plants and animals.

So when plant life moved, animal life also moved. In the last part of the Ice Age, whole groups of people moved too. These people were herders and hunters. Where the animals went, the people followed. And the animals followed the plants.

Of these animals, some kinds survived the Ice Age.

Some kinds survived in one place and died out in another. Still other kinds died out everywhere.

The saber-toothed tiger was one of the animals that died out everywhere. A big, fierce killer, the saber-tooth ruled wherever it lived. No other animal was its match. Yet the ice wiped it out, while animals that served the saber-tooth as food survived.

The giant ground sloth also died out. There is reason to think that early people tamed the sloths, which were harmless plant-eaters. The people survived, but the sloths did not.

The end of the mammoths is even more puzzling. Mammoths were huge animals of the elephant family. As cold spread over the land, some mammoths grew thick, shaggy fur. They became cold-loving animals that hugged the northern borders of the land. When the Ice Age ended, mammoths changed again. They survived the flood and the warmer times. Then they died out. Perhaps they were killed off by early hunters, who killed herds of animals by driving them over cliffs. Perhaps something else happened. No one knows.

To many people the greatest mystery of all has to do with horses. During the Ice Age, big herds of horses grazed the plains of North America, Europe, and Asia. In Europe and Asia horses survived both the Ice Age and its end. In America they did not. Yet American bison grazed the same plains as the horses, and the bison survived. No one knows what happened to the horses. But there were no more horses in the Americas until, long after, explorers and settlers brought them in from Europe.

There are also great gaps in what we know about the people who lived during the Ice Age. So far we do not know whether people came to North America during the Ice Age or only as it was ending. We do

298

know, though, that 20,000 years ago there were people living in Europe. These people were cave dwellers, and they were skilled hunters and herders. They could not write, but they drew pictures on the walls of their caves, and they made carvings. Their paintings, like their carvings, tell a story of animals. To these people, animals were both food and clothing.

On the walls of the caves, long-dead animals parade. There are woolly rhinoceroses. There are mammoths and bison and horses. There are lions, bears, hyenas, and saber-toothed tigers.

A whole Ice Age village has been uncovered in Czechoslovakia.[1] Here Ice Age hunters camped. They made shelters and warmed themselves with fires. Piles

[1] Czechoslovakia (chek-ə-sloh-VAH-kee-ə)

299

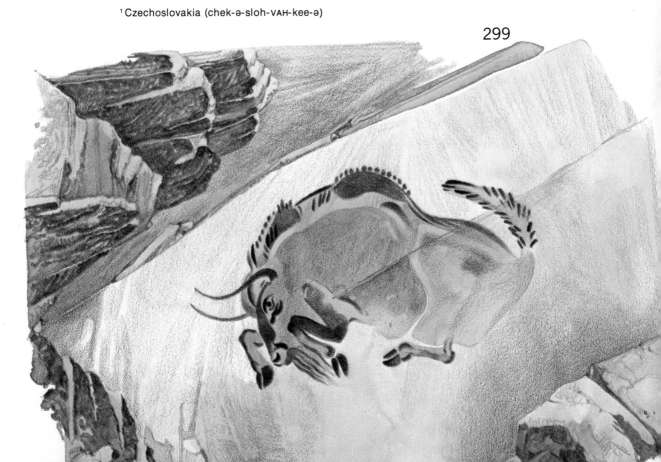

of bones show that they hunted mammoths, rhinoceroses, lions, horses, arctic foxes, and reindeer. They killed small animals with spears. They trapped big animals by digging deep pits and covering these over. When a mammoth or a rhinoceros fell into the pit, the hunters killed it with huge stones.

Most Ice Age people lived well south of the glaciers. Some hunted near the edge of the glaciers. Perhaps some even lived near the edge of the ice. Certainly, they *could* have.

They had fire, which they would have needed for warmth. They would have found animals, which they needed for food. From the same animals they could have gotten warm furs for robes and clothing. With their tools of bone and hard stone, the people could have made clothing like that worn today by Eskimos.

Fire, food, clothing. The people would have needed one more thing—shelter. There were some caves, but not enough. Still, the people had the skills and tools to make tents. They could have felled and trimmed poles. They could have skinned animals, dressed the skins, and laced the skins around tent poles. There are tribes in cold parts of the world that use such tents today.

Did these people live near the edge of the glaciers? Did they see the ice move forward or shrink back? We do not know, but we are still learning. Perhaps the surprising thing is that we know so much.

—*Patricia Lauber*

What do You Think?

1. What were the titles of the three sections in "The Ice Age"? Which section did you find the most interesting? Why?

2. Choose one of the mysteries that still remains about the Ice Age. Think of some answers that might explain it.

3. Skim the first section of "The Ice Age." Find some words and phrases that describe what the ice did as it slowly crept forward. Which words or phrases do you like the best? Why?

Taking A Closer Look

1. Think about this sentence: "The Ice Age made itself felt in many ways." Reread the first part of the section titled "The Secrets of the Wintry Past," and find four facts that explain this statement.

2. In the section titled "The Secrets Are Unlocked," find two of the marks that the glaciers left upon the land.

3. Are we living in the Ice Age today? Explain your answer. Then check what you have said by reading the last three paragraphs in "The Secrets Are Unlocked."

4. Skim the last two pages of the selection and find the things the Ice Age people would have needed to live near the edge of the glaciers. Do you think you could ever live near a glacier? Explain your answer.

5. The people who lived during the Ice Age did not write. How did they leave their story?

During the Ice Age, the area that is now the city of Los Angeles in California was warmer than the lands to the north, just as it is today. Animals living during that period came to this area for protection from the terrible cold. Some of the animals, however, did not fare so well, as you will see.

TRAGEDY OF THE TAR PITS

Imagine time turned back almost a million years. That was the beginning of the Ice Age in America. Great fields of ice covered much of the northern part of the continent.

The country near Los Angeles, California, looked much as it does today. In the wide valley at Rancho La Brea, trees and bushes were scattered through tall grass.

To the east, the thread of a river could be seen. Nearby lay several strange pools. Around each was a bare black patch of ground on which nothing could grow. The pools were half-liquid asphalt, or tar. Through them broke bubbles of oil and smelly gas. After a rain the surface may have been covered with a few inches of water. It was not good water, but one could drink it.

302

During dry weather a film of dust made the tar look like hard ground. The pools, the valley, and distant mountains shimmered in the hot summer sun.

A saber-toothed "tiger," just rising from sleep, looked over the valley. She stood at the top of a shaded hill. She was a powerful beast, the most feared killer of the country. She had a short tail and large front limbs. From either side of her upper jaw, two long teeth pointed downward. They were nine inches long, curved like sabers, and very sharp. No animal could stand against her. She wasn't really a tiger. She looked so much like one, however, that tiger is what she is usually called.

The saber-toothed tiger was ruler of the country. All of it belonged to her by right of strength and her terrible teeth. She stretched like a giant house cat and yawned. The lower jaw dropped, lying almost flat against her neck. This allowed her mouth to open widely. It gave her free use of her teeth as knives or daggers. Those teeth could cut through skin, flesh, and even bone.

The saber-tooth was hungry, but the sun beat down with blazing heat. Food in plenty moved about in front of her. She had only to select. But the day was hot, and she didn't want to push herself. A herd of mammoths lumbered along the skyline. They were like our living elephants, but larger. Their great ivory tusks, curving inward, were like bars of polished steel.

But mammoths were not favorites of the saber-toothed tiger. They were too big, their skins too thick, their strength too great. At any time they would give a powerful fight. Only a baby mammoth was worth the trouble.

At one side, camels were feeding among the bushes and small trees. They were big animals, larger than camels of today. Their hair was thick. But they had no humps of tissue and fat on their backs.

The saber-tooth looked at them without interest. It would take effort to track one down and make the kill. She wasn't hungry enough. It was a lazy day. A little more sleep would be very good. She stretched out on the rock. Her eyes closed, and her chin rested on her paws.

Half an hour later she waked suddenly. Some strange instinct brought her to her feet. In the valley below, her eye saw something move. Two huge, golden-brown animals were pushing through the brush.

Instantly the tiger's body stiffened. Her yellow eyes blazed. This was her favorite prey — the big, slow ground sloths. They were cousins of the small sloths living today in South America. Today's sloths hang with hooked claws beneath tree branches.

These ground sloths were larger than a grizzly bear. All through their skins were little pieces of bone. It gave them a kind of armor. Also, the hair was very thick and long. And they had great curved claws.

The sloths moved about, sure that they were safe. They were safe enough from most animals, but not from the saber-tooth. She could cut through their skin with blows of her sharp teeth. She must be careful of their claws, but that wasn't hard. The ground sloths were too slow to worry her. But their flesh was very good.

The beasts were working their way toward the black pools. They were thirsty. Water from the rain of the night before shone in the sun. They crossed the bare, black ground around the largest pool. Then they splashed in to drink. For a few moments nothing happened. Then slowly the bottom began to give way. Their feet sank into sticky tar. Struggling in fear, they tried to pull themselves out. But their hind legs only went deeper and deeper into the black tar. Escape was impossible.

The saber-toothed tiger had left her hill. She crept silently through the brush. Belly down, chin almost touching the grass, her body seemed to flow across the ground. It was like the smooth movement of a snake. With eyes blazing she watched the great beasts stuck in the pool. The time had come. In one jump, she leaped on the back of the nearest sloth. With a sharp turn the animal threw her off. She rolled over in the asphalt. Roaring, the saber-tooth turned to bite the neck beside her. But she couldn't raise her feet. The sticky tar held them in a clutch of death. For the first time in her life, fear gripped her heart. She tried to drag herself out. But it was too late. She was sucked down slowly into the deep black pool.

In the bare branches of a tree waited half a dozen great black vultures. They were watching the tragedy taking place below them. Huge birds they were, with bare red heads, large beaks, and wings ten feet wide. They were like the California condor that lives today.

Like all vultures, they fed on dead flesh or helpless animals. They didn't kill as eagles and hawks do. They waited until an animal died or had been caught.

While the sloths were still struggling, the vultures circled over them. One dropped down upon the surface of the pool. Then another and another. Croaking, they gathered around the exhausted beasts. In a moment their great beaks would tear out pieces of living flesh. But as each bird tried to move, the sticky tar gripped its feet. Like insects on flypaper, their wings and feathers were caught. Soon the vultures were only black balls of tar. Long before the sun went down, all trace of birds and beasts had gone. The pools shone like silver. The traps were ready for new victims.

The story you have just read is true. It is imaginative only in details. We know it is true because of the bones buried in the asphalt. Also because we can see the same tar traps today. The pits are not so large as they were a million years ago.

One morning I stood on the edge of one of the La Brea pools. A rabbit and a heron were struggling in the black tar. A hawk circled overhead, coming lower and lower. I watched it dive for the rabbit. It sank its claws in the animal's body and tried to lift it out. In two minutes the bird itself was caught. Such has been the fate of many animals and birds through the years. Often cattle, horses, and dogs have been caught. Some were dragged out with ropes. Others, not seen in time, died.

308

By this time the pits have been shut off so that animals cannot be trapped by the deadly tar.

The pools were first formed by oil that rose up from the earth in springs. Around the springs the tar remains soft. Elsewhere it becomes hard when mixed with earth and dust. In the Ice Age, the oil springs were more active than now.

Then people began to take asphalt out of the La Brea pits to make roads. They discovered thousands of bones buried in the tar. For a time, little was done about it. Then scientists at the University of California began to study the strange bones. Thousands of skulls and tens of thousands of other bones have been dug out. The bones are filled with asphalt, but they have changed very little. Of course, nothing remains of the flesh, skin, horns, and hoofs. The bones are mixed up so that the skeletons are never together.

The La Brea tar pits are the richest fossil deposit ever discovered anywhere. Nowhere else are found the remains of so many different kinds of animals. Nowhere else are the bones so well preserved. Nowhere else are they so easy to dig out and study.

In studying the La Brea fossils, people have discovered more than fifty different kinds of birds. They have found at least that many kinds of mammals, too. There are remains of elephants, camels, and sloths; of deer, bison, horses, and wild pigs. Three thousand skulls of the "grim wolf," and two thousand of the saber-toothed tigers, have been found. Also there are

309

bones of bears and lions and other beasts. Most of these animals have been extinct for thousands of years.

Most of the bones are those of flesh-eating mammals, birds of prey, and wading birds. The story of the saber-toothed tiger, the sloths, and the vultures gives the reason. The larger animals, caught in the asphalt, set the trap. They drew the others into the tar. Day after day this has gone on for a million years.

The remains of ducks, geese, and herons are numerous. Perhaps they were fooled by the sheets of shimmering water on the tar. They may have thought these were pools in which to swim.

The La Brea tar pits tell a wonderful story about the animals that lived in southern California during the Ice Age. It is a whole chapter in the past life on this earth, written in black asphalt tar.

—*Roy Chapman Andrews*

What Do You Think?

1. How does the word "tragedy" apply to this story?
2. There are two parts to this selection. One is completely factual. The other is partly imaginative. If the author didn't tell you, how would you know the difference? Think up good titles for the two different sections.

Taking A Closer Look

1. How was the Ice Age in Europe, as described in "The Ice Age," the same or different from the way it was at the La Brea tar pits in California?
2. Do you agree or disagree with the author when he calls the saber-toothed tiger the "ruler of the country"? Why?
3. Name four prehistoric animals and four modern animals that may be compared to one another. How are the pairs of animals alike? How are they different?
4. How were the tar pits formed? How are they different now from the way they were a million years ago? Why are they different today?
5. Find three reasons why scientists call the La Brea tar pits the richest fossil deposit anywhere.

This story tells about a girl who made a great discovery. At first, some experts did not believe that her discovery was important. As you read, *you* will discover how later events proved the experts wrong.

A Girl and the Altamira[1] Cave

A girl only five years old discovered the amazing paintings in the Altamira Cave. This cave, in Northern Spain, holds important clues about prehistoric cave people. The story of how it was discovered is a famous and interesting one.

The girl's name was Maria. She was a daughter of Spanish nobility. Her family lived in a gray stone castle in the tiny village of Santillana del Mar.[2] The village is among the limestone hills that rise up along the Bay of Biscay.

The story really begins in 1878, when Maria's father, Don Marcelino de Sautuola,[3] visited Paris. There he

[1] Altamira (ahl-tah-MEE-rah)
[2] Santillana del Mar (sahn-tee-YAH-nah del MAHR)
[3] Don Marcelino de Sautuola (dawn mar-say-LEEN-oh day SOW-TWOH-lah)

312

saw some prehistoric stone tools and carved antlers found in France. He was so interested that he decided to search for clues about cave people. He also decided that a cave near the castle would be a good place to begin. Northern Spain was near a place in France where many cave homes had already been discovered.

Before Don Marcelino left Paris, he asked about the proper way to explore a cave. He learned that he might have to dig through many feet of earth before reaching any signs of a cave home. He was told to dig very carefully. He must sift every bit of soil. He must be sure not to miss the tiniest scrap of bone or the smallest bit of chipped stone. Don Marcelino returned home determined to follow the directions carefully. He would be proud if he could find even a few stone tools or bits of bone. Then he would be adding to the world's knowledge of our prehistoric ancestors.

There was only one entrance to the cave Don Marcelino had chosen. It was a narrow crack in the earth in a rocky meadow. No one had known about the crack, or the cave, until a few years before. A hunter's dog had fallen into it and was not seen again. The crack was covered over so that children could not crawl in and be hurt or lost.

But now, when Don Marcelino reached home, he opened up the old cave. He went down a sloping passage. At the foot of it was a cave room of fairly good size. A passage only a few feet high led off the room. The passage was too low to work in. So Don Marcelino

313

started digging slowly away at the floor at the front of the cave.

Months went by. He was beginning to think he had made a poor guess. Perhaps no prehistoric people had ever lived in that cave. But one day in November, 1879, he found several interesting stones. They were neatly chipped into the shape of spearheads. That night he hurried home to show the stones to his family.

Little Maria saw the spearheads too. She couldn't understand why everybody thought the stones were so important. But she could see that her father was very excited. She decided that the cave must be a wonderful place. She told Don Marcelino she wanted to go with him.

At first Don Marcelino shook his head. He felt sure Maria would quickly grow tired of playing in a dark cave. But he was very fond of his little daughter. It was hard for him to refuse her anything. So he finally agreed to take her into the cave. She must promise, however, not to disturb him at his work.

Maria was disappointed in the cave, as her father had known she would be. There was nothing to play with. It wasn't much fun to watch her father scraping away in the dirt. After a time, with a candle in her hand, she crept into the low passage.

Soon the little tunnel grew broader. But it was still very low. Even a small child like Maria had to be careful. She might bump her head on the rough ceiling as she moved along.

Suddenly, glancing up at that ceiling, Maria stopped still. The candle wavered in her hand. All around her, in the flickering yellow light, there seemed to be animals. She thought she saw huge beasts with curving horns and staring eyes.

"Father!" Maria screamed. "Bulls! Bulls!"

Her voice echoed against the stone.

Don Marcelino dropped his tools, grabbed a candle, and crawled into the tunnel.

"I'm coming, Maria!" he called. "Don't be frightened."

But when he saw Maria, he knew she was quite safe. She was not frightened at all. She was pointing at the ceiling.

"Look, Father!" she cried. "Look!"

315

At first Don Marcelino couldn't understand what he was supposed to look at. He turned about to look up at the ceiling. It was very close above his own head. He could see at first only some black lines, and some splotches of red and yellow.

Then slowly, one after the other, the splotches and lines took on shape. He turned this way and that. Finally, he was lying flat on his back to see more clearly. Don Marcelino now knew why Maria had shouted out the word "Bulls!" Some of the shapes did look like bulls. They were huge staring beasts with curving horns.

Don Marcelino blinked his eyes. The more he stared, the more real the animals seemed. He could see that the paintings were skillfully done. The red and black and yellow creatures appeared to be alive.

There was one great beast with head down and hind legs bent under it. It looked as if the huge animal had been struck a mortal blow just before Don Marcelino first saw it.

Not far away was a red horse with a black mane and a black tail. It looked as if it had just touched the ground after a long leap.

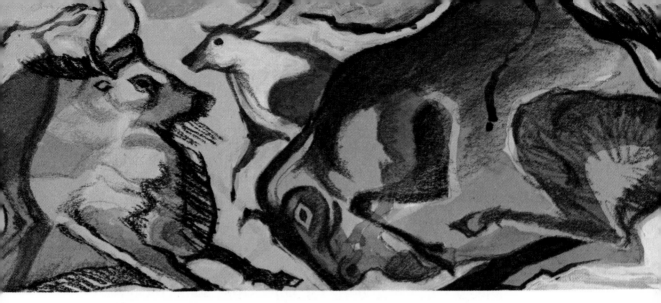

Amazed, Don Marcelino looked from one picture to another. Red animals had been painted over animals outlined in black. A red creature was half covered up by another animal. The second one was painted in black and yellow. Its legs were set as if it were about to spring.

How had these paintings come to be made? The ceiling was so low that an adult couldn't sit up straight in it. Who had made the paintings? And when? Don Marcelino knew that only he and a few of his workers had entered the cave since he had opened it.

He tried to puzzle out an explanation for the figures leaping and striding across the rock ceiling. He began to see that the ones that looked like bulls were not bulls at all. He studied them more carefully. Suddenly he caught his breath. The bull-like animals were really bison. Bison were horned and humped animals that had disappeared from Europe thousands of years before.

317

The other figures on the ceiling were prehistoric animals too. There were wild horses, reindeer with long antlers, and huge wild boars. The animals were of a kind no living person had ever laid eyes on.

That was when Don Marcelino saw how important little Maria's discovery was. That very evening he wrote a long letter about the cave paintings. He sent the letter to scientists in the Spanish capital, Madrid.

He wrote that the paint on the ceiling of the cave looked fresh and new. He noted that some red even came off on his finger when he touched it. But, he said, no one skillful enough to paint these figures had entered the cave since it was discovered. And it was discovered only a few years earlier. Besides, he wrote, the animals were prehistoric animals. None of Don Marcelino's neighbors knew what such animals looked like. He felt sure that the pictures had been painted when there were bison in the Spanish hills. They had been painted, he said, by the same people who hunted those bison. They had been painted by the cave people of prehistoric times.

His letter brought a geologist hurrying to the little village of Santillana del Mar. He wanted to see the cave, which Don Marcelino called Altamira. At first the geologist thought Don Marcelino must be playing a joke on him. No prehistoric people, he said, could have painted those pictures. But when he questioned Don Marcelino, the geologist began to change his mind. When he saw the cave himself, he found some more of

318

the chipped stones Don Marcelino had found. He also found some bones of prehistoric animals. So the expert decided the amateur was right. At once he returned to Madrid to make a public announcement of Maria's discovery.

Maria and the little village in which she lived became famous. Every day people came to visit the Altamira cave. Even the King of Spain arrived to admire the paintings. He wished to praise the little girl who had found them. Copies of the paintings were prepared for a great meeting of scientists from all over the world. The meeting was soon to be held in Lisbon,[1] Portugal. Those coming to the Lisbon meeting were invited to visit Altamira.

[1] Lisbon (LIZ-bən)

Then that meeting took place, and suddenly every-thing changed. The scientists in Lisbon said they didn't even have to look at the pictures. They were sure that the story of Altamira was a hoax.

Once more Santillana del Mar became a quiet village. No one came to visit it after the experts had their say. The newspapers that had been praising Don Marcelino and his little daughter now made fun of them. Experts refused to answer Don Marcelino's letters. They also refused to let him attend their meet-ings to tell them about Altamira.

Finally Don Marcelino sealed up the opening to the cave.

Years passed. Maria de Sautuola grew up. After Don Marcelino died, she was one of the few people who even remembered the cave. She was also among the few who remembered when Altamira had been the pride of Spain.

In the meantime, French prehistorians were explor-ing caves in their country. They were discovering more and more about cave people. They dug down through the layers of debris that filled some of the caves. There they found hundreds of bones and stone tools. Sometimes their digging even exposed drawings on the walls. But the drawings were so simple that they could have been made only by cave people. In fact, these drawings were exactly what most people expected of cave people. Nobody connected them with the paint-ings the King of Spain had admired as works of art.

320

Then, in 1901, French experts began to clear the debris from two caves close to the village of Cro-Magnon.[1] This is the village where young Louis Lartet[2] first found the five skeletons of Cro-Magnon people. Each inch of soil revealed another inch of cave wall. In time they reached the original floors of the two caves. They had dug away debris that had been undisturbed for thousands of years. The walls they now saw had been covered up all that time. And the walls were decorated!

On the walls of the Les Combarelles[3] cave were hundreds of figures of prehistoric animals. These figures were carved into the rock. The animals seemed to run and leap like living beasts.

On the walls of the Font-de-Gaume[4] cave, there were only a few paintings in red and black. But everybody agreed that the red rhinoceros and the black-and-red reindeer looked alive too.

Many experts had been present while the caves were being cleared. They knew that the decorations had been put on the walls before the caves became filled up. They had to face the fact that those painted and carved walls proved two things.

They proved that the cave people had discovered the idea behind all art. That idea is that lines and colors, on a flat surface, can give the impression of an animal, or of some other real thing.

[1] Cro-Magnon (kroh-MAG-non)   [2] Louis Lartet (loo-EE lahr-TAY)
[3] Les Combarelles (lay kawm-bah-REL)   [4] Font-de-Gaume (FOHN-də-GOHM)

The paintings and drawings also proved that the cave people were really good artists. Some pictures were so simple they looked like the work of a small child. But in almost every case the animals on the cave walls seemed alive. Only a skillful artist can give the appearance of life to lines and splotches of color.

One expert who saw the works of art in the French caves was Emil Cartailhac.[1] He was a well known French paleontologist. As he stood before them he remembered something he had done almost twenty-five years earlier. He had refused to visit a certain Spanish cave called Altamira. He had refused because he couldn't believe that what its discoverer said was true. Now Cartailhac knew that the Spanish amateur must have been right.

Cartailhac was an honorable person. He blamed himself for having questioned Don Marcelino's word without even seeing the Altamira paintings. Then he packed his bags and set out for Spain.

[1] Emil Cartailhac (ay-MEEL kahr-tay-YAK)

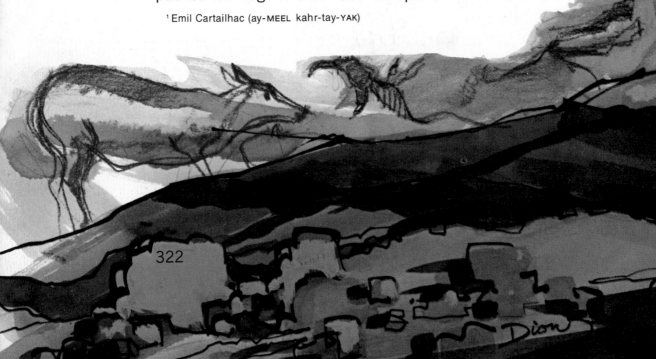

A few days later Maria de Sautuola met the French-
man. She led him up to the sealed opening of Altamira.
She turned the key in the rusty lock, pushed the door
open, and took him inside. Quietly she lit candles. She
then showed him the pictures she had first seen when
she was five years old.

Cartailhac could hardly believe his eyes. The paintings had been so well preserved in the cool cave! They
looked as if they had been made only an hour before.
But Cartailhac knew at once their true age. And he
knew that they were by far the greatest example he
had ever seen of prehistoric art.

From that day on, the village of Santillana del Mar again became a famous place. It was always crowded with eager visitors. Experts came from every quarter of the world. Those who couldn't come asked that copies of the pictures be made. Then they too could see the paintings that had suddenly become so famous.

A book was published showing all the drawings and paintings on the Altamira ceiling. The floor of the cave was dug away so that the works of art could be better seen. In time the Spanish government took over responsibility for the cave. Now its paintings, one of Spain's greatest art treasures, would always be protected. Every year, Altamira becomes more famous. More people go there to admire the pictures little Maria de Sautuola first saw by the light of her candle.

Maria de Sautuola lived to hear all the experts admit that her father had been right. She lived to hear her own name spoken in praise all over the world. She had discovered the clue proving that some of the greatest artists of all time were cave people. These were the people who lived among bison and mammoths during the Ice Age.

—Sam and Beryl Epstein

What Do You Think?

1. Pretend you are deep in the cave with Maria when her candle flickers on the ceiling. Tell what you see and how you feel.

2. What could have been Don Marcelino's feelings as he sealed up the cave? How would Maria have felt twenty-five years later when the cave was reopened?

3. If Don Marcelino had not searched for prehistoric tools, do you think the Altamira paintings would ever have been discovered? Explain your answer.

Taking A Closer Look

1. List the directions for the proper way to explore a cave. How do you know that Don Marcelino did or did not follow them correctly?

2. Name two other caves besides Altamira that are mentioned in this story. Where are they? What has been found in each one?

3. Why were the experts so sure the Altamira paintings were a hoax? If you had been in Lisbon, what would you have thought about the cave?

4. How did Cartailhac show he was an honorable person?

5. What has been done to the Altamira cave to make it easier to see the paintings? Why was this necessary?

CAVE ART FROM THE ICE AGE

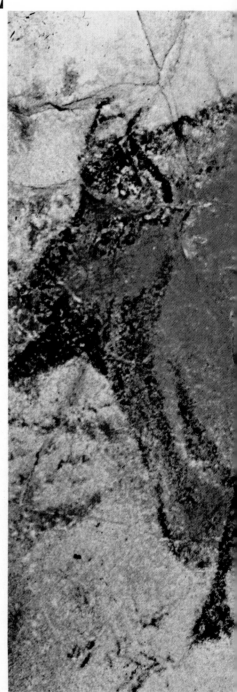

Deep, deep in caverns, in places almost impossible to find or reach, cave artists of the Ice Age decorated rock walls and ceilings with paintings of animals they saw and hunted. Many of these creatures have long since disappeared from the earth. For tens of thousands of years the magnificent Ice Age paintings have been sealed up and preserved by nature in the cool caves. Until they were discovered only a century ago, perhaps no one, except the cave dwellers themselves, ever knew they existed. How fortunate we are today to be able to see these great art treasures from so long ago!

As you look at some of the colorful cave paintings, try to imagine how the cave artists might have created them. What tools do you think they used? How do you think they created the different colors? Try also to picture in your mind what the daily life of the cave dwellers might have been like. Do you find any clues in these paintings?

326

Young Maria might have seen this red and black bison when she looked up at the ceiling in the Altamira cave.

Courtesy, Istituto Editoriale Italiano

One of the most beautiful of the animal murals in the Altamira cave is in the Picture Gallery. Animals are painted life-size on a part of the roof.

Here is a painting of part of a hind, which is a kind of deer. The entire hind is painted in the Altamira Picture Gallery.

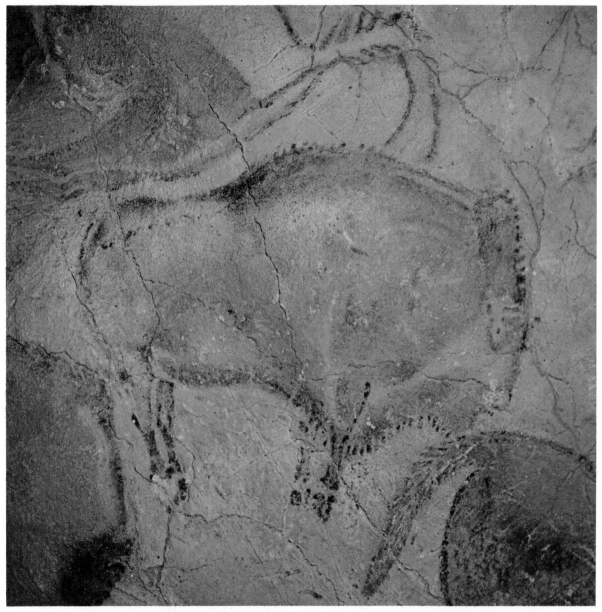

Here is another bison from Altamira. The roof has many rocky bulges. The cave painters used these bumps to make animals seem real. Some parts of the bison seem to stand out.

In 1920 a child climbed down an underground
passage and broke into the cave at Pêche-Merle,[1]
France. Two years later the hall with pictures was
discovered.

In this picture you see one of the ten paintings of
mammoths found at Pêche-Merle. Notice the long
hairs covering the trunk and legs of the mammoth.

[1] Pêche Merle (PESH MAIRL)

Almost opposite the paintings of the mammoths is a room with pictures of polka-dotted horses and outlines of hands. These are painted on rock walls. Do you see the hand in this picture? How do you think the cave painters made prints of their hands?

331

Some of the most famous of the Ice Age paintings are in the caves of Lascaux,[1] France. These were discovered in 1940 by four children chasing a dog down a hole in the ground. After going down a twenty-foot tunnel, they found themselves in a big hall whose walls were covered with paintings. Passages from this cavern led to other rooms with murals.

Here is a picture of a wall painting at Lascaux. A leaping cow is shown with little horses underneath. The box-like figure near the cow's head may be a fence or trap.

[1] Lascaux (las-KOH)

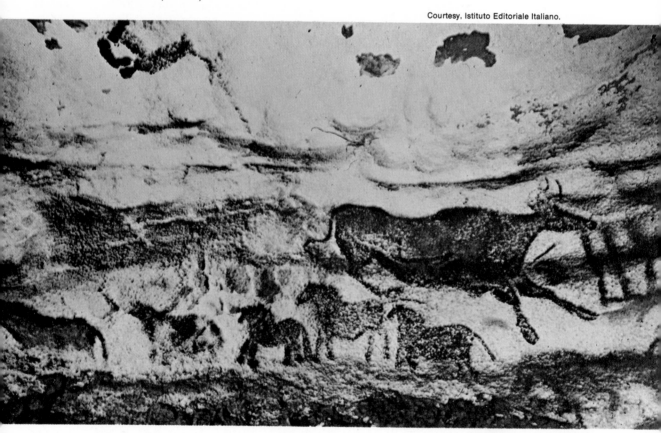

The heads of cows and a horse are grouped on the ceiling. Notice the "trap" in the middle.

A large bull is painted over an earlier figure.

334

This painting seems to tell a story. It is at the bottom of a deep pit at the end of a passage at Lascaux. A bison is seen with horns lowered and eyes wide open. A spear has gone through its body. Nearby is a simple drawing of a person who appears to be lying on the ground or falling backwards. On the other side is a bird on a stick. Is this a hunting scene, or is it a dance of the hunt with people in masks? What story do you see in this strange painting?

335

Failure in the hunt would mean no food for the tribe of cave dwellers. But the hunt this day brings unexpected adventure for Marek[1]-son. As you read this story, what do you learn about how the cave people hunted, and how they may have lived?

THE GREAT HUNT

A hunting party is following a path down from its cave to the valley below. At the head of the line of hunters is Marek, the shaman.[2] Right behind him is his young son, Marek-son.

By late morning, the hunting party has reached the other side of the valley. The party comes to a pass leading into a land of plains and hills. This is a grazing land. Here game can be found in good times.

The sun, which was pale at dawn, is now partly hidden by clouds. A wet, raw wind bites into the faces of the hunters.

As the weather gets worse, Marek studies the sky. He knows that the sudden storms of spring can be most dangerous.

And now, in the rugged pass, the storm breaks upon the hunters.

Hurriedly they seek cover, climbing up the steep walls of the ravine. They seek places high enough to be safe

[1]Marek (MAR-ek)   [2]shaman (SHAH-mən)

336

from the flash flood. The flood, they know, will soon come rushing upon them.

A loud rumble of thunder echoes in the ravine. Lightning flashes against the low clouds. Gusts of wet, icy wind lash against the hunters, hidden behind the rocks.

The clouds burst. A wall of water roars down the narrow pass. Trees, rocks, and trapped animals are carried along in the rushing stream. It is well that the cave dwellers have chosen high places in the storm.

Now, as suddenly as it came, the storm is over. Marek has left his place of safety. The others climb down from the rocks. Only a trickle of water runs along the floor of the ravine.

Carefully Marek leads the party ahead. Suddenly, just in time, he stops them. A huge rock hanging out from the cliff comes crashing down. Swiftly the hunters draw back, but only for a moment. When the small rocks and mud have stopped falling, they move forward.

Marek-son climbs to the top of the ravine and studies the landslide. He looks all about him. He looks back to the way

the party has come and ahead to the flatlands. He hopes bison will be grazing there. Far off, across the plains, he can see black specks growing smaller. He strains his keen eyes to make them out.

Something has frightened the game. The storm? The coming of the hunters? It is true that bison become harder to track the more often they are hunted. But this is the first time Marek-son has found the prairie bare of game.

This, he knows, means failure for the hunters and for his father. His eyes narrow as he carefully searches out the answer.

There is something strange out in the middle distance. One huge form seems to lean against a grove of trees. Forgetting the hunters still below him, Marek-son sets out to see this strangeness. Moving down to the flatlands, the boy

loses sight of it. But his sure sense of direction takes him toward one grove of trees.

His sense of smell, sharp as an animal's, adds to his excitement. There is a strong, musky smell in the air. It grows stronger as he nears the grove.

Marek-son knows he must come near any game only with much care. All animals are alert. They are easy to anger, and can be dangerous. His nose tells him this is no animal he has seen before. He moves toward the grove more carefully than usual.

As he enters the grove, he nearly bumps into a living mountain of flesh. He can't believe that a thing so huge can be alive. He knows that if he makes a mistake, he will die.

Now a sudden excitement shakes the hairy creature. It towers into the branches of the trees around him. The

beast roars with anger as it senses Marek-son in the grove. Its huge head comes down almost in reach of the young hunter. Something like a snake reaches toward him. Long tusks root wildly in the earth.

The son of the shaman has been trained to stand strong against fear. Swiftly, he darts into the bushes where he is safe. The beast is too huge for him to attack. The whole party of hunters would be hard put to kill it. Yet there must be a way.

Suddenly the boy remembers the painting he has seen in the magic cave. This is the great mammoth! Marek-son remembers, too, the spear in the leg of the painted animal. This beast is as huge as ten bison. If it can be killed, there will be food for all his people. If he can only wound the beast! Then, perhaps the hunters, when they come up, can somehow kill it.

Marek-son weighs his spear in his hand. To throw it here among the trees would do little harm to such a huge beast. Yet he does not dare to leave the grove that protects him.

If he could only strike the mammoth in the lower leg! He works his way behind the animal. Its sight appears to be poor. It continues to beat the bushes the hunter has just left. Marek-son comes very close to the beast. He can see the bugs crawling in its long, matted hair.

With all his strength, the boy drives his spear deep into the heavy leg. Almost with the same movement, he throws himself back into the bushes. But at that very instant he feels a hard blow across his back. For a moment, Marek-son feels as if he is part of the landslide back in the ravine. He feels as if he is being thrown down a long rocky slope.

The hunters arriving from the ravine have come near the grove. They can hear the roars of the big beast as it fights to get at Marek-son. They speed up their steps to a run. When they reach the grove, they immediately attack the mammoth. All afternoon they fight it. Some throw their spears, then watch their chance to rush in and grab their weapons. They draw their spears out of the beast's flesh as it whirls to face yet another attacker. Now the sky grows dark. But the mammoth stands at bay near the edge of the plain. It seems as powerful as ever.

As the day ends, the hunters are growing desperate. They may lose this prize if night falls before they have killed it. Their attacks become more daring. Yet the great beast fights back with its powerful trunk.

Marek has remained in the grove with his son. Marek-son moves restlessly in pain. Marek has cleaned the boy's wounds. He has covered the red streak across his back with a comforting herb.

The shaman, like the hunters, is worried about the coming of night. It is his task to bring the hunt to a successful end. Even more than the hunters, he knows that the dark is full of danger. It can mean escape for the beast.

He bends over his son. The boy's eyes, still dull with shock and pain, meet his father's. Suddenly Marek-son remembers something, something very important. Painfully, he speaks the word for "landslide."

The landslide! The falling rock had left a gaping pit at the edge of the cliff.

Marek understands what his son means and his face brightens. He places a spear beside the boy for protection against animals. Then he leaves quickly, for he must return to the hunt.

He comes again to where the hunters are still fighting the mammoth. They all shout with joy as they see their shaman. Most of them do not have weapons now. They can only throw rocks at the great beast.

Quickly Marek tells the hunters of his plan. He sends half the party on ahead. Next he makes a small fire with flint and leaves. The others make torches out of branches and grasses.

Then, waving their flaming torches overhead, the hunt-

342

ers frighten the mammoth with fire. It roars wildly in great terror. Of all the weapons of the hunters, fire is the one most feared.

Night comes quickly now. Moving clumsily in the dark, the beast climbs toward the top of the ravine. It is hurried on by the burning torches on all sides. Reaching the top, it turns to face the hunters. They cannot come near it from below. But Marek grabs

a flaming branch and throws it into the woolly face of the beast.

Roaring loudly, its hair burning, the mammoth steps back.

The hunters who have gone ahead have lined a path with fires. The others drive the beast along the path with their torches. At the end of the path the pit has been hidden with brush. On the edge of the pit, the mammoth stands for a long moment. Its feet seek firm ground. But the earth crumbles away beneath its great weight. With a loud roar, it slides into the hole. There is an earthshaking thud. A howl of victory goes up from the hunters.

The great mammoth is theirs!

The sun has risen and set three times over the valley. And now it is evening again. There has been a long line of

men, women, and children bearing back the meat from the mammoth. There has been a funeral for two hunters killed in the hunt. There have been both joy and sadness in these three days.

The torches light the magic room where Marek-son lies. His spear, brought from the battle, has been placed beside him. Marek has taken care of him during these long days and nights. Now the shaman raises a torch to light the ceiling above his son. The boy's eyes grow wider. For the first time his attention seems caught. In his eyes a gleam of health tells the father that his boy will recover.

It is something above the young hunter that holds his attention. It is there on the ceiling of the magic cave. Painted on the ancient drawing is a figure driving a spear into the mammoth. In that figure Marek-son sees with growing pride his part in the hunt. The painting tells him all he needs to know about the outcome of the great hunt of his people. His people are the cave dwellers of thirty thousand years ago.

—*Richard M. Powers*

What Do You Think?

1. What part of the hunt do you think the most exciting? Tell about it as if you were there at the time.
2. What two important facts did the cave painting tell Marek-son? How was each fact important to the great hunt?
3. Tell at least three facts you learned about cave dwellers. Which fact was the most interesting to you? Why?

Taking A Closer Look

1. Tell two important ways Marek-son helped in the great hunt.
2. Pretend you are Marek, the shaman, and explain to the hunters your plan for killing the mammoth.
3. Why was the landslide important to Marek's plan for capturing the mammoth?
4. Why do you think the word *magic* was used to describe the room where Marek-son saw the painting of the mammoth?
5. Look back to the next to the last page in the story. Find the sentence, "The sun has risen and set three times. . . ." What does the sentence tell you?

Putting Ideas to Work

Art can tell a great deal about how people live. Pretend you are planning an exhibit. Make a list of the things the paintings would show.

Under One Sun

You are about to take a trip to other lands, with stops in Morocco, Nigeria, Mexico, Japan, and China. Though the boys and girls you will meet have different customs from you own, they, like you, face problems, have adventures, and dream dreams.

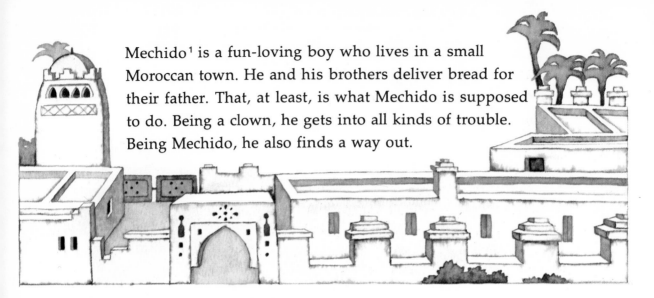

Mechido[1] is a fun-loving boy who lives in a small Moroccan town. He and his brothers deliver bread for their father. That, at least, is what Mechido is supposed to do. Being a clown, he gets into all kinds of trouble. Being Mechido, he also finds a way out.

MECHIDO

Mechido lived in a small Moroccan town. When he was nine, the time had come for him to go to work, as his older brothers had done, delivering bread for their father. Their father was a baker. He owned a small oven in the town.

"He has finished his training," said his brother Mohammed. "He can make his way home blindfolded."

"Can he balance the breadboard on his head?" asked their father.

"Yes. And he can come around corners without letting it fall."

"Good," said his father. "And can he climb up and down stairs and still keep it on his head?"

"Yes," said the brothers, and winked at each other.

"Then he is ready. And if he is ready, why are you laughing?" Mechido's brothers were laughing very hard.

[1] Mechido (mə-SHEE-doh)

"Stop laughing at once and answer," commanded their father.

"Mechido is a clown," said his brother Driz. "I am weak thinking of the trouble he will cause."

Mechido hung his head in chagrin.

And everyone became serious. They all stood around him in a little circle, staring, his brothers solemn and a massive frown on the father's face. Mechido wilted.

He began work the next day. From then on he was called the Tarah,[1] as all Moorish boys are called who deliver dough to the oven. The women make their batter at home; and it is the Tarah's job to run with the breadboard from house to house, collect the dough and uncooked pastries and, balancing them all on the breadboard, carry them to the oven. When they are baked, it is the Tarah who delivers them again from house to house. Morning and afternoon the women bang their door knockers and call, "Tarah!", and the Tarah goes running.

Mechido's father had his oven in a semicellar. A long slanting chute opened into the cellar from the street. It was here that Mechido would send the loaded breadboard sliding down to his father. It was here, craning his neck up the chute to listen, that Mechido waited that first morning for the first woman to call.

But it was not a glad Mechido. He felt apprehensive, more than anything else because of his father. Mechido's father had once been a wrestler, and he still had plenty of muscle. He also had a close, black beard. When he was dressed in his best burnoose and fez, Mechido thought the beard made him look like a prince. But somehow, it had a different effect in the

[1] Tarah (tə-RAH)

cellar. There he wore only full white pants. Seeing him with the long bread paddle in his hand and those old wrestling muscles shining, his face glowing from the heat and that little beard glistening, Mechido thought he looked very much like someone to be feared.

"Tarah!" There it was. Mechido grabbed the breadboard.

"Tarah!" Mechido darted into the street.

"Tarah!" Mechido dashed up a stairway, burst through a door and fell into a pair of floury arms.

That first day, the hardest thing for him to get used to was the piercing cries of "Tarah" that followed him everywhere. He was in such a state of alarm that every time he heard the call, he fell down.

Around a corner he came with two dozen cakes on his head. "Tarah!" He stumbled and two dozen cakes took off in the air.

He sped through a hall with eight loaves of bread piled up on his head. "Tarah!" A shadowy figure swelled out on a wall. He leaped and eight loaves rolled away.

He tore past a fountain. "Tarah!" from above. "Allah!" from Mechido, and sixteen sweet cakes lit in the water.

This happened near the close of the day, and it was almost too much for Mechido. It had already been a very bad day. He tried to fish out the cakes but they were sinking fast. Unhappily, he watched them settle on the bottom. His father! What was he going to tell his father?

That was something he could not understand about grown-ups. Why were they so earnest? So drastic! They hardly ever saw the bright side of things. Mechido could not see why. He often wondered about it.

350

The cakes were disintegrating. What had shortly before been so crisp was now so flabby. Mechido was sure his father would not take this well.

It was too depressing to think about. A few minutes later, to cheer himself up, with twenty-four rolls of fresh dough on his board, he slid down three flights of bannisters backward. He did not see the woman waiting at the foot of the stairs.

"Tarah," she hissed in his ear as he sailed to the bottom.

"Ay!" he cried, threw his hands in the air, and the breadboard fell over flat.

"Smashed," said his father when he saw the twenty-four rolls of dough. "Sit down, Mechido, my son. Let us take the toll."

There was a cloudy look in his eyes.

"Out of thirty-five deliveries today, my son," began his father, "thirty-one were incomplete and four were not made at all. What happened, my son?"

"It is their voices, my father," answered Mechido. "Such shrieks! Such screams! I drop everything."

His father took two pieces of dough and put them in Mechido's ears.

"Tarah!" he thundered. "Can you hear that?"

"Yes. But it is not piercing."

There was a snort from Mechido's father. It was plain that he was not long on patience.

"You will plug your ears every day," he said in a thick voice. "That is one thing. Here is another thing. Where are your Aunt Zorah's[1] cinnamon wafers? Can you answer me that?"

Mechido felt more and more apprehensive.

"There is a wall in front of Abdelkrim[2] the candlemaker's house," he began cautiously. "Do you know that wall?"

His father grunted.

"It's not high. I was walking on top of it with the wafers on my head. I was walking on it, sir, as the scarecrows walk at night, with their eyes tight closed. I did not see the end of the wall. I fell."

"You fell. And the wafers?"

[1] Zorah (zə-RAH)   [2] Abdelkrim (AHB-dəl-kə-REEM)

Mechido bit his lip. "In Abdelkrim's pigpen."

The cloudy look in his father's eyes had grown to a storm.

Then followed a scolding. But there were so many scoldings in Mechido's career as bread boy, I think it's kinder to leave them out.

That night, from his bed, Mechido could hear his parents' voices in the front room, next to his. His father was raging.

". . . down a bannister . . ."

Mechido's eyes danced.

". . . into a fountain . . ."

Mechido's stomach was heaving.

". . . and over a wall . . ."

Mechido held his sides and wheezed.

That was only the first night. His father went on in a similar way night, after night, after night.

As the days passed, Mechido got into so much more trouble, his brother took over the job of Tarah.

It was a very contrite Mechido who appeared before his father one night.

"I beg," said Mechido, "for one more chance."

Mechido's father was unmoved.

"Your last chance," he said somberly, "your last chance is gone. Finished and gone."

"Oh, my father, only one more chance, I beg of you."

"Finished and gone. *I* am *almost* finished and gone," said Mechido's father, and he pounded the table.

Mechido pressed his kness together, took a deep breath, and said in a rush, "There is something I want to do, and it will take only a week. You will not see me during that week, and if at the end of it you like what I have done, perhaps you will forgive me and allow me to be Tarah again. That is all I beg of you, my father."

His father brightened visibly. "If it means that I shall not lay eyes on you for one week, yes! One thousand times, yes!"

And the next day, and the next, and the next, not a hair of Mechido's curly head was seen. At night, he came home to climb into bed after everyone else had eaten, and in the morning he left before breakfast.

"Where does Mechido spend his time?" his father asked at the dinner table.

No one knew.

"Where does he eat?"

No one knew.

"But is he eating?" his father demanded.

"I heard him counting his money last night," said his brother Driz. "He was saying, 'Oranges, nuts, and cheese,' and I heard his money clink."

"I think," said Mohammed, "he is buying his own food with the coins he took as tips while he was Tarah."

"Mohammed," announced his father at the end of the meal, "tomorrow you will find out where Mechido goes."

"I have seen him!" Mohammed exclaimed at dinner the following night.

Their father's eyes gleamed.

"He was at Abdul[1] the cabinetmaker's; and I saw him there as I was on the way to Aunt Zorah's with bread. He was sitting

[1] Abdul (AHB-dəl)

354

at Abdul's workbench, sandpapering something. He had his tongue clenched between his teeth. On the way back from Aunt Zorah's he was hammering something. I called to him, but he jumped up and looked very angry and closed the door."

Their father said nothing. The next morning, on the pretext of an errand, he left his son Driz at the oven and went by the cabinetmaker's. Through a window he could see Mechido bent over a sheet of tin. He was honing the edges and measuring them, sliding them back and forth over something. Mechido's father stepped away from the window and puffed out his chest.

"My poor little Mechido," said his mother at dinner, looking at his empty place. "And what is it that he is doing?" she asked.

"One of his pranks, you'll see," said Driz.

"I believe it is not a prank," his father said proudly. "Perhaps Mechido is not the dunce you think," he said in rolling tones. "Two days more, Driz, my son, and you shall see."

The evening of the seventh day, at the end of dinner, Mechido ran into the room. His cheeks were flushed and his eyes were shining. In his hands he carried a box.

"It's finished!" he cried. "Look what I have made!" And he set it on the table for them to see.

It was rather long, some four feet, and a foot or so high. The sides were made of fine, thin sheets of wood, and on one end of it was a little door with hinges and a small latch. It was quite plain, except for the little door, which had inlays of different colored pieces of wood arranged in the pattern of a star. "Look inside!"

Mechido's father and mother and his two brothers crowded around while Mechido unlatched the door. Inside were three shelves of bright tin. "You see," explained Mechido, "they slide in and out." He slid each of the shelves out and in again.

"Do you like it? Isn't it beautiful!" Mechido hugged himself. "Isn't it just the most beautiful thing?"

"It is very nice, Mechido," said his father. "But what is it?"

"It is," said Mechido, "a breadbox."

"What, Mechido, my son, do you mean?" his father said slowly.

"I mean, it is a breadbox for carrying bread. Instead of a board, you see. It is very light, much lighter than the board." He put it on his head. "And it balances." He tipped it from side to side. "And nothing, nothing can ever happen to the bread again. If I fall in the street, let me fall! The bread is safe. No more garbage in the dough. If they throw mud at me, let them throw! The bread is safe. Look. I go to Aisha's[1] house." He walked around the table. "She piles on the dough. Whisk, I go to Abdelkrim's, more dough. Then to Aunt Zorah's for more." He marched back around the table. "And off to the oven, all baked at once!" Mechido clapped his hands. "And the best is this. When I deliver the bread again, it will still be hot!"

[1] Aisha (AH-ee-shə)

Driz and Mohammed stared first at their brother and then at the box and then at their brother again. Who would have guessed that such a clown could make such a box?

"Oh, my dearest Mechido." His mother swept him into her arms and covered him with kisses. "How hard you have worked! See the tiny nails you drove in. How many times you must have hammered your little fingers!" She kissed him again.

"Not once!" cried Mechido. "Oh, I did it very well. It's the most wonderful work in the world. It is the most exciting thing I have ever done. I would rather do that than any—" He stopped short. He was afraid he had offended his father.

But Mechido's father stood silent. There was something stubborn in the set of his shoulders.

"No, Mechido, my son." He spoke stiffly, "It cannot be. The art of the Tarah is in his board. The way he handles it. That is his merit; that is his skill. There will be no breadbox. It was not a good idea."

357

"But, Father! It is better. It has three shelves. It carries far more than a board. And now the bread will be safe!" Mechido's voice was rising. "Now there can be no mistakes. The bread will not fly off into the fountain. The bread will not fall to the pigs."

"No. No. One thousand times no!" His father's face had turned a dark red. "For seven generations the boys of this family have carried a simple board. I will not have my son parading around town with a fancy box on his head. A box with a door! No."

"Father—" Mechido's throat was closing—"the bread will still be hot."

"No!" said his father and brought his hands palm down on the breadbox.

Mechido made a choking sound and fled from the room. He did not want his brothers to see him cry.

From his bed he heard his mother berating his father. It was the only time in his life that he had heard them fight on his account, but it did not console him at all.

"You are cruel," he heard her cry out. "Obstinate and cruel. And you have broken his heart. It is a beautiful box. I would like to see you try to make such a box."

For once Mechido did not hear his father shout. He answered something in such a low rumble that Mechido could not make it out.

He sat on his bed with his cheeks flaming.

"It is not just," he said to himself again and again. Tonight he did not care to peek through the hole. And, "Tomorrow I am going to fill the hole with putty. I will never look at my father again. So help me, I will never even look into his eyes again." At that sad thought, tears welled over and down his hot cheeks.

358

He was about to give over into sobs when he heard a murmur in the next room. It was Abdul the cabinetmaker's voice. Abdul had been very kind to him; this might be worth seeing after all. Mechido dried his face, lifted the poster, and looked through the hole.

Abdul was crossing the room. He was a big clumsy man who shuffled when he walked. He had heavy, sloping eyes that were full of humor, and when he was amused they seemed to slide down the sides of his face. Mechido thought that was a marvelous sight, and during his week with Abdul he had tried to say all kinds of funny things, just so he could watch what happened to Abdul's eyes.

Abdul bowed a deep bow. "I see you have the box," he said with a smile.

"We have it," answered Mechido's father.

"I have come to congratulate you," said the kindly Abdul, "on your remarkable son. A man is blessed to have such a son."

Mechido's father was immediately on guard. He observed Abdul with veiled eyes.

Abdul rubbed his fingers over the top of Mechido's box. "Never have I seen a boy work so hard. Such devotion and such concentration! Do you know, my friend, that your son sat for six hours at a stretch, morning and afternoon, without stirring?"

"That is interesting," said Mechido's father. "Very interesting."

"Look at the workmanship." Abdul bent over the box. "He has sanded it like satin. The shelves are measured to a fraction of a fraction. This is a nine-year-old boy! Do you realize that? Never have I seen a boy with such a gift. And the inlays in the door—they require the craft of a grown man." Abdul folded his arms across his stomach and rocked slowly on his feet. "My friend, your son Mechido could become a master cabinetmaker and I would consider it an honor if you would allow him to become my apprentice."

Mechido gave a start. "It's too good," he whispered into the wall.

Mechido's father apparently could not find his tongue.

At last he said, "Is it so fine a box as that?"

"For a nine-year-old boy, it is an extraordinary box," said the genial Abdul.

"But, Abdul, you have an apprentice. Your own son is your apprentice."

Abdul's jovial smile faded. "My son. My own son is the nightmare of my life. My son!" Abdul clutched his stomach. Then he clutched Mechido's father by the nape of his burnoose. "My own son wants to be a juggler. Or a weight lifter. The bane of my life is my own son. Do you know—no, how can you know—what he does when I leave the workshop? He piles everything on his head—planks, blocks of wood, tools, as many things as he can, the more the better. My half-made cabinets on top of the planks, sideboards on top of that, and when I come back I find him walking up and down the stairs, balancing it all on his head, all my beautiful work piled up, and with his hands he is throwing nails into the air and catching them. Oh, my own son, the bane of my life!" Abdul drooped.

Mechido's father was fascinated. "He likes to carry things on his head?"

A dejected nod from Abdul.

"The more the better?"

"Yes." A sigh.

"And does he not often drop the things?"

"Drop my cabinets! Should he dare, indeed that would be too much." The more Abdul sagged the more pleased Mechido's father grew.

"Surely he must get into trouble in the streets?"

"Who, Hamed?[1] Have you never seen my large son, Hamed? He walks like an ox." Abdul wagged his head sadly from side to side. "Woe to him who goes near Hamed in the streets."

"Rejoice, my friend! Hamed has found his destiny!" Mechido's father gave a sudden cry and embraced him. "If ever there was

[1] Hamed (hah-MED)

a born bread boy, Hamed is he. He will be my apprentice! And Mechido will be yours!"

Mechido smothered a shout.

Abdul's sunken frame rose back into shape. "My greatest friend!" he cried, and they embraced again. "I am doubly honored. It will be a privilege and a pleasure. What's more—" through the hole Mechido saw to his delight that Abdul's eyes were beginning to slide—"apart from his skill, Mechido amuses me. The jokes he makes. He is a nice boy."

Mechido's father smiled. There was an expression in his face that Mechido had never seen before, something fond and deeply tender.

"Yes, there is no one like Mechido," he said softly. "My Mechido, he is a very fine boy."

And Mechido felt his cheeks grow hot again, but this time from joy.

—*Giggy Lezra*

What Do You Think?

1. When people say someone is like "a square peg in a round hole," what do you think they mean? How might any of the characters in "Mechido" be called "a square peg in a round hole"?

2. Describe in your own words each of the characters given below.

     Mechido   Mechido's father Abdul
     Mechido's mother Hamed

3. When Mechido left home during the daytime hours for a week, why did he not tell his family where he was going and what he was doing?

Taking A Closer Look

1. Many accidents happened to Mechido on his first day as Tarah. Name some of them. Which accident do you think mattered most to his father?

2. In what ways did Mechido's parents feel differently from one another about the breadbox Mechido made?

3. Write a help-wanted ad for an apprentice to a baker or a cabinet maker. Be sure to list the tasks to be done and the skills needed for the job.

4. How did Mechido's father act, and what did he say, while talking with Abdul? How do his actions and words at that time prepare you for the end of the story?

363

Taiwo[1] and her twin brother
Kehinde[2] live in Nigeria. One
day, as they go out into the
bush looking for palm nuts,
they suddenly hear a strange
sound. What can it be?

The Creature in the Bush

One afternoon, Taiwo went to the bush to hunt for
palm nuts. But she was not alone, for Kehinde, her
twin brother, went with her.

"They frisked through the bush as free as young goats,
Taiwo this way, Kehinde that way, calling out to each
other as they went. Each claimed boastfully to have
found more nuts than the other." The bush was so shady
and pleasantly cool.

Suddenly Taiwo heard a loud rustling sound. Some
big creature was pushing through the bush. It sounded
very close.

Taiwo stiffened. Still as a stone, she listened. What
could it be? Goats and sheep did not wander so far
from the village. It sounded too big to be a rat or rabbit
or bird.

[1] Taiwo (TIGH-woh)   [2] Kehinde (KAY-in-day)

364

Then she heard a cry, a strange scolding cry, coming from the same direction as the rustling. Taiwo remembered the fearful tales she had heard about the bush.

"Kehinde!" she called. "KEHINDE!"

Kehinde was searching around a palm tree not far from Taiwo's. At the sound of Taiwo's cry, he ran quickly to see what the trouble could be.

"Listen, Kehinde!" Taiwo's voice was all trembly. "Do you hear it?"

Kehinde listened. He too heard the loud rustling. He too heard the scolding cry. But the cry did not sound strange to Kehinde. In fact, it sounded very familiar.

"That is very odd," Kehinde answered, looking quite puzzled. "Surely it sounds exactly like the Bale's[1] turkey. But how would the turkey come to be here in the bush?"

Taiwo did not answer. If it was indeed a turkey, how silly Kehinde would think her if he knew how frightened she had been.

Kehinde pushed through the bush toward the noise. "It is the turkey!" he shouted back. "It has broken its string again. Come, help me catch it!"

Taiwo ran toward her brother's voice. And there indeed was the turkey, flapping through the bush with the end of string dangling behind it. Kehinde was thrashing and crashing after it.

"Come!" he called again. "Help me catch it!"

The twins chased and chased, but they were no match for that turkey. Their crashing and thrashing

[1] Bale (BAH-lay)

365

frightened it and made it quite frantic. They could not get close, for when they did, the turkey rose from the ground and flapped away out of reach. Soon they were stinging with countless scratches and puffing for breath, and still no closer to catching the turkey.

"Wait! Let us stop a bit," Taiwo puffed. "I just cannot run any more."

"Oh, no," Kehinde protested. "If we stop, then he will run away!"

Taiwo dropped to the ground. "Run away!" she exclaimed, leaning her back against a tree trunk and trying to catch her breath. "Run away! What is he doing now? Sleeping?" Taiwo shook her head. "We will have to think of a better way to catch him. We are just frightening him and tiring ourselves."

Kehinde shrugged his shoulders and dropped down beside Taiwo. He was quite as breathless as she. It

did feel good to sit back against the tree. It was so pleasant and quiet. Very quiet.

Each of the twins realized the same thing at the same time. The turkey was no longer flapping about. When they had stopped chasing, he had stopped fleeing. He was probably as tired as they were. And hungry too. They could hear him scratching about in the bush nearby.

Thinking of the turkey's hunger reminded Kehinde that he was hungry too. "I wish I were a turkey and could scratch for my food," he said. "How I would like something to eat now!"

"My head is surely empty today," Taiwo said. "I brought some *eko*[1] for us to eat and forgot all about it."

Taiwo pulled the leaf-wrapped packets from their hiding place in her wrapper. Kehinde reached eagerly for his. Already he could taste the smooth corn porridge sliding over his tongue and into his empty stomach.

But, just as Taiwo was handing the packet of *eko* to Kehinde, the idea came to her. Of course! This was the way! In Taiwo's excitement, the words came sputtering out.

"Listen, Kehinde! We must not eat it! We must not eat the *eko*! We can use it for bait. For turkey bait. I have a plan that . . ."

"Not eat it!" Kehinde protested, the tempting green packet practically in his hands. "Turkey bait? Whatever are you raving about?"

[1] *eko* (EK-KAW)

367

"It is such a good plan. Just listen. You will see."

Kehinde looked very doubtful, but he listened nonetheless.

Taiwo explained her plan carefully. "When we ran after the turkey and made much noise, he just got frightened and ran away. But if we go slowly and quietly, perhaps we can make him come after us instead of us going after him. This is what we must do . . . ."

The more Kehinde listened, the less doubtful he looked. It did sound like a very good plan.

Kehinde stayed where he was, crouched very still near the trunk of the tree.

Taiwo crept quietly toward the turkey. She moved slowly and cautiously, careful not to let twigs snap or branches slap. At last only a small shrub was between her and the great black bird. She could almost reach out and touch him.

Her fingers broke off a small bit of the pasty corn porridge. Slowly, careful not to rustle the bush by her movement, she threw the small ball of corn porridge toward the bird. The *eko* landed near the turkey's head.

Peck! Peck! With a pick and a peck and a shake of his head, the turkey gobbled up the *eko*. Then he scratched eagerly about, turning his head this way and that, searching for more of this treat.

Quickly Taiwo broke off another piece of *eko* and threw it to the turkey. Again the gobbler gobbled it up and hunted about for more. Taiwo threw the third piece,

368

but so gently that it landed quite close to her feet. The bird pushed eagerly through the brush to get it.

Taiwo moved slowly away from him, back toward the tree where her brother was crouching. Every few steps she dropped a small piece of *eko* to the ground.

The turkey followed the trail of *eko*. He came nearer and nearer to Taiwo. The string dangled from his leg

369

so temptingly! Taiwo could have bent down and grabbed it so easily! But she knew that this would not do. The turkey would only pull away.

The first portion of *eko* was almost finished. Thank goodness! Here was the tree where Kehinde waited. Taiwo stopped. She crumbled the last of the *eko* and dropped the crumbs in a small heap near the base of the tree.

Such a feast! The great bird pecked and swallowed, pecked and swallowed. Here a crumb, there a crumb, everywhere crumbs. The turkey paid no attention to Taiwo, standing there so still. He did not notice Kehinde reach out quietly from behind the tree and take hold of the end of the dangling string.

Now it was Kehinde's turn to move quietly and cautiously. He pulled the string gently toward him — very gently. He must be sure not to tug on it or he would alarm the bird. Now! He had hold of enough string. Quickly Kehinde wrapped the string around the trunk of a small sturdy sapling that grew beside the big tree. Once around. Twice around. Quickly he tied the string with the tightest knots he could. At last! The turkey was their prisoner.

Some villagers, out searching for the turkey, helped the twins return it to the Bale, the chief of the village. He was so pleased, he rewarded Taiwo and Kehinde for their good work.

—*Letta Schatz*

370

What Do You Think?

1. How well do you think the twins get along with one another? Which sentences in the story make you think so?
2. Why do you suppose the twins bothered to catch the turkey instead of letting it go? How do you think the bird got into the bush in the first place?

Taking A Closer Look

1. When Taiwo said, "My head is surely empty today," what do you think she meant? Think of other ways to express the same idea.
2. Look up the word *eko* in the Glossary. How do you think *eko* would taste? In what way is it like some of the foods you have eaten? Try to describe *eko* to someone who has never heard of it.
3. "If at first you don't succeed, try, try again." How does this saying apply to the twins? What could have been wrong with their first plan? Why did they finally succeed?

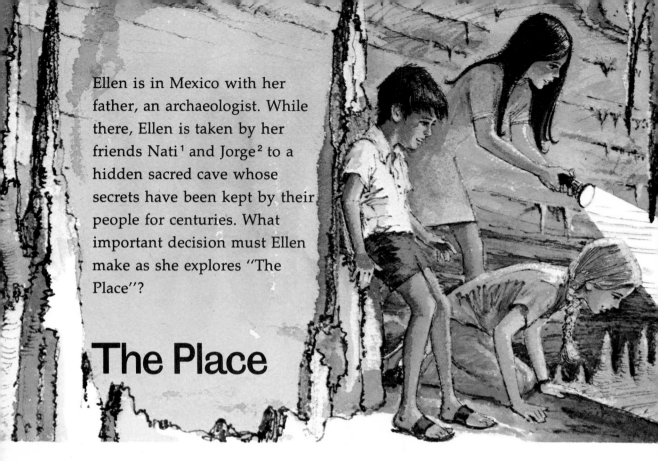

Ellen is in Mexico with her father, an archaeologist. While there, Ellen is taken by her friends Nati[1] and Jorge[2] to a hidden sacred cave whose secrets have been kept by their people for centuries. What important decision must Ellen make as she explores "The Place"?

The Place

"Keep close to the wall," whispered Jorge. "The water's deep here, and the path is slippery."

Ellen obeyed and walked with one hand touching the limestone surface beside her. It was wet and slimy under her fingers.

"Hold the torch down a moment and let me see the water," she begged Nati, who stopped, a little impatiently, and threw a circle of light into the stream below them. There were fish there, very small fish which paid no attention to the glare, but went on swimming about. Ellen sat down on her heels, so that she could see them better. One rose to the surface for a drowning midge.

[1] Nati (NAH-TEE)   [2] Jorge (HOR-hay)

372

"Look," she whispered. "Look! It has no eyes! It must know there's something to eat near it by the vibration in the water."

"Didn't I tell you this is a wonderful place?" Jorge answered, delighted by Ellen's surprise, but Nati murmured urgently, "Come along!" and started off again with the torch and Ellen had to follow.

The air grew colder and colder and the stale odor of bats grew stronger. When Nati for a moment swept the light upwards, bats' eyes glared back, studding the roof above them. Ellen knew she had nothing to fear from bats, but suppose a jaguar had a den somewhere in the cave? Suppose the next eyes that shone in the beam of their light should be a jaguar's eyes?

But if Nati dared lead the way, Ellen would follow. On down the narrow passage they went and into another great chamber

filled with more strange shapes, and always the air grew colder, as they went deeper and deeper into the earth. By now they must have come nearly half a mile, Ellen thought.

"I love it," she said, between chattering teeth. "It's wonderful, but let's go back now."

"No," whispered Nati. "This is not yet the Place. There is nothing to hurt you here."

Ellen gritted her teeth. She wouldn't suggest going back again. It was Jorge who murmured excitedly,

"We're almost there."

Again a handmade wall appeared to one side of the cave and the passage which they entered was very winding, while the ground sometimes rose steeply underfoot. They had left the stream behind them, and there were no bats here to hang like fungus from the roof. Once, in a quick spurt of light, Ellen saw hollows in the stone wall, made to hold pitch-pine torches, for the limestone above them was blackened with old smoke stains.

And then they came to the Place.

Once more there was a handmade wall and a narrow entrance. This time it was not a cavern they entered, but a room floored by flagstones, with plastered walls reaching up to the natural ceiling. There were the remains of frescoes on these walls, where the damp had not destroyed them. Priests and warriors and women formed a procession towards an altar, or so Ellen thought in the glimpse she had, before Nati directed the light to the center of the cave, from which rose what appeared to be a shining seated figure, at least ten feet high.

It was a stalagmite like the others they had seen, but instead of having taken the shape of a mushroom, tower, or animal, it was like a human with bent head and arms close to the sides of the body. There seemed even to be hands laid in the lap. And all this shone and glistened, in white darkening to amber, like a moist and living thing.

While Ellen stared, the other two children dropped to the ground, crouching, rather than kneeling, before the figure. They were praying, but in their own language. Their prayers seemed to be earlier prayers than any said in the village church. Jorge was repeating the same words, over and over, like a lesson, but Nati, Ellen guessed, was begging for forgiveness for having brought a stranger into this holy place.

When Nati had finished, she went forward on her hands and knees to put some copal[1] in an earthenware incense bowl standing on a stone altar before the god. She must have broken it from the lump she had bought for her mother at the market. There wasn't much, but there was enough. Nati lighted a match and held it to the copal, but for a moment the incense refused to catch fire; then, at last, it slowly began to burn and the fragrant smoke drifted into the air.

Nati, satisfied, sat back on her heels.

"It's all right," she said to Ellen in quite an everyday voice. "The god is satisfied and has accepted my offering. But you'd better make one, too. Why don't you offer your watch?"

Ellen's silver watch was the only thing of any value she had with her, but she didn't hesitate. As, lighted by the torch, she and her shadow were stooping a little to lay the watch on the stone slab, she saw that all around her were ancient bowls and jars, such as her father and his workers sometimes dug up, but

[1]copal (кон-pəl)

375

these were unbroken and sat in a thick circle, facing the god.
There were jars shaped like chiefs, and some like market
women with their little children. There were laughing cripples,
and old men, and prisoners with their arms tied behind their
backs. There were parrots and doves, and a jaguar with white
eyes, and a fat pot-bellied puppy, on four wheels like a toy. There
were toads and snakes and a baby playing with its toes and tall

376

ears of corn. A few of the jars held large jade beads. All faced towards the image, as they must have faced for hundreds and hundreds of years, ever since they were first brought to the Place as offerings.

And the god? The cavern itself had made the image from limestone, drop by heavy drop, as it had made the columns and chandeliers and waving curtains.

And suddenly the jaguar spoke, not from the shadows of the shrine, but from its den in Ellen's heart. If only she had not promised! In all her father's explorations, he had never found anything like this. If he should write an account of the Place for some scientific magazine, he would be famous among archaeologists, and everyone would know that it was his daughter, Ellen, who had brought him here, so she would be famous, too. Better still, she would be given the reward, which the Society offered for new archaeological sites. And that meant she could buy Centavo,[1] the red horse!

Centavo and the Place! The Place and Centavo! Almost from the beginning, the two had combined to fill her heart with longing. Two things which she had supposed could never be hers. And now . . .

Ellen shook her head until her braids stung her cheeks.
No!

She had sworn on her life to tell no one and to bring no one here, but even if she had not sworn, she would never, never never take from these people the last secret which bound them to their ancestors. Smiling, they dug out old temple foundations for her father; politely, they took him to forgotten terraces.

[1]Centavo (sen-TAH-voh)

Hoping to please him, they brought him the beautiful things they had found in their fields. But this they did not show him, although they all knew about it. This was theirs and theirs alone! What would be left of its mystery after the frescoes had been photographed? When the jars and bowls had been taken away to museums? When the figure had been measured and copied, perhaps even chipped from its foundation? No! No! No! No! Jorge was right. The Place was the most wonderful place in the world and it should remain so! What did she and Centavo or even her father matter compared to these people and this old god, hidden away in the depths of the earth?

"I'll never tell," Ellen promised the figure. The air was so still that she could hear her watch ticking, the sound echoing back from the stone altar. For a little while it would go on and then the hands would stop. But what was time to a limestone deity created, drop by drop, over so many centuries?

Nati touched her arm.

"We must go now, Ellen," she said out loud. From the moment the copal had begun to burn, Nati had been at ease, as though the image and she understood one another.

"Snap on the torch again, please, Nati," Ellen begged. "Let me see everything: the pictures and the jars and the god. I want to remember the Place as long as I live."

"I told you it was the most wonderful place in the world," said Jorge. "Wasn't I right, Ellen?"

"Yes," said Ellen. "It's the most wonderful place in all the world."

—*Elizabeth Coatsworth*

378

What Do You Think?

1. How might the information about the Place be of value to Ellen's father? Do you agree with her decision not to tell him about it? Explain.

2. Why do you think the Place is considered sacred by Nati and Jorge's people? Why do you think they kept the Place a secret from outsiders?

3. Jorge and Ellen describe the Place as "the most wonderful place in all the world." What place would you describe in this way? Explain why you would choose that place.

Taking A Closer Look

1. List in two columns some of the things Ellen saw in the Place. In the first list things that were made by people. In the second list things that were formed naturally.

2. What are some of the kinds of jars and bowls in the Place? Why do you suppose they are in different shapes?

3. Explain the following sentence in the story: "And suddenly the jaguar spoke, not from the shadows of the shrine, but from its den in Ellen's heart."

4. Compare Ellen's feelings about the Place at the beginning of the story with her feelings at the end.

5. Tell what you have learned in this story about the work of archaeologists.

Putting Ideas to Work

Would you like to be an archaeologist? Write a paragraph telling why or why not.

379

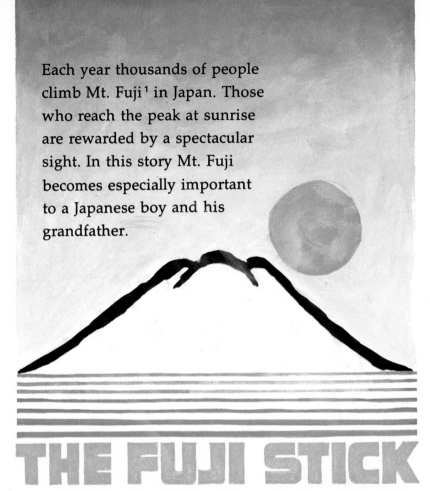

Each year thousands of people climb Mt. Fuji[1] in Japan. Those who reach the peak at sunrise are rewarded by a spectacular sight. In this story Mt. Fuji becomes especially important to a Japanese boy and his grandfather.

THE FUJI STICK

Fujio pushed his bowl of rice away from him and put down his chopsticks, his dark eyes thoughtful. The evening meal was usually a happy time in the Toyama[2] home. The family sat on the *tatami*[3] covered floor around a low table and Mama-san served the rice from a large wooden bowl. The tea was strong and hot, and the talk around the table was good. Usually. But today Fujio's forehead creased in a frown—today there was something wrong.

[1]Fuji (FOO-jee)   [2]Toyama (TOH-YAH-MAH)   [3]*tatami* (Tə-TAH-MEE)

He looked around the table. Mama-san smiled her
same gentle smile as she ladled rice into their bowls
and poured the tea. Papa-san sat straight and proud,
smacking his lips as he enjoyed the rice in his bowl.
Obaa-san[1] sat primly, as a grandmother might, nibbled
her rice and sipped her tea in silence. And small sister Michiko,[2] with her bobbed black hair and impish
black eyes, pushed the rice around in her bowl with
the ends of her chopsticks. Now and then she giggled
at the way the tiny bits of rice skidded around the
slippery china and found their way down into her lap.

[1] Obaa-san (oh-BAH-ah-sahn)　　[2] Michiko (MEE-chee-koh)

At last Fujio's glance fell upon his aged grandfather. His dark eyes narrowed. That was where the trouble was! Ojii-san[1] wore his old, mended kimono instead of his newest one. He sat with his balding head bowed to his chest. His rice sat untouched in his bowl. The bitter green tea he usually loved cooled in the cup in front of him. Fujio scowled. What was the matter with Grandfather? Couldn't the others see that he was acting strangely?

At last Grandfather raised his head and looked around. His black eyes seemed narrower than usual. It was then that the family knew he wished to speak. Immediately everyone was silent.

"My birthday is two days from now," he announced. "Seventy-two years have passed by swiftly. There is much I want to do before I become tired and stiff. I have one very strong wish, and that is to climb to the top of the great mountain." Now his eyes seemed to hold a vision. Fujio felt his own heart thump faster at Grandfather's words. He leaned forward to hear the old man. "I want to stand proudly at the top of Fuji-san and greet the sunrise as my own honored father once did. I wish to look down upon my beautiful country and see the blue lakes and the green valleys and the mountains."

Fujio's own eyes widened as he watched the effect of his grandfather's words upon Mama-san and Papa-san. "You are too old to climb so high," Papa-san said. "Climbing is for the young."

[1]Ojii-san (oh-JEE-ee-sahn)

382

The old man shook his shiny head. "Some of the pilgrims who climb the sacred mountain are as ancient as I. If they can do it, I can do it!" His jaw was set in determination. Fujio watched his grandfather shake his head indignantly. "I have listened too long now to my friends talk about climbing the mountain," the old man said. "And too many times I have had to look upon the seals of Fuji-san on their walking sticks. Soon I will be much too old to climb. I must do it now!"

Grandmother nodded and smiled in agreement. Fujio found himself nodding too. Surely the family would understand Grandfather's wish. It was very clear to him.

But no more was said about it then. Silence fell over the table like a cloud. When the meal had ended, Grandfather placed his cushion-like *zabuton*[1] on the floor in front of the television and prepared to watch an American western. Fujio sat on his heels beside the old man. He felt a tingle of excitement go up his back as he spoke.

"Ojii-san . . . I wish to talk to you about your dream to climb Fuji-san." He spoke as quietly as he could. "I have this same dream. Some of my older friends have already seen Lake Kawaguchi[2] from the top of the mountain. They make fun of me because I have only seen the lake from the foot of the great mountain. They say I am too small to climb—a baby! I have been thinking. We could climb to the top together. We would

[1] *zabuton* (zah-BOO-TON)   [2] Kawaguchi (KAH-WAH-GOO-CHEE)

show everyone that you are not too old—and I am not too young."

He sat back, waiting breathlessly for his grandfather's reply. The old man stared at the bright television screen for a long time. Fujio rocked on his heels, frowning. Hadn't his grandfather heard him? He opened his mouth to repeat his words, but his grandfather nodded.

"I think your idea is good, Fujio. You were named for the great mountain. It is right that you climb to the top while you are young. Yes . . ." he nodded again. "It is a good idea. We will help each other and enjoy the climb together. The family will see our dreams come true when we show them the seals of the great mountain on our walking sticks." He sat taller. "We must make our plans. Perhaps it can be a secret journey." A smile spread over his wrinkled face. "Do you think so?"

Fujio bounced on his heels, holding back a shout of joy. "Oh, yes! We will climb to the top the very day of your birthday. Tomorrow we will plan what clothes to wear on our journey up the mountain."

Grandfather slapped his knee in happiness. "We will need strong walking sticks—and a camera to take many pictures."

"And rice cakes to eat when we get hungry!" Fujio jumped to his feet, wishing he could spin around the room to show how good he felt. But this was not allowed in the house.

384

He went out the open door to the garden. There, beside the pool, he spun around. The stones tickled his feet, reminding him that he was still in his soft cotton *tabi*[1] and had forgotten to put on his sandals to come outside. It didn't matter! Nothing mattered now. He and Grandfather were really going to climb to the top of Mt. Fuji! The day after tomorrow! Nothing would spoil their dream now.

He stepped across the pool on the large flat stones and stood beside the stone lantern at the edge of the path. Little Michiko toddled into the garden, scuffing her wooden *geta*[2] as she walked. She carried her favorite *kokeshi*[3] doll clutched tightly in her small fist. When she reached Fujio, she held the armless wooden doll out to him. "See what Mama-san bought for me from the doll peddler on the street."

[1]*tabi* (TAH-bee)   [2]*geta* (gay-TAH)   [3]*kokeshi* (koh-KAY-shee)

385

Fujio nodded, sighing in disgust. He had seen the wooden doll with the painted face endless times. He couldn't be bothered about dolls now. Now he wanted only to think about the journey to Mt. Fuji.

Michiko's small mouth pouted. "I heard," she said impishly. "You and Ojii-san will climb the mountain."

Fujio whirled to face her, his eyes showing his alarm. "It is a secret, Michiko."

She shook her dark head and turned back to the house. Fujio watched her go. She was little. Perhaps she didn't understand about secrets, he told himself. Perhaps if he gave her a present, she would forget. His eyes darted about the garden. What would she like? "Michiko . . ." he called softly, "come back . . ."

And as Michiko turned back, Fujio's eyes came to rest on the small cage beside the bench near the path. Of course! He hurried over to the bench and picked up the tiny cage, peering inside. "Hello, my happy singer," he greeted his pet cricket. "I think you will soon have a new owner. . . ." He motioned to Michiko. "I will give you my cricket if you keep the secret."

Michiko's dark eyes looked at the insect in the cage. Her tiny nose wrinkled and she shook her head. "No! I do not want your bug!" With that, she clip-clopped over the path toward the house.

A frown creased Fujio's forehead. Now Mama-san and Papa-san would know the secret he and Grandfather shared. Would they forbid him to go on the journey up the mountain? The cricket in the cage chirped and

386

Fujio sighed. "I am not sure this is the time to sing, my friend."

He stayed in the garden until Mama-san's soft voice called to him. "It is time for bed, Fujio."

Fujio hung the cricket cage on a tree branch and went inside. Mama-san and Grandmother closed the sliding doors, dividing the big room in two for the night. Mama-san spread the heavy quilt-like *futon*[1] on the floor—one for each to sleep on and one to cover with. Fujio slept in the same room as Grandfather and Grandmother. Michiko slept in the second room with Mama-san and Papa-san. There was no time to talk to Grandfather alone. No one metioned Mt. Fuji again that night. Fujio sighed. They would have to talk about it in the morning—before breakfast, when Grandmother and Mama-san put the beds away in the closets,

[1]*futon* (fə-TON)

opened the sliding doors, and cleaned the house. Papa-san would go off to work in the bakery. Then he and Grandfather could walk in the garden and talk. And they would know if Michiko had told their secret.

Fujio snuggled down under his quilt and stared up at the ceiling. Grandfather's snores filled the room. "How could he sleep?" Fujio wondered. In another day they would journey to the foot of the great mountain! They would start their climb! No matter what anyone said, they would get to the top! Butterflies danced in his stomach at the very thought.

The next morning when the family gathered around the table for their breakfast of soybean soup and rice, Fujio had the feeling again that something was wrong. This time he looked straight at his grandfather. Ojii-san's bald head was again bowed. The silence in the room made Fujio shudder. He looked at Michiko. She grinned impishly at him. "I have told about your trip," she said sweetly.

"We do not like the idea, Fujio. It would be too long a climb for your grandfather's tired legs—and too long a climb for your short legs." Mama-san shook her dark head.

Grandfather looked up. His dark eyes were glowing. "I *must* go up the mountain. How many more years will I be able to climb? Would you have me the only aged one in all Japan who hasn't seen the sunrise from the top of Fuji-san?"

Fujio watched his mother and father look at each

388

other. Papa-san shrugged his shoulders. "Father, if you feel that strongly about it, you must certainly try to climb the mountain. With a strong stick, and Fujio to help you, you might reach the summit."

Fujio felt his heart speed up. "Thank you, Papa-san."

"I will drive you to the mountain tomorrow morning. It will take you all that day and night to climb. But if you tire, you must come back down. Agreed?"

Fujio and his grandfather both nodded. "Agreed!" Fujio exclaimed. And he began to count the hours until the next morning.

Early the next day Papa-san drove Fujio and his grandfather across the many miles to Mt. Fuji. He helped them adjust their packs on their backs and then said good-by.

"And much luck in your climb," he told them. As he gazed up the slope to the top of the mountain towering in the clouds, he shook his head. "You will not do it," he muttered. "It is too far to climb."

Fujio saw his grandfather straighten up as tall as his thin frame could go. "We will! You go home now, my son, and work in the bakery. Return tomorrow and you will see our seals of Fuji-san."

Fujio watched his father drive off. Then they started up the mountain. The trail wove gently up the slope and many people walked upward. Now and then Fujio saw a pair of worn straw sandals by the side of the trail. He pointed toward one of the pairs. "Someone has lost his shoes, Grandfather."

The old man shook his head. "The pilgrims who climb the sacred mountain carry many pairs of sandals. They throw them aside when they become worn and they put on a new pair." He pointed to another pair of the straw sandals farther up the slope. "They mark the trail for climbers."

Bells tinkled ahead and behind them. Fujio saw the pilgrims dressed in white. For them, the summit of the sacred mountain was a shrine, a place to visit and worship. He saw that they had bells tied to the ropes which they wore around their waists to help pull each other up the slopes. Each climber had a lantern. "I am glad we have flashlights," he told his grandfather.

Onward up the slope they walked, slowly on the uneven parts. When they reached a small temple, they

390

bought strong walking sticks to help them on their climb. There were many climbers. Young people passed by Fujio and Grandfather. Climbers the age of Papa-san walked more slowly, Fujio noticed. Wives and husbands climbed beside each other. But Fujio did not see anyone as ancient as Grandfather. And he didn't see another child as young as himself.

Now and then they had to stop along the path to rest. Grandfather shaded his eyes and looked upward toward the summit. "It is still a long way to the top, Fujio."

How tired Grandfather sounded! Fujio's dark eyes showed his concern. "Perhaps we were wrong to come after all, Grandfather. We can turn back."

Grandfather stood tall and straight. "We will go to the very top and see the sunrise from there in the early morning."

Fujio slipped his pack off his back and took out the rice cakes Mama-san had packed for them. "Here. We will eat, Grandfather. Then we can go on."

As they sat beside the trail, other climbers went by them. Some sang happy songs. The people wound along the path as far up the slope as Fujio could see. He watched Grandfather eat the rice cake. Could the old man go on to the top? He sighed. Could *he* go on? Even now his legs ached. He brushed dust off his heavy shoes. He could go back down and climb again another year when he was taller and stronger. But Grandfather's bones were already stiff with age. If he went down now, he might never be able to say that he had climbed the great mountain. Grandfather would be ashamed to tell his friends that he could not climb the mountain. That must not happen!

Grandfather got slowly to his feet, using his walking stick to push himself up. "We must go on, Fujio. We will almost reach the top by dark."

Fujio nodded. At least Grandfather had not given up. Up and up they went, more and more slowly with each step. Fujio found himself breathing hard. He watched his grandfather closely. Now and then the old man stopped to take a deep breath and mop his forehead. Fujio's legs throbbed from the climb. He watched his grandfather in wonder. How could one so old climb so well? What a strong man his grandfather was!

They climbed through the long afternoon and stopped again to eat. The sun began to set and the climbers

put on heavier clothing and lit their lanterns. Fujio took their flashlights out of the pack to light the path ahead of them. Soon the slope was twinkling with hundreds of lights. Fujio heard his grandfather puffing. Once the old man stumbled and fell to his knees. Fujio helped him to his feet. On they went. Now Fujio put his arm around Grandfather's waist to help him along the darkened path. The old man's footsteps became slower and slower. Fear clutched at Fujio. How far could they go? "We should have listened to Mama-san and Papa-san," he thought.

At last they reached a hut near the top of the mountain. Many of the climbers went in and stretched out on the floor to sleep. Grandfather motioned Fujio inside and they too stretched out on the floor. Soon

393

Grandfather was snoring. Fujio sighed and closed his eyes. Now they were too far to return home. So of course they would go on. He smiled in the darkness. In the morning they would be standing on top of the world!

Shuffling feet and hushed voices woke Fujio. The first faint light of dawn filtered into the open doorway of the hut. Quickly he shook his grandfather. "It is almost morning, Ojii-san. We must go on."

Grandfather tried to rise, but fell back to the floor. "I cannot get up!" he moaned. "Your mother and father were right. Old bones were not meant to climb mountains."

Fujio's heart pounded. If Grandfather couldn't go up, he couldn't go down either! What would become of them? He looked anxiously at Ojii-san.

The old man looked sad. "If you want to see the sunrise, go on without me," he told Fujio.

Fujio shook his head. "I will not go on without you, Grandfather. Come, I will help you. Your dream to go to the top of the mountain will come true. It will!"

He took his grandfather's thin arm and pulled him to his feet. The old man leaned on Fujio, and on his heavy walking stick. "I will try," he said finally. And slowly they started out, up the slope of the mountain.

Grandfather's weight seemed to push Fujio down. The mountain air was thinner than that below. He puffed for breath. Each step became painful. Ojii-san's feet dragged. Often he would stop, mop his forehead,

394

and sigh. "I will wait for you here, beside the path," he said.

Stubbornly, Fujio shook his head. "No! We have come this far. We will go on together." As he spoke, Fujio tripped on a loose stone. He felt a sharp pain in his ankle as it turned. He cried out as he sank to the ground. Grandfather bent to help him to his feet. Fujio gasped, "My ankle! I twisted it."

Ojii-san pushed Fujio gently to a rock. "Then we must sit here and rest," he said. "I am afraid we have come as far as we can. This great mountain is too much for us." He rubbed his grandson's ankle as he spoke. They sat quietly, neither one speaking. The light in the eastern sky was beginning to brighten. Fujio could see the pink and gold sunlight peeking through the clouds. In just a few more minutes the sun would be

up. He saw his grandfather's eyes searching the sky. How much he wanted to see that sunrise! They must get to the top before the sun rose.

With an effort, Fujio got to his feet. "Come, let us go on, Grandfather. Now I must lean upon you. We won't give up now. We are near the top and the sun is coming up."

His grandfather nodded. He put his arm around Fujio. Suddenly his fading strength seemed renewed. Up they went. Slowly . . . very slowly. Soon they could hear chanting voices and shouts of joy ahead of them. The end of the trail was near! On they went. Fujio's ankle hurt. Grandfather moaned under his breath. But—they were there!

The sun slid out from under a cloud blanket and rose, a giant red ball in the sky. Fujio shouted a loud hurrah, and Grandfather's eyes filled with tears. They stood together, quietly watching the beautiful sight before them. "We have done it!" Grandfather exclaimed. "We will get a seal of the mountains to put on our walking sticks. Those waiting for us below will want to see them."

Fujio nodded. His heart throbbed with happiness. "The way down is easier, Grandfather. We can go slowly and ask for help if we need it. We will have no trouble." He sighed and breathed the clear air. It was, he thought, like standing on top of the whole world. He clutched his walking stick tightly. "We climbed well, Grandfather. And we will have the proof."

—Virginia K. Smiley

What Do You Think?

1. Explain why you would agree or disagree with this saying: "One who climbs Mt. Fuji once is wise; one who climbs it twice is a fool."
2. Why do you think Grandfather hadn't climbed Mt. Fuji as a young man? Why couldn't he wait any longer?
3. What did the Fuji stick stand for? If you had earned a Fuji stick, what would it mean to you?

Taking A Closer Look

1. What problems did Fujio and Grandfather have to solve before they could climb Mt. Fuji? How did each show his determination to succeed?
2. Find four ways the author tells you the story takes place in Japan. What clues tell you it happens in modern Japan?
3. Fujio's father said, "Climbing is for the young." Tell why you agree or disagree with him.
4. Think of a word or phrase to describe how each person in these sentences felt.
    a. Butterflies danced in Fujio's stomach.
    b. Grandfather's jaw was set.
    c. Fujio's heart thumped faster.
    d. Grandfather's rice sat untouched in his bowl.
5. Tell about a time when you were determined to do something that others felt you were too young to try? Did you succeed?

398

YONDER HANGS THE MOON

Yonder hangs the moon
eating an orange,
and throwing the peeling
into the lake.

—*Traditional Mexican*

399

There are many ways to "see"—as Hwei Ming was quick to discover. Sometimes it is not the eyes that see best of all. It is the heart and the mind.

The Seeing Stick

Once in the ancient walled citadel of Peking
there lived an emperor who had only one daughter,
and her name was Hwei Ming.[1]
Now this daughter had carved ivory combs
to smooth back her long black hair.
Her tiny feet were encased in embroidered slippers,
and her robes were woven of the finest silks.
But rather than making her happy,
such possessions made her sad.
For Hwei Ming was blind,
and all the beautiful handcrafts in the kingdom
brought her no pleasure at all.
Her father was also sad
that his only daughter was blind,
but he could not cry for her.
He was the emperor after all,
and had given up weeping over such things
when he ascended the throne.
Yet still he had hope
that one day Hwei Ming might be able to see.
So he resolved that if someone could help her,
such a person would be rewarded
with a fortune in jewels.

[1]Hwei Ming (WAY MING)

401

He sent word of his offer
to the inner and outer cities of Peking
and to all the towns and villages
for hundreds of miles around.
Monks came, of course,
with their prayers and prayer wheels,
for they thought in this way
to help Hwei Ming see.
Magician-priests came, of course,
with their incantations and spells,
for they thought in this way
to help Hwei Ming see.
Physicians came, of course,
with their potions and pins,
for they thought in this way
to help Hwei Ming see.
But nothing could help.
Hwei Ming had been blind from the day of her birth,
and no one could effect a cure.

402

Now one day
an old man, who lived far away
in the south country,
heard tales of the blind princess.
He heard of the emperor's offer.
And so he took his few possessions —
a long walking stick,
made from a single piece of golden wood,
and his whittling knife —
and started up the road.
The sun rose hot on his right side
and the sun set cool on his left
as he made his way north to Peking
to help the princess see.

At last the old man,
his clothes tattered by his travels,
stopped by the gate of the Outer City.
The guards at the gate
did not want to let such a ragged old man in.
"Grandfather, go home.
There is nothing here for such as you," they said.
The old man touched their faces in turn
with his rough fingers.
"So young," he said,
"and already so old."
He turned as if to go.
Then he propped his walking stick
against his side
and reached into his shirt
for his whittling knife.
"What are you doing, grandfather?"
called out one of the guards
when he saw the old man bring out the knife.
"I am going to show you my stick,"
said the old man.
"For it is a stick that sees."
"Grandfather, that is nonsense,"
said the second guard.
"That stick can see no farther
than can the emperor's daughter."

"Just so, just so,"
said the old man.
"But stranger things have happened."
And so saying,
he picked up the stick
and stropped the knife blade back and forth
three times to sharpen its edge.
As the guards watched
from the gate in the wall,
the old man told them
how he had walked the many miles
through villages and towns
till he came with his seeing stick
to the walls of Peking.
And as he told them his tale,
he pointed to the pictures in the stick:
an old man,
his home,
the long walk,
the walls of Peking.
And as they watched further,
he began to cut their portraits into the wood.
The two guards looked at each other
in amazement and delight.
They were flattered at their likenesses
on the old man's stick.
Indeed, they had never witnessed such carving skill.

"Surely this is something
the guards at the wall
of the Inner City should see," they said.
So, taking the old man by the arm,
they guided him
through the streets of the Outer City,
past flower peddlers and rice sellers,
past silk weavers and jewel merchants,
up to the great stone walls.
When the guards of the Inner City
saw the seeing stick,
they were surprised and delighted.
"Carve our faces, too,"
they begged like children.
And laughing,
and touching their faces
as any fond grandfather would,
the old man did as they bid.
In no time at all,
the guards of the Inner City took the old man by his arm
and led him to the wall of the Innermost City
and in through the gate
to the great wooden doors of the Imperial Palace.

Now when the guards arrived
in the throne room of the Imperial Palace
leading the old man by the arm,
it happened that the emperor's blind daughter,
Hwei Ming,
was sitting by his side,
her hands clasped before her,
silent, sightless, and still.
As the guards finished telling
of the wonderful pictures carved on the golden stick,
the princess clapped her hands.
"Oh, I wish I could see that wondrous stick," she said.
"Just so, just so," said the old man.
"And I will show it to you.
For it is no ordinary piece of wood,
but a stick that sees."
"What nonsense," said her father
in a voice so low it was almost a growl.
But the princess did not hear him.
She had already bent toward
the sound of the old man's voice.
"A seeing stick?"

The old man did not say anything for a moment.
Then he leaned forward
and petted Hwei Ming's head
and caressed her cheek.
For though she was a princess,
she was still a child.
Then the old man began to tell again
the story of his long journey to Peking.
He introduced each character and object—
the old man,
the guards,
the great walls,
the Innermost City.
And then he carved the wooden doors,
the Imperial Palace,
the princess, into the golden wood.

408

When he finished,
the old man reached out
for the princess' small hands.
He took her tiny fingers in his
and placed them on the stick.
Finger on finger,
he helped her trace the likenesses.
"Feel the long flowing hair of the princess,"
the old man said.
"Grown as she herself has grown,
straight and true."
And Hwei Ming touched the carved stick.
"Now feel your own long hair," he said.
And she did.

409

"Feel the lines in the old man's face," he said.
"From years of worry and years of joy."
He thrust the stick into her hands again.
And the princess' slim fingers
felt the carved stick.
Then he put her fingers onto his face
and traced the same lines there.
It was the first time
the princess had touched another person's face
since she was a very small girl.
The princess jumped up from her throne
and thrust her hands before her.
"Guards, O guards," she cried out.
"Come here to me."
And the guards lifted up their faces
to the Princess Hwei Ming's hands.
Her fingers,
like little breezes,
brushed their eyes and noses and mouths,
and then found each one on the carved stick.

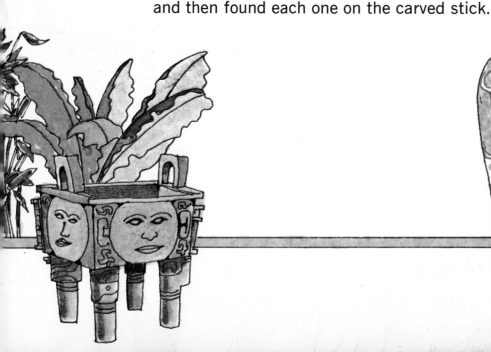

Hwei Ming turned to her father,
the emperor,
who sat straight and tall
and unmoving on his great throne.
She reached out
and her fingers ran eagerly
through his hair
and down his nose and cheek
and rested curiously on a tear they found there.
And that was strange, indeed,
for had not the emperor
given up crying over such things
when he ascended the throne?

411

They brought her
through the streets of the city, then,
the emperor in the lead.
And Princess Hwei Ming
touched men and women
and children as they passed.
Till at last
she stood before the great walls of Peking
and felt the stones themselves.
Then she turned to the old man.
Her voice was bright
and full of laughter.
"Tell me another tale," she said.
"Tomorrow, if you wish," he replied.

412

For each tomorrow
as long as he lived,
the old man dwelt
in the Innermost City,
where only the royal family stays.
The emperor rewarded him
with a fortune in jewels,
but the old man gave them all away.
Every day
he told the princess a story.
Some were tales as ancient
as the city itself.
Some were as new
as the events of the day.
And each time
he carved wonderful images
in the stick of golden wood.
As the princess listened,
she grew eyes
on the tips of her fingers.
As least that is what
she told the other blind children
whom she taught to see as she saw.
Certainly it was as true
as saying she had a seeing stick.
But the blind Princess Hwei Ming
believed that both things were true.
And so did all the blind children
in her city of Peking.

414

And so did the blind old man.

—*Jane Yolen*

415

What Do You Think?

1. Why do you think the old man came so far to see Hwei Ming?

2. In what ways did the old man's carved stick "see"? Did it only tell a story, or did it tell more than just facts? Explain your answer.

3. Do you think Hwei Ming could "see" as well as the sighted people around her? Why or why not?

Taking A Closer Look

1. What was the emperor's greatest hope?

2. Who tried and failed to cure Hwei Ming?

3. What did the place guards think of the old man at first? What changed their minds?

4. How did the Seeing Stick teach Hwei Ming to see?

5. How did Hwei Ming show her eagerness to learn?

6. How did Hwei Ming help other blind children?

7. Why did the old man seem to have a special understanding of Hwei Ming?

THE SUN THAT WARMS YOU

Is it not so, brother?

The sun that warms you

                warms me,

The fate that forms me

                forms you,

The irk that frets you

                frets me,

The rain that wets me

                wets you,

The hour that tries you

                tries me,

But the sun that dries me

                dries you.

It is so, brother.

—Eleanor Farjeon

418

Boston Bells

by Elizabeth Coatsworth

Long ago, when George Washington himself was
only fifteen years old, and no one had as yet dreamed of
freedom for our country, there lived in Boston a little
boy named John Singleton Copley.

John was nine years old. He was a quiet boy, rather
shy and easily frightened. But he had a courage of his
own, especially when anyone else was in trouble. His
father was dead and he lived with his mother in a pint-
sized house built on Long Wharf right out over the
water of Boston Harbor.

Often when a ship was coming to her mooring and
pushed against the dock the whole wharf shook, and
the Copleys' little house shook too, so that the dishes
clattered and the beds trembled. At any time of the day

420

or night John had only to stop what he was doing, and
listen, to hear beneath him the lisp and slap of the little
waves against the green seaweed-covered piles on
which the wharf stood. The air smelled salt, and fogs
often drifted up from the surface of the water. Instead
of looking out at other houses, John looked out at ships'
masts and sails. Instead of grass, he saw the water,
pewter gray or green or sometimes blue as the sky.
Instead of robins and wrens, John was accustomed to
seagulls circling and circling overhead, mewing against
the sky, or squabbling together over something which
they had found floating on the tide. Instead of coaches
and riding horses, he was accustomed to sailing vessels
and boats of all kinds.

Their house was squeezed between two larger buildings. Upstairs there were two bedrooms, and all the downstairs except for the kitchen ell was taken up by a little tobacco shop. Of course the shop being on a wharf, most of the customers were sailors. When Mrs. Copley had to be away for a few hours John took her place behind the counter. But he was always afraid of the rough men who came in, and glad when his mother returned and he could go back to his drawing.

For John drew pictures whenever he got the chance. It was strange that he never drew pictures of the ships moored at the wharf opposite his own door, or of the sailors lowering the great white sails or lounging on the decks. What he liked to draw were princes and princesses, and knights and ladies and dragons, and sometimes his mother or her friends or the merchants on the wharf. He liked quiet, gentle faces.

Mrs. Copley, who was a practical woman, thought that all this drawing was a waste of good time.

"You're old enough now to earn your own keep," she told John more than once. "Next spring I'm going to apprentice you to Mr. Green, the tailor. I never yet knew a tailor to starve. There's always enough money comes through the eye of a needle."

John hated the idea. Imagine sitting all his life cross-legged on a table, cutting and stitching!

"I want to be a sign painter!" he cried.

"But that takes a special gift," his mother said with a sigh. "If there was such a gift in the family it would have shown before this. You're only a little boy scribbling away at nothing."

John had a friend, Alexander, who was eleven years old. Alexander understood how John felt about drawing. He felt the same way about music. He wanted to play the violin, but he was apprenticed for seven years to old Mr. Southard, whose sail loft stood next door to John's house. But Mr. Southard was a good master. He had four older apprentices, and sometimes he would allow Alexander to go off with John on an errand or perhaps just to see what was going on.

Long Wharf was always exciting, too exciting to please John when he was alone, but with Alexander he felt safe, and could look about him and enjoy what he saw. On one side lay the ships from all the ports of the world, and facing them stood the houses and shops which sold things to the ships or the sailors.

The wharf itself was like a street, running a long way out into the harbor. There were carters snapping their whips, merchants and apprentices, the old woman with a basket on her arm filled with gingerbread, or a boy selling ballad sheets about some shipwreck or bold robbery. Everywhere were the sailors, talking half a dozen languages, but all alike, pig-tailed, smelling of tar, loud-voiced and heavy-handed. And always overhead the seagulls circled or sat in wooden rows along the ridgepoles or warmed their wide feet on chimney tops.

Sometimes the two boys fished from the wharf. Usually they found an out-of-the-way place to sit, and tied their lines, so that Alexander might play on the whistle which he carried in his pocket and John might draw on the planks with an old stub of chalk or even a charred piece of wood.

One cold November day Mrs. Copley went to market and John was left in charge of the shop, as usual much against his wish, though he said nothing about his dread of the hours which lay ahead.

"Don't go off with Alexander, mind you," his mother warned him. "It should be a good day for customers. With the English fleet in from taking Louisburg and prize money in their pockets, the sailors should be feeling like kings and we'll have our share of the general good fortune."

But after Mrs. Copley went away and John was left alone in the shop, for a long time no one came in. He felt uneasy with no sound of his mother stirring in the kitchen, knowing that at any moment a dozen men might burst in, shouting and laughing, all giving their orders at once and paying in shillings or Spanish pieces-of-eight or Portugese joes, and disputing over the change and scaring him with their scowls and brandished fists.

If only no one would come!

And for a long time no one did.

Then suddenly there was the dreaded warning from the little bell over the door.

John looked up, his heart beating faster. In the doorway stood two British sailors acting even more strangely than usual. They were holding open the door while a third sailor, a thickset man with red hair, boisterously shooed a little gray cat into the shop.

The door slammed shut with a bang and a jangle. "Now we have her cornered!" one of the sailors shouted, and they all set out to catch the cat.

But the frightened cat did not want to be caught.

She was almost beside herself with terror.

Round and round the room she ran, and round and round the room the sailors ran after her.

They knocked over stools.

They knocked over chairs.

They knocked over one another.

John watched, and as he watched, pity fought with

fear in his heart. The hullabaloo frightened him almost as much as it did the cat, but when, in her frantic efforts to escape, the animal dodged away from the redheaded sailor's hands and jumped up on the counter near John, he did not hesitate. Seizing her in his arms, he ran to the kitchen door and, putting her through it, quickly shut the door and turned to face her pursuers.

He was shaking from head to foot with excitement and fear. A short, black-haired sailor caught him by the shoulder with fingers that hurt.

"I say! That's our cat! Stand out of the way!" he shouted.

"Must get us a mouser," said the second sailor, coming close. "Rat stole the biscuit out of my hand only yesterday."

"Can't stop a press gang, boy," the thickset sailor with the red hair explained, wiping his face with a bandanna handkerchief as he came up, puffing.

"Press gangs don't come to Boston," John protested in a shaky voice, hoping and praying that his mother or someone, anyone, would come in.

"They'll be coming sooner than you expect if any more of our sailors take French leave." The second man laughed, showing a mouth full of broken teeth. "We've scarcely enough crew as it is to sail the fleet back to England."

"Why don't we take this young fellow along with us right now?" said the dark-haired sailor, grinning, his fingers biting into John's shoulder more painfully than

427

ever. "We haven't had a cabin boy since the last one took to his heels."

"Good," agreed the tall sailor. "I'll take one arm and you take the other and between us we'll march him off to see the world."

John's heart almost stopped beating. He was too frightened to shout for help. A sailor had him by each arm and now he was being dragged across the shop toward the door.

But at that last terrible moment help came—and from an unexpected quarter. It was the heavy red-haired sailor who stepped in front of the door, barring the way.

"Enough of that!" he exclaimed, still smiling. "The boy's got spunk and I like spunk. Let him be, Dan'l! And you, there, Jack! Cast off, I say! If you want to take him, you'll have to put up your fists and fight Tom Lightfoot."

The men didn't seem to want to fight Tom Lightfoot, so after a little more talk they dropped John's arms and at last the three went out.

John woke from a daze of terror to find them all gone and the shop as empty as before. The whole thing was over like some dreadful nightmare.

Later his mother came back and John, trembling again as he talked, told her what had happened.

As usual she tried to take the sensible view.

"It was only their rough fun. No one would *dare* steal boys from Boston, although they do often enough in England, poor young things! Give the cat some milk and then put her out. There's no one to trouble her now."

The cat was thin, with a heart-shaped gray face and big green eyes. When she smelled the milk, she began to purr and knead the floor with her paws.

She drank every drop and licked the last one from her chin.

"Now put her out," said Mrs. Copley again.

"But she has no place to go," cried John.

Perhaps John's account of the visit of the three sailors had disturbed his mother more than she realized, for without much urging she agreed to let the cat stay, though in the past she had always maintained that two mouths were all that she could manage to keep filled.

"What will you name her?" she asked.

"Lucy Locket."

" 'Lost her pocket?' Well, the name fits her. She'll be pretty later on, I shouldn't wonder."

And so Lucy Locket became a member of the household of the little shop on Long Wharf. She seemed to know from the first that it was John to whom she belonged. Fear had brought them together and affection strengthened the bond. When he drew pictures she sat close beside him, looking interested. Sometimes she would reach out a white paw to play with the moving pencil. Then at last she would curl up nearby and purr, her gray sides going in and out like a little bellows.

Feeling how soft her fur was, John brought a pair of scissors and, cutting a little where it scarcely showed, made a hair brush from it with a split stick for a handle.

Now he needed paint and he was pretty sure that Mr. Cushing, whose ship-painting shop was farther out on the wharf, would help him.

But what was he to paint on? John remembered the white plaster walls of his room. Often and often he had lain in bed making up pictures out of the cracks which

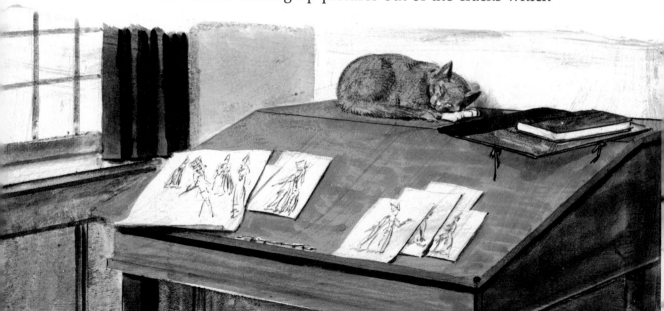

appeared here and there in the plaster. Would his mother let him paint real pictures on the wall? He had never before got up his courage to ask her, but today everything seemed different. With Lucy Locket under one arm and the new brush in his hand, John hurried off to find Mrs. Copley.

When his mother heard what he wanted she surprised him by nodding right away. But to make up for being so easygoing, she tried to sound as practical as ever.

"You might as well try to paint," she said, "then you'll find out for yourself that you can't do it. You're like someone with a fever, and it will have to burn itself out before you're well again. But I do hope to goodness that you'll get painting out of your system soon!"

John made no answer. He was sure that wanting to paint was as much a part of him as were his hands and feet.

He thanked his mother and, leaving Lucy by the fire, went off into the chill November air to find his friend Alexander, first looking about carefully to make sure that there were no sailors between him and the sail-loft door.

Old Mr. Southard was a good friend, and when he heard what John wanted he smiled and pushed back his spectacles and said that Alexander might go.

"But mind now, ask Mr. Cushing when he'll have the *Two Sisters* painted. I've promised a full set of sails for

431

her but I'm distracted with work and hope he won't have her done for a while yet."

The east wind was blowing, and the boys walked with their heads down, butting against it. But just the same Alexander managed to blow on his whistle. Now John felt safe again, for Alexander was two years older and afraid of nothing. Once they stopped to buy apples from the old woman whom they found sheltered in a doorway, wrapped in her worn cloak. And once they lingered to talk with a cabin boy lounging on the deck of a moored vessel. He had been in a sea fight with the Algerine pirates, he told them proudly, and had once almost been shipwrecked, and he even invited them to come into the cabin to see the captain's pet monkey.

But John was anxious to find Mr. Cushing and, promising to come some other time, the two friends went on. The ship painter was even kinder than John had hoped and gave him five old crocks with a little paint in each. Best of all, he added two brushes.

"These are small enough for what you want," he explained. "We need them mostly for scroll work. A fur brush has its uses but it's too delicate for most things. These are half worn-out but they'll last for a while. Good luck. And you there, tell Mr. Cushing I count on having the *Two Sisters* finished in a fortnight."

Alexander helped John carry the crocks and left him at his door. Inside everything continued to go well.

433

John's mother didn't want him for anything, so a few minutes later he was hard at work, painting his first picture on one of the walls, while Lucy Locket purred sleepily from the middle of his bed.

John learned very quickly how to handle his paints, but he was not at all pleased with the picture itself. He was sure that the next one would be better.

"Have you noticed," his mother asked the following day as she stood in the open door after seeing a customer out, "there are no British sailors on the wharf this morning? I wonder why."

John would have been happy if he never saw another sailor—especially a British one—but he did not say so. Instead he remembered, "One of the crew said yesterday that a number of the sailors are running away from the fleet."

"Poor fellows!" Mrs. Copley shook her head. "Life on a warship is hard, they say. But of course the commodore has to have sailors. I suppose the fleet will soon be off for England."

But the fleet did not sail immediately. It needed sailors and knew only one way to get them, a way never tried before in Boston.

Early next morning, Mrs. Copley happened to look out on the wharf as she and John were eating breakfast.

"That's strange!" she exclaimed. "Here are some of the British sailors back, but look! They're all carrying sticks and clubs!"

John went uneasily to join her at the window and

434

Lucy Locket, thinking no doubt that they were looking at a bird, jumped up on the sill to see, too.

Outside, through the morning mist, the early sun was casting long shadows of masts and spars across the wharf and up the pale fronts of the buildings. Through these shadows the British sailors were moving, like shadows themselves.

Mrs. Copley and John and Lucy Locket watched them until they came to the foot of King Street.

"Whatever are they up to now? Half of them have lined themselves across the foot of the street and the others are coming back," Mrs. Copley murmured, plucking at her apron nervously.

"Look! Look! They're chasing someone!" John cried out all at once.

Suddenly the silence was broken. People were shouting, windows and doors were slamming open, someone yelled, and the cry, "Press gang! Press gang!" was taken up and ran the length of the wharf, like a train of powder set alight at one end.

But escape was not easy with half the press gang making a wall between wharf and town.

As the Copleys watched, frozen at their window, they saw an unknown apprentice rush past, pursued by two sailors. They were overtaking him when the boy dodged desperately to one side and jumped off the edge of the wharf into the water.

"Get him!" John could hear the pursuers shouting, but no one on the moored vessel seemed in a hurry to fish the boy out of the water, and in the end the sailors came away without him.

"Thank goodness he escaped!" John was trembling all over as he had trembled when the two sailors were dragging him out of his mother's shop, but he could not leave the window. With horror, he saw more men coming out of the sail loft driving Mr. Southard's apprentices ahead of them as dogs drive sheep.

"Alexander! They've got Alexander!" And forgetting his own fears John ran toward the door, but his mother caught his arm and held him back.

"You can't help Alexander!" she cried. "No! No! John! They'd take you too!"

She let go his arm and the boy stumbled blindly back to the window, rapping on it hard with his knuckles.

Alexander looked up, gave a sort of smile, and shouted, "Tell my family."

But the press gang was hurrying him along, and now Mrs. Copley was pulling John away from where he stood.

"Keep out of sight!" she exclaimed. "They mustn't see you!"

Dejectedly John stood by the hearth while his mother, at the window, told him what was going on.

"They're taking all the young men and boys," she mourned. "Four more just went by and one had a cut on his forehead. Poor lad! There's a crowd now, gathered at the foot of King Street, but the guard there won't let them by. Hear how they shout!"

Suddenly Mrs. Copley was silent as though a hand had been laid at her throat. John, looking up, heard a heavy knock on their own door.

This was the end.

The press gang had come for him.

Again came the knock, like the blow of a cudgel.

"Open up in there!" someone shouted.

And the blows began to rain down on the panel, filling the little house with a deafening din.

Lucy Locket, appalled, leaped down from the sill and hid under the table, but no one else in the kitchen moved. Mrs. Copley was praying out loud. John stood by the hearth, one hand thrust tight in his pocket holding onto a bit of pencil as though his life depended on it.

438

The blows stopped as suddenly as they had begun and a voice was heard saying jovially, "I know the people in there, mates! Come on. There's only a woman and a child too young for us. No need to scare them out of their wits!" and a moment later three men passed by the window arm-in-arm, and the man in the middle was Tom Lightfoot.

"Oh, God be praised!" exclaimed Mrs. Copley softly. "The good soul! The kind soul!"

"He's the one I told you about, Mother, the one who helped me the other day. Shall I run out a minute to thank him?"

"No! No! Get back there by the fire! They've put their prisoners in the barge and now they're coming for more, hunting out the poor men who've hidden away."

Terrified though he was, John could not keep away from the window. Hidden behind his mother, he looked out shivering into the misty morning, and there he saw a hurrying figure. It was a young gentleman, so shabby that John felt sure that the press gang would not hesitate to gobble him up. That must have been what the gentleman thought too, for he was slipping along, looking from side to side for some place where he might hide, and finding none. John knew just how hunted and helpless he felt.

Before Mrs. Copley could call him back again, the boy had unbarred the door and slipped through. He ran up to the stranger and, taking his hand, led him quickly into the shop, two shadows among the shadows.

439

Mrs. Copley met them. Like her son, she could think quickly in an emergency.

"Hurry, sir!" she said almost in a whisper. "Get into John's bed and pull the sheets up to your chin. There's no place to hide in this thimble of a house. John, show the gentleman up, and be sure to get his hat out of sight," and while they hurried upstairs she straightened her white cap and kerchief and took her place behind the counter, followed by Lucy Locket, who jumped up beside a tobacco jar and began to wash her whiskers.

A moment later the bell above the door gave a furious jingle and in strode an officer, followed by three sailors, their footsteps covering the last sounds from upstairs.

"Did a man come in here?" the officer demanded sharply.

Mrs. Copley tried to appear surprised.

"There's no one here but my husband, sir. He came home only last week from the West Indies and he's upstairs now, cruelly sick with the fever."

Probably the officer noticed the quaver in her voice, which she could not quite hide, and would have searched the house and carried off the fugitive and John, too, as a punishment, but at that very moment Boston came to the rescue.

From over the roofs a church bell began to ring, and then another answered and another and another took up the cry. The angry crowd at the foot of King Street had not been able to break through the armed guard which held them away from the wharf, but the people had found a voice for their fury and now from belfry to belfry the warning rolled with the swinging bells, rousing the citizens.

"Clapper up!
Clapper down!
Guard yourself,
Boston town!"

The menacing sound frightened the British.

"They'll be around our ears like hornets, sir," said one of the sailors.

The officer nodded. "We've enough prisoners," he agreed. "Better get back to the barge while we can." And without another look at Mrs. Copley he hurried out, followed by the sailors.

A moment later the people inside heard a whistle blown three times, and the press gang rallied at their door with what new prisoners they had. When the captives and captors were in the barge with the lines ready to be cast off and the sailors at the oars, the guard at the foot of King Street was recalled and retreated down the wharf followed by the mob. Sticks and broken bricks were beginning to fly but the barge got off safely.

The moment the danger was over, the stranger jumped up, fished his hat out from under the bed, and with John close at his heels, ran out onto the wharf to join the shouting mob.

"Keep up heart, boys!" "We'll have you back!"
people were calling to their friends, who with every
stroke of the oars were being carried farther and
farther away. John, too, shouted: "Alexander!
Alexander!" He couldn't tell which was Alexander, nor
if Alexander heard him. But louder than any shout —
threatening the captors, encouraging the captives —
sounded the endless din of the Boston bells, calling
over the steep roofs of the town, out, out, far out
among the islands behind which the barge was
already disappearing.

443

When John and the stranger returned to the shop
they found old Mr. Southard drinking a dish of tea in
front of the kitchen fire, where Mrs. Copley had
brought him. He kept talking about his lost apprentices.
"And the rogues even took little Alexander," he said
again and again. "I'm glad you got away, sir," he
added to John's gentleman, who now introduced
himself as Peter Pelham, engraver by trade. Mrs. Copley
poured another cup of tea for him, and as he sat
sipping it from the deep saucer he thanked her and
John for having saved him from the press gang.
Later, when he was leaving, he turned at the door to
add, "While I lay in bed, I noticed a picture painted on
the wall. Will you tell me, madam, who painted it?"

"That's just some of John's foolishness. He's a good boy in other ways, but he wastes his time scribbling. And now he must paint, it seems. I wish you would tell him, sir, to turn to something of more use in this world."

Peter Pelham looked at John.

"How old are you, John?"

"Nine, sir."

"Has anyone taught you to paint?"

"No, sir."

"That was your first painting on plaster?"

"Yes, sir."

"Your next one will be better." And with a smile and a few more grateful words, Peter Pelham was gone.

All that day and night and the next day and night the bells rang. There was no getting away from their angry clamor, and while their din shook the air the citizens rioted in the streets against the royal governor and all things British.

No one came to buy tobacco.

Even Lucy Locket was at first disturbed by the uproar and went about the house mewing uneasily.

> "Clapper up!
> Clapper down!
> Return our sons
> To Boston town!"

demanded the bells, hour after hour, from their cold November belfries.

John went back to his painting. Noise or no noise, bells or no bells, he was so upset by the coming of the press gang and the carrying off of Alexander and the others that he had to do something, and the only thing he could do was to paint.

He wanted to paint a picture which would express his feelings. *Alexander was coming back.* Like the bells, John would hold to that idea through thick and thin. Even King George upon his throne couldn't hold Alexander when the bells of Boston ordered him to let his prisoners go. No, John wanted to paint a picture of triumph and, knowing his Bible well, he knew just what it would be.

All that day he painted. This time it must be a large picture. It must be good.

"You're wasting your time," said Mrs. Copley, shaking her head. But she spoke mostly from habit.

Lucy Locket was glad to have John busy upstairs. As usual she played with his brushes, dipped her paw into a paint pot, drew it hastily out and shook it, and at last went to curl up in the middle of the bed, licking her paint-covered paw and making faces.

But John never noticed. He was painting. When his mother called him to come down to eat, he was surprised. He didn't feel hungry or thirsty. While he washed his hands in cold water at the bowl in his room, Lucy Locket stretched herself, looking at her master, but for once John did not even see her.

Downstairs he ate his dinner, answered when he was

446

spoken to, folded his napkin, and slipped away upstairs.

"It isn't as though he had a gift," his mother thought, impressed in spite of herself by his absorption in his work. "That young man, Peter Pelham, didn't seem to think much of his daubing the other day. I can see that the poor boy doesn't want to be a tailor, but beggars can't be choosers. There's always something to keep the rabbit's tail short, especially in a widow's house. I'll let him finish this picture and then I *must* put my foot down."

The afternoon darkened. Twilight comes early in November. John painted while he could, and Lucy Locket slept. If a cat has nothing else to do she can always sleep.

John woke the next morning to the din of bells, and at once he remembered his friend.

"Where is Alexander?" he thought. "When will he come home?"

And thinking of Alexander, he jumped up to see his picture. How much there remained to be done! But his mother heard him moving about and called him down to breakfast.

The second day was like the first. The bells of Boston rang hour after hour without stopping. No one came to the shop, and John painted while Lucy Locket slept. Outside in the streets the rioting went on, and rumors spread that the commodore was going to shell the city.

"It's a time for wise people to keep to their houses," Mrs. Copley thought. "I suppose John might as well work at his picture as suck his thumb. I shall bake some pies."

But on the next morning a strange silence lay over the town. It was as ominous as the uproar had been. What was happening? What did this silence mean?

"They had to stop sometime," John said to himself. "The bell ringers must have been very tired."

And as always his thoughts went to Alexander, a prisoner on some English warship down the harbor, and his eyes went to his picture, almost finished now. But as he stared at it his heart sank.

The day before in the sunset light it had seemed wonderful. But now everything was wrong. No wonder his mother said that he had no gift! No wonder he was to be apprenticed to a tailor!

But John set his jaw. His mouth looked very firm and his hazel eyes very bright. With his bare feet on the cold floor, he took up his brush and began to paint, trying to correct the faults he saw.

Lucy Locket wandered in and walked with high steps, purring, round and round his ankles, feeling soft and tickly. Noticing her at last, John reached down and patted her and then went back to his painting. Lucy Locket waited to see if he would pat her again, but when he did not she shook out her fur and jumped on the bed, landing neatly in the smoothest part of the bedclothes.

449

Soon his mother called him down to breakfast.
"I wonder why the bells aren't ringing," she said in a
worried voice. "I don't hear any shouting in the
town. Later we must go out. There may be news."

"Let me finish my picture first," begged John. "It's
almost done."

"I'm certainly glad to hear that!" Mrs. Copley
exclaimed. "These last two days you've been like a
sleepwalker. You hardly know even what you're
eating. This is the very last time I shall give in to your
foolishness."

John finished his breakfast and went back to work.

Now that the bells had stopped ringing the sounds of
the wharf again made themselves heard. There were
footsteps and voices, perhaps more than usual, but
John never noticed. If he had looked out he would have
seen people climbing the riggings or perched astride
the spars with hands shading their eyes as they
stared eastward down the harbor. But John never
glanced at the window.

In the middle of the morning the shop bell rang and a moment later Mrs. Copley called up the stairs, "John! John! Mr. Pelham and another gentleman are coming up to see you!"

Then, indeed, John pulled back from his work. How terrible it looked! And how untidy his bed was, unmade, with Lucy Locket in the midst of it! And he was just as bad, covered with paint, with one stocking half down!

But before John could move, the gentleman had come in, followed by Mrs. Copley.

"John," said Mr. Pelham, looking rather solemn, "this is my friend, Mr. Smibert. We stopped in on our way to see what you were painting."

Way to what? John never wondered.

He was looking at Mr. Smibert, who, after the briefest of nods, had walked into the middle of the room and now stood staring at John's painting with his feet well apart and his hands behind his back.

He stared and he stared but he said nothing. Peter Pelham said nothing.

Outside people were running along the wharf, but no one in the little room over Mrs. Copley's tobacco shop heard them.

John looked at his picture and felt ashamed of it. He had painted the escape of the children of Israel through the Red Sea out of their Egyptian bondage. There they stood on a green bank, safe and sound, looking back at the Red Sea, which was closing over the

Egyptians who had pursued them in their chariots. The nearest figure was of a boy with a long Scotch face and sandy hair. He certainly looked like Alexander, and Pharaoh in his chariot, with the big red wave coming down over him, had a profile like King George's head on a penny.

But it was the faults that John noticed. Pharaoh's head was much too large and the Red Sea was too red. And Alexander's leg bent the wrong way and one of his arms was longer than the other.

Now there came a shouting from the end of the wharf, but all that John noticed was the silence in the room.

Why didn't anyone speak?

John looked at Peter Pelham but Peter was looking at Mr. Smibert and Mr. Smibert was looking at John's picture.

At last the boy could bear the silence no longer.

"It's no good," he said in a choked voice.

"A waste of time," added his mother. "But he'll be all right as soon as he's apprenticed to the tailor."

John felt very unhappy.

"I can do better next time," he began.

But at last the stranger was speaking.

"You need do no better!" he exclaimed, looking now at John. "There aren't five grown men in Boston who could do as well!"

Peter Pelham smiled.

"I thought you'd say that, Smibert. You see, madam,"

he explained to Mrs. Copley, "I am only an engraver, but my friend here is the best portrait painter in Boston."

For once Mrs. Copley found nothing to say. She had never been so surprised in her life.

Now the man was speaking to her.

"It would be a true waste to try to make your son a tailor," he was saying. "By the time he is twenty-one he will be the greatest artist in America. Perhaps before that. I have never seen such promise."

"Fancy that!" cried Mrs. Copley, her eyes wide with pleasure and astonishment. "The greatest in America!"

Suddenly John came back to life. He was aware again of Lucy Locket stretching herself and yawning on the bed. He saw a boy in the rigging almost outside his window. He heard the shouts.

"Hurrah! Hurrah! Hurrah!" yelled the boy in the rigging.

The two men hurried to the window.

"They must be coming!" exclaimed Peter Pelham. "The governor has persuaded the commodore to send our people back."

Alexander was coming back! And he himself was going to be a painter! Snatching up Lucy Locket, John joined the others at the window. Why, the masts were filled with people, and the other windows, like theirs, were crammed with people, and a great crowd darkened the wharf.

There were loud shouts now and people were tossing

their hats into the air. Where was the barge among all
the boats and ships stirring in the harbor? Suddenly
John saw it, nearer than he had expected. It had
almost reached the wharf, and the cheering, which had
at first been scattered, now came in a steady roar.

Which was Alexander? John could not be sure among
all the crowd in the barge. But Alexander was there.

John knew that. For suddenly between the cheers he heard from the approaching boat the shrill gay tooting of a penny whistle.

And now the Boston bells again began to ring. But this time there was no anger in their note. Boston had fought for its citizens, and see, they were coming home again.

> "Ding ding,
> Dong dong,
> Ding ding,
> Dong dong,
> All is right
> Where all was wrong,"

cried the bells, until the air throbbed with joy. Fear and anger were forgotten. Only joy remained.

John, holding Lucy Locket tight in his arms, leaned far out from the window and shouted, "Alexander! I'm going to be a painter!"

No one heard him. Certainly not Alexander. But like an answer, John again caught the sound of the penny whistle as the crowd surged forward to meet the returning men.

Afterword

John Singleton Copley was brought up on Long Wharf where his widowed mother kept a tobacco shop.

In 1748 Mrs. Copley married Peter Pelham and went to live near the upper end of King Street next to the Quaker Meeting House. There John could watch his stepfather work at his engravings, and he probably spent much time in Smibert's studio. But when he was fourteen his stepfather died, and John began to support himself and his mother and half-brother as a professional portrait painter.

I have chosen to write about a few days in John's ninth year during the course of the Knowles Riots while the Copleys still lived on Long Wharf. Thirty years before the Boston Tea Party the independent and fearless little city of Boston fought for its rights against the royal governor and the royal navy and succeeded in forcing the return of its stolen young men. This was a popular and democratic uprising, a forerunner of the revolution which was to come. Living as they did on Long Wharf where the riot began and ended, John and his mother were necessarily in the midst of it all. Years later, when he was famous throughout England and America, he liked to tell his children how as a little boy he had painted on the plaster walls of his room on the wharf a picture of Moses and the children of Israel coming out of the Red Sea.

Although I have read many details of the riot in *The Transactions of the Colonial Society of Massachusetts* and in Caleb Snow's charming old *History of Boston* published in 1828, I owe my initial interest in the subject entirely to James Thomas Flexner's vivid *Short History of American Painting*, fortified by his biography of John Singleton Copley.

—*Elizabeth Coatsworth*

John Singleton Copley's portrait of Paul Revere,
famous silversmith and patriot.

459

Key to Pronunciation

Letter Symbol for a Sound	Key Word and Its Respelling	Letter Symbol for a Sound	Key Word and Its Respelling
a	pat (PAT)	oo	boot, rule (ROOL)
ah	far (FAHR)	or	for (FOR)
ai	air (AIR)	ow	power (POW-ər)
aw	jaw (JAW)	u	put, book (BUK)
ay	pay (PAY)	uh	cut (KUHT)
e	pet (PET)	ch	church (CHERCH)
ee	bee (BEE)	hw	when (HWEN)
ehr	berry (BEHR -ee)	ks	mix (MIKS)
er	term (TERM)	kw	quick (KWIK)
i	pit (PIT)	ng	thing (THING)
igh	sigh (SIGH)		finger (FING -gər)
ihr	pier (PIHR)	sh	shoe (SHOO)
o	pot (POT)	ss	case (KAYSS)
oh	oh, boat (BOHT)	th	thing (THING)
oi	oil (OIL)	<u>th</u>	this (<u>TH</u>IS)
		zh	pleasure (PLEZH -ər)

y used in place of (igh) before two consonant letters as in child (CHYLD)

ə represents the sound for any vowel spelling when a syllable is sounded very weakly, as in the first syllable of about, or the last syllables of item, gallop, or focus, or the middle syllable of charity.

Glossary

ac•cu•sa•tion (ak-yoo-ZAY-shən) *noun.* A charge of wrongdoing.

ac•knowl•edge (ak-NOL-ij) *verb.* 1. To admit to be true or correct: Alex *acknowledged* that he was responsible for the damage. 2. To give recognition to the authority of: The prince *acknowledged* the king to be his ruler. 3. To respond or reply to (a greeting or message): Jenny *acknowledged* my greeting with a wave of her hand. 4. To show gratitude or give praise for something. **acknowledged, acknowledging.**

aisle (IGHL) *noun.* The space for walking between rows of seats in a classroom, auditorium, or church.

a•lert (ə-LERT) *verb.* To warn, caution. **alerted, alerting.** —*adjective.* Wide-awake, watchful.

Al•lah (AH-lə) *noun.* Name of God in the Mohammedan or Moslem religion.

al•ler•gic (ə-LER-jik) *adjective.* Affected badly or irritated by certain substances: John is *allergic* to cat fur; it makes him sneeze.

Alp *noun.* A high mountain. —**Swiss Alps.** *noun.* A mountain range in south-central Europe.

al•tar (AWL-tər) *noun.* A raised block or table, usually at the front of a church, at which religious services are held.

The pronunciation system and word entries are adapted from *The Ginn Intermediate Dictionary*, © Copyright, 1977, 1974, 1973, by Xerox Corporation, published by Ginn and Company (Xerox Corporation).

am·a·teur (AM-ə-chər) *noun.* 1. A person who uses his or her skill for fun and not to make money. 2. An athlete who has never received money for playing.

am·ber (AM-bər) *noun.* 1. A substance of yellow-brown color used in costume jewelry. 2. (Also *adjective*). A yellow-brown color.

An·ky·lo·sau·rus (an-ki-lə-SAWR-uhss) *noun.* A plant-eating dinosaur. Since its body was covered with plates that were thick and bony, it is sometimes called the "armored dinosaur."

an·noy (ə-NOI) *verb.* To bother, irritate, make displeased: The buzzing of that fly *annoys* me. **annoyed, annoying.**

ap·ply (ə-PLIGH) *verb.* 1. To request formally: Nan *applied* for a position on the school newspaper. 2. To put or spread on: Jim *applied* two coats of paint to the house. 3. To relate (to): Traffic rules *apply* to everyone. 4. To devote; put effort into: Ann *applied* herself to drawing because she wanted to be an artist. **applied, applying.**

ap·pre·hen·sive (ap-ri-HEN-siv) *adjective.* Uneasy or worried about the future.

ar·chae·ol·o·gist (ahr-kee-OL-ə-jist) *noun.* A person who studies ancient people and cultures by examining tools, pottery, pictures, clothing, and other relics.

arc·tic (AHRK-tik or AHR-tik) *noun.* 1. [Often capital A] The geographic area around the North Pole. 2. [Capital A] The Arctic Ocean. —*adjective.*

1. Related to, from, or of the area around the North Pole: An *arctic* fox turns white in winter. 2. Very cold; frigid: Joe feared an *arctic* winter.

ar·id (AR-əd) *adjective.* 1. Dry; without life: A desert is an *arid* region. 2. Boring; uninteresting.

as·cend (ə-SEND) *verb.* 1. To rise to a higher rank or position: Herb *ascended* to the rank of Eagle Scout. 2. To travel upward: The climbers *ascended* the mountain. **ascended, ascending.**

as·phalt (ASS-fawlt) *noun.* A dark subtance similar to tar that is used with sand or gravel to pave roads and cover roofs. —*verb.* To cover with asphalt. **asphalted, asphalting.**

ath·lete (ATH-leet) *noun.* A trained, skilled person who competes seriously in sports that require qualities like speed and endurance. **athletes.** —**athletic** *adjective.*

at·ten·tive (ə-TEN-tiv) *adjective.* 1. Alert; paying attention: The student was *attentive* during the history lesson. 2. Considerate of the needs and desires of others. —**attentively** *adverb.*

aus·tere (awss-TIHR) *adjective.* 1. Stern; harsh. 2. Extremely simple; without luxury. —**austerely** *adverb.*

ban·di·coot (BAN-di-koot) *noun.* A small, ratlike Australian animal.

bane (BAYN) *noun.* 1. A person or thing that harms or ruins something: The destructive dog was the *bane* of Mildred's existence. 2. A poison.

bane·ber·ry (BAYN-ber-ee) *noun.* 1. A plant with small black poisonous berries. 2. Berries from this plant.

ban·nis·ter Also **banister** (BAN-i-stər) *noun.* A railing with supports, usually running alongside a stairway.

ban•yan (BAN-yən) *noun.* A kind of fig tree, found in East India, with branches that grow down to the earth and take root.

bar•na•cle (BAHR-nə-kəl) *noun.* A salt water shellfish that attaches itself to anything solid and under water, such as rocks, or the undersides of ships.

ba•sic (BAY-sik) *adjective.* Main; essential; necessary or required: Food and water are *basic* needs for human life. —**basically** *adverb.*

ba•zaar (bə-ZAHR) Also **bazar** *noun.* 1. A fair or a festive occasion at which goods are sold and entertainment is provided to raise money for a special purpose. 2. A section of a town, especially in countries of the Orient, where goods are sold at shops or marketplaces.

be•drag•gled (bi-DRAG-əld) *adjective.* Worn-out; soiled; limp, as with wetness: Bob's clothes looked *bedraggled* after his hike in the rain.

be•rate (bee-RAYT) *verb.* To rebuke or scold harshly. **berated, berating.**

be•seech (bi-SEECH) *verb.* To plead with; to beg for. **besought** or **beseeched, beseeching.**

be•wil•der (bi-WIL-dər) *verb.* To confuse: The difficult instructions on the machine *bewildered* my cousin. **bewildered, bewildering.**

bil•lion (BIL-yən) *noun.* The cardinal number 1,000,000,000 in the United States or 1,000,000,000,000 in Great Britain.

bi•son (BIGH-sn) *noun.* A large animal of the ox family with short horns and a shaggy head; the American buffalo. —**bison** *plural.*

bor•der (BOR-dər) *noun.* 1. The edge or rim of anything. 2. The line which separates political divisions or private property.

boul•der (BOHL-dər) *noun.* A large, rounded, smooth rock: There was a huge *boulder* in front of the cave.

boun•ty (BOWN-tee) *noun.* 1. Generosity 2. A reward: There was a bounty for capturing the killer. **bounties.** —**bountiful** *adjective.* —**bountifully** *adverb.*

bread•fruit (BRED-froot) *noun.* A large eatable fruit that grows on a tree found in tropical regions.

bur•eau (BYUR-oh) *noun.* 1. A chest of drawers used for storing clothes. 2. A business office that performs a special duty: a travel *bureau.* 3. A department of the government.

bur•noose (ber-NOOSS) *noun.* A long cloak with a hood: *Burnooses* are worn by the Arabs. **burnooses.**

car•na•tion (kahr-NAY-shən) *noun.* 1. A fragrant flower with fringed petals. 2. A pink or light-red color.

carve (KAHRV) *verb.* 1. To form or decorate by cutting: The artist *carved* a statue of marble. 2. To slice; cut into slices. **carved, carving.**

cas•se•role (KASS-ə-rohl) *noun.* 1. A dish usually with a cover, in which foods are baked. 2. Food baked and served in a deep dish. **casseroles.**

cau•tious (KAW-shəss) *adjective.* Careful; watchful. —**cautiously** *adverb.*

cha•grin (shə-GRIN) *noun.* A feeling of shame or disappointment.

chal•lenge (CHAL-ənj) *noun.* 1. An offer to take part in a fight or contest: a *challenge* to a chess game.

2. A questioning; a demand for evidence or proof. **challenges.** —*verb.* 1. To offer to engage in a contest of any type. 2. To question the correctness of or to demand evidence for. **challenged, challenging.**

cham•ber (CHAYM-bər) *noun.* 1. A room, especially a bedroom. 2. Any enclosed space.

chan•de•lier (shan-də-LIHR) *noun.* A lighting fixture that hangs from a ceiling.

char•ac•ter (KA-rik-tər) *noun.* 1. A person's individual manner of thinking and acting; the qualities of a person or thing that make it different from another. 2. A person in a novel, play, or other work. 3. Moral or spiritual quality; moral strength: It takes *character* to face problems. 4. (Informal) An odd or unusual person.

chem•i•cal (KEM-i-kəl) *adjective.* Of or related to chemistry, the science concerned with the make-up of substances. —*noun.* Any substance that results from or is used in the processes of chemistry.

chord (KORD) *noun.* 1. A combination of musical tones made in harmony. 2. A feeling or emotion: The bitter remark struck a sensitive *chord.*

chore (CHOR) *noun.* 1. An odd job or task. 2. A burden or difficulty: Studying is a *chore* for some students. **chores.**

chute (SHOOT) *noun.* 1. A slope or channel down which things may flow, slide, or be rolled. 2. (Informal) A parachute. **chutes.**

cit•a•del (SIT-ə-dl) *noun.* A fort, especially one protecting a city: Foot soldiers defended the *citadel.*

clash (KLASH) *noun.* 1. A conflict, as of ideas or opinions. 2. A battle or collision. **clashes.** —*verb.* 1. To conflict: Jim's desire to leave the party *clashed* with Tom's wish to stay. 2. To collide or to do battle with. **clashed, clashing.**

clutch (KLUHCH) *verb.* 1. To grip or hold tightly. 2. To snatch or catch hold of: The drowning sailor *clutched* at pieces of driftwood. **clutched, clutching.** —*noun.* A grip or grasp.

co•coon (kə-KOON) *noun.* A silky case or covering spun by some insects when they are in the larval or early stage of their development.

comb (KOHM) *noun.* 1. A device with a row of teeth or prongs, used to arrange or clean the hair. 2. Any device used to clean, untangle, or arrange fibers, hair, or fur. 3. A crest or outgrowth on the head of a rooster or other bird. 4. A honeycomb. —*verb.* 1. To untangle, clean, or arrange with a comb or similar device. 2. To search or look through thoroughly: Doris *combed* the library to find a special book. **combed, combing.**

com•pas•sion•ate (kəm-PASH-ən-it) *adjective.* Showing pity; sympathetic. —**compassionately** *adverb.*

con•ceit (kən-SEET) *noun.* 1. A vain or too-high opinion of one's own ability, attractiveness, or importance. 2. A whim or imaginary notion.

con•cen•tra•tion (kon-sən-TRAY-shən) *noun.* 1. Undivided attention: To understand the instructions requires *concentration.* 2. The act or process of concentrating.

con•dor (KON-dor) *noun.* A large vulture found in South America and in parts of California.

con•fuse (kən-FYOOZ) *verb.* 1. To bewilder, perplex. 2. To mistake for another; fail to see a difference. **confused, confusing.**

con•sole (kən-SOHL) *verb.* To give comfort, relief, or encouragement. **consoled, consoling.**

con•stant (KON-stənt) *adjective.* 1. Not stopping; continual. 2. Faithful; loyal: David was *constant* in his friendship with Jonathan. 3. Not changing; regular. *—noun.* Something that does not change. **—constantly** *adverb.*

con•ti•nent (KON-tə-nənt) *noun.* 1. One of the seven major masses of land areas on earth. 2. [Capital C] The mainland of Europe; Europe not including the British Isles.

con•tra•dict (kon-trə-DIKT) *verb.* 1. To state the opposite of something already stated: The witness *contradicted* the story of the accused person. 2. To be contrary or opposed to. **contradicted, contradicting.**

con•tra•ry (KON-trehr-ee) *noun.* The opposite: I thought that Joan beat Sue in the race, but the *contrary* was true. *—adjective.* 1. Completely different; opposite. 2. (kon-TRAIR-ee) Inclined to have an opposite viewpoint; tending to argue. **—contrarily** *adverb.*

con•trite (kən-TRIGHT or KON-tright) *adjective.* Having or showing sorrow or regret. **—contritely** *adverb.* **—contrition** (kən-TRISH-ən) *noun.*

con•ven•ience (kən-VEEN-yənss) *noun.* Comfort; ease; assistance. **conveniences.**

con•ver•sa•tion (kon-vər-SAY-shən) *noun.* Talking, especially in an informal way.

co•pal (KOH-pəl) *noun.* A hard resin that comes from the sap of any of several tropical trees.

count•less (KOWNT-liss) *adjective.* More than anyone can or will count; innumerable.

cour•age (KER-ij) *noun.* Bravery

when faced with something frightening or dangerous.

cray•fish (KRAY-fish) Also **crawfish** *noun.* 1. A shellfish similar to a lobster but smaller in size. 2. A small, spiny lobster. **— crayfish** or **crayfishes** *plural.*

crease (KREESS) *noun.* 1. A fold, line, ridge, or wrinkle: The old man's face was lined with *creases* of age. 2. The fold pressed into clothing. **creases.** *—verb.* 1. To make a fold or ridge. 2. To graze or wound slightly. **creased, creasing.**

cred•it (KRED-it) *noun.* 1. Honor, recognition, or praise for some deed, quality, or accomplishment. 2. A source of honor or praise: Sue is a *credit* to her Girl Scout troop. 3. Belief in a person's promise to pay a debt: Al bought a coat on *credit.*

crit•i•cism (KRIT-ə-siz-əm) *noun.* 1. The act of judging or testing something, particularly a performance, a piece of writing, or a work of art: The newspaper's *criticism* of the new play was favorable. 2. The act of making an unfair or rash judgment.

Cro-Mag•non (kroh-MAG-non) *noun.* 1. A prehistoric form of human beings who lived in the Stone Age. 2. The village where some Cro-Magnon skeletons were found.

Czech•o•slo•va•ki•a (chek-ə-sloh-VAH-kee-ə) *noun.* A country in Central Europe.

dan•gle (DANG-gəl) *verb.* 1. To swing or hang loosely: A broken wire *dangled* from the telephone pole. 2. To hold (something) so that it hangs loosely. **dangled, dangling.**

de•bris (də-BREE or day-BREE) *noun.* Litter, rubbish, waste.

de•i•ty (DEE-ə-tee) *noun.* 1. A god or goddess: Apollo was considered a *deity* by the Greeks. 2. [Capital D] God. **deities.**

de•jec•tion (di-JEK-shən) *noun.* Low spirits, discouragement, unhappiness. **—dejected** *adjective.*

des•ti•na•tion (dess-tə-NAY-shən) *noun.* The place to which someone or something is going: Mars may be the *destination* of future space travelers.

de•tail (di-TAYL or DEE-tayl) *noun.* 1. One small part of a whole. 2. Many or all of the small parts of something.

de•ter•min•a•tion (dee-tər-min-AY-shən) *noun.* Strength of purpose; firmness of decision.

di•nar (də-NAHR) *noun.* The money used in several Middle East and Eastern European countries.

dis•guise (diss-GIGHZ) *verb.* 1. To change so as to appear to be something else: The robbers *disguised* themselves as window washers. 2. To hide or conceal: Tim tried to *disguise* the fact that he had broken a lamp. **disguised, disguising. —***noun.* A make-up or costume used to change one's appearance. **disguises.**

dis•in•te•grate (diss-IN-tə-grayt) *verb.* To come apart, separate into pieces. **disintegrated, disintegrating. —disintegration** *noun.*

dis•po•si•tion (diss-pə-ZISH-ən) *noun.* 1. Placement; arrangement. 2. The power to use or manage as one wishes: All the boats were at the captain's *disposition*. 3. Basic or general nature.

dor•mi•to•ry (DOR-mə-tor-ee) *noun.* 1. A large room with many beds. 2. A building with a number of rooms for sleeping and living, especially for students.

down•heart•ed (DOWN-HAHR-tid) *adjective.* Dejected, sad, depressed. **—downheartedly** *adverb.*

drake (DRAYK) *noun.* A male duck. **drakes.**

dra•ma (DRAH-mə or DRAM-ə) *noun.* 1. A story or poem written to be acted out on the stage; a play. 2. The art of writing or presenting plays. 3. An exciting or moving experience in real life.

duck•ling (DUHK-ling) *noun.* A young or baby duck.

dy•nam•ic (digh-NAM-ik) *adjective.* Having power and force: a *dynamic* personality. **—dynamically** *adverb.*

ea•ger (EE-gər) *adjective.* Having a great desire or wanting something. **—eagerly** *adverb.* **—eagerness** *noun.*

earth•en•ware (ERTH-ən-wair) *noun.* (and *adjective*). Any article made of baked clay.

ef•fect (ə-FEKT) *noun.* A result: The *effect* of so much rain was a flood. **—***verb.* To make happen; bring about: The rain will *effect* a change in the temperature. **effected, effecting. —in effect.** In use or active: The rules have been *in effect* since last week.

e•ko (EK-KAW) *noun.* A solid food made from cooked cornmeal, like cornmeal mush.

el•dest (EL-dəst) *adjective.* The oldest one of more than two persons or things.

em•brace (em-BRAYSS) *verb.* 1. To hug or hold in the arms. 2. To take up eagerly: Marion *embraced* the fight against pollution. 3. To include: The school recreation program

465

embraces many different sports and activities. **embraced, embracing.** —*noun.* A hug. **embraces.**

em•per•or (EM-pər-ər) *noun.* The ruler of an empire.

en•cour•age (en-KER-ij) *verb.* 1. To give hope or confidence to. 2. To help; to support: Cold weather *encourages* the sale of warm clothing. **encouraged, encouraging.**

en•cour•age•ment (en•KER-ij-mənt) *noun.* Something that urges a person on.

e•nor•mous (ih-NOR-məss) *adjective.* Huge; very large; vast in size or number. —**enormously** *adverb.*

en•ter•tain (en-tər-TAYN) *verb.* 1. To amuse. 2. To have as guests. 3. To consider. **entertained, entertaining.**

en•vy (EN-vee) *verb.* To be jealous of. **envied, envying.** —*noun.* 1. Jealousy. 2. Something that causes jealousy.

es•cape (eh-SKAYP or ih-SKAYP) *verb.* 1. To get away; get out; get free: The prisoner *escaped* three times but was always caught. 2. To avoid; keep free from: Susan was the only one to *escape* the measles. 3. To leak out: The gas *escaped* from the balloon. **escaped, escaping.** —*noun.* 1. The act of getting away. 2. A way of escaping. **escapes.**

Es•ki•mo (ESS-kə-moh) *noun.* One of a people who live in the Arctic regions of North America.

ev•i•dent (EV-ə-DENT) *adjective.* Plain to see; easy to understand; obvious. —**evidently** (ev-ə-DENT-ly) *adverb.*

ex•pen•sive (ek-SPEN-siv) *adjective.* Very costly; high in price. —**expensively** *adverb.*

ex•pert (EK-spərt) *noun.* A person who knows a lot about a particular subject. —*adjective.* Highly skilled or trained. —**expertly** *adverb.*

ex•pla•na•tion (ek-splə-NAH-shən) *noun.* 1. Act of explaining; what is

said or written that explains. 2. Meaning, reason.

ex•pose (ek-SPOHZ) *verb.* 1. To reveal; uncover; open. 2. To leave open to the effects of sun, wind, or rain. 3. To tell or reveal something that was secret or unknown. **exposed, exposing.**

ex•pres•sion (eks-PRESH-ən) *noun.* 1. Act of expressing: an *expression* of opinion. 2. Show of emotion on the face: Pete's *expression* showed how sad he was. 3. Words of explanation: I know how I feel but I can't give it *expression.* 4. The act of showing or representing feeling: An actor must be a master of *expression.* 5. A special word or words: "23 skidoo" was a popular *expression* around 1900.

ex•tinct (ek-STINGKT) *adjective.* 1. Having died out completely. 2. Burned out; dead.

ex•traor•di•nar•y (ek-STROR-də-nair-ee) *adjective.* More than ordinary; unusual; special. —**extraordinarily** *adverb.*

fas•ci•na•tion (fass-ə-NAY-shən) *noun.* Very strong attraction.

fawn *noun.* 1. A light brownish color. 2. A young deer. —*verb.* 1. To show affection or fondness. 2. To act like a slave. **fawned, fawning.**

fer•ti•li•zer (FERT-l-igh-zər) *noun.* Manure, chemical compound, or anything worked into the soil to make it produce more richly.

fes•ti•val (FESS-tə-vəl) *noun.* 1. A special occasion or time marked by feasting, celebration, and rejoicing. 2. A group of related events, exhibits, entertainments: an arts and crafts *festival.*

fes•tiv•i•ty (fess-TIV-ə-tee) *noun.* 1. A joyous party or festive occasion. 2. The joyousness of a festival or party. **festivities.**

fez *noun.* A man's hat, of Turkish origin, and usually made of red felt. **—fezzes** (FEZ-iz) *plural.*

fil•ter (FIL-tər) *noun.* 1. A device or substance used to strain out bits of solid matter from a gas or liquid. *—verb.* 1. To pass through a device used to strain out particles of solid matter. 2. To move through a screen: The sunlight *filtered* through the thin drapes. **filtered, filtering.**

flick•er (FLIK-ər) *verb.* To burn or shine unevenly; to make an unsteady flame or light. **flickered, flickering.**

fore•see (for-SEE) *verb.* To expect, know something before it happens. **foresaw, forseeing.**

for•tress (FOR-triss) *noun.* 1. A fort; a place built to be defended. 2. Any protection or safe place. **fortresses.**

for•tu•nate (FOR-chə-nit) *adjective.* Lucky. *—noun.* Those who have good luck. **—fortunately** *adverb.*

foun•da•tion (fown-DAY-shən) *noun.* 1. The base or ground on which something is built: The *foundation* of their friendship is trust. 2. The lowest part of a building, set in or on the ground.

frank (FRANGK) *adjective.* 1. Honest and open in speech; forthright. 2. Without cover, disguise, or hidden motive: Her *frank* report did not omit a single detail.

fres•co (FRESS-koh) *noun.* 1. A painting done on wet plaster (walls or ceiling). 2. The method of painting on wet plaster. **—frescoes** or **frescos plural.** *—verb.* To paint on wet plaster. **frescoed, frescoing.**

fringe (FRINJ) *noun.* 1. A trimming of loose or bunched threads on the edge of clothing, curtains, tablecloths, and the like. 2. (Plural) Borders: People are moving to the *fringes* of big cities. **fringes.**

fu•ner•al (FYOO-nər-əl) *noun.* A ceremony in honor of a dead person followed by burial or cremation of the body.

fun•gus (FUHNG-gəss) *noun.* Any of several plants, such as mushrooms and molds, that do not have green color, leaves, or flowers. **—fungi** (FUHN-jigh) or **funguses** *plural.*

fun•nel (FUHN-l) *verb.* To pour or go through a small opening or funnel: The nurse *funneled* cough syrup from a large bottle into several smaller ones. **funneled** or **funnelled, funneling** or **funnelling.** *—noun.* 1. A cone-shaped device with a tube at one end, used to pour liquids or powders into a narrow opening. 2. A chimney or smokestack as on a steamship or locomotive.

gape (GAYP) *verb.* 1. To open the mouth wide. 2. To stare or gaze with the mouth open. 3. To become wide open. **gaped, gaping.**

gap-toothed (GAP-tootht) *adjective.* Having spaces between the teeth.

gar•ment (GAHR-mənt) *noun.* Anything worn as clothing.

gen•er•os•i•ty (jen-ə-ROSS-ə-tee) *noun.* 1. Willingness to give or share; unselfishness. 2. Abundance: Nature's *generosity.*

gen•ial (JEEN-yəl or JEE-nee-əl) *adjective.* 1. Cheerful, kindly. 2. Healthy; favorable for growth. **—geniality** *noun.* **—genially** *adverb.*

ge•ol•o•gist (jee-OL-ə-jist) *noun.* A person whose field of study is geology, the science of the history and structure of the earth's crust.

ges•ture (JESS-chər) *noun.* 1. A motion of the hand or other part of the body that expresses a feeling or emphasizes something spoken: The girl shook her fist in a *gesture* of anger. 2. An action, often only for effect, performed as a sign or token of some attitude or feeling. **gestures.** —*verb.* To indicate or show (something) with a gesture. **gestured, gesturing.**

gnarled (NAHRLD) *adjective.* Twisted and knotted.

gouge (GOWJ) *verb.* To cut into with a digging motion; to dig with a gouge. **gouged, gouging.** —*noun.* 1. A tool with a curved blade used for digging into wood. 2. A hole or mark made by gouging.

green•house (GREEN-howss) *noun.* A building, usually made of glass, in which plants are grown; a hothouse. **greenhouses.**

ground sloth (GROUND-slohth) *noun.* An extinct animal that lived on the ground; It is thought to be an ancestor of the modern tree sloth.

guard•ed (GAHR-did) *adjective.* 1. Protected or watched. 2. Very careful and cautious: *guarded* answers. —**guardedly** *adverb.*

guard•i•an (GAHR-dee-ən) *noun.* 1. One who protects. 2. A person appointed to take care of a minor until he or she is old enough to assume legal responsibility. —**guardianship** *noun.*

gust (GHUST) *noun.* 1. A sudden and forceful rush of wind: A violent *gust* tipped over the small sailboat. 2. A sudden rush of emotion: Maria felt a *gust* of anger over the insult. —*verb.*

To rush or flow suddenly, as a wind or strong feeling. **gusted, gusting.**

hab•it (HAB-it) *noun.* 1. A usual or regular practice or action: Getting up early is one of my *habits*. 2. A special outfit, such as that worn by some nuns.

halt•ing (HAWLT-ing) *adjective.* Hesitant; uneven: The frightened child told his story in a *halting* manner. —**haltingly** *adverb.*

harsh (HAHRSH) *adjective.* 1. Cruel or unkind; demanding. 2. Unpleasant to the senses. **harsher, harshest.** —**harshly** *adverb.*

haunch (HAWNCH) *noun.* 1. The upper part of a leg, including the hip. 2. (Always plural) The hindquarters of an animal. **haunches.**

hemp *noun.* 1. A tall plant with strong, tough fibers. 2. Fibers used to make rope and heavy cloth. 3. A drug made from the flowers and the leaves of some kinds of hemp.

hes•i•tant (HEZ-ə-tənt) *adjective.* Undecided; holding back; tending to hesitate. —**hesitantly** *adverb.*

hinge (HINJ) *noun.* The movable jointed device by which a door, gate, or lid is joined to a frame. —*verb.* 1. To install or apply a hinge or hinges. 2. To depend (on): The success of the team *hinged* on the hard work of all. **hinged, hinging.**

hoarse (HORSS) *adjective.* 1. Scratchy, weak, or harsh in sound. 2. Having a harsh, rasping voice. **hoarser, hoarsest.** —**hoarsely** *adverb.*

hoax (HOHX) *noun.* Something that tricks or deceives. **hoaxes.** —*verb.* To cheat, deceive, or mislead. **hoaxed, hoaxing.**

hon•est (ON-ist) *adjective.* 1. Honorable; truthful; fair. 2. Sincere; open: an *honest* smile. 3. Genuine; pure: *honest* merchandise. **—honestly** *adverb.* **—honesty** *noun.*

hor•ror (HOR-ər) *noun.* 1. Terror; great fear. 2. Disgust; great dislike.

hy•e•na (high-EE-nə) *noun.* A wild dog or wolf of Africa and Asia that has a shrill, laugh-like bark: A *hyena* looks like a wolf.

ice•box (IGHSS-boks) *noun.* 1. A box containing ice to cool food. 2. A refrigerator. **iceboxes.**

im•age (IM-ij) *noun.* 1. A picture or statue. 2. Something seen through a lens or reflected as in a mirror.

im•ag•i•na•tion (ih-MAJ-ə-nay-shən) *noun.* The ability or act of creating in the mind. **—imaginative** *adjective.*

im•ag•in•a•tive (im-A-jin-ə-tiv) *adjective.* 1. Having the ability to picture or invent vividly. 2. Original, creative: an *imaginative* painting.

Im•pe•ri•al Pal•ace (im-PIHR-ee-əl PAL-iss) *noun.* A building that is the official dwelling of an emperor or empress. **palaces.**

imp•ish (IMP-ish) *adjective.* Mischievous; playful.

im•pres•sion (im-PRESH-ən) *noun.* 1. Imprint made by pressing: The FBI keeps files of fingerprint *impressions.* 2. A feeling: I got the *impression* Al didn't like me. 3. An effect made on someone: Politeness makes a good *impression.*

in•cense (IN-senss) *noun.* 1. A substance such as gum or spices that gives a sweet or fragrant smell when burned. 2. A pleasing smell or perfume. **incenses.**

in•ci•dent (IN-sə-dənt) *noun.* 1. A happening or event. 2. An event that is not very important.

in•dig•na•tion (in-dig-NAY-shən) *noun.* An angry reaction to unjust acts. **—indignant** (in-DIG-nənt) *adjective.* **—indignantly** *adverb.*

in•i•ti•ate (ih-NISH-ee-ayt) *verb.* 1. To begin; start: The school will *initiate* a hot lunch program. 2. To introduce or teach the basics of a subject. 3. To admit a person into a club, organization, or society, often by a secret ceremony. **—initiated, initiating.** **—initiation** (ih-nish-ee-AY-shən) *noun.*

in•scribe (in-SKRIGHB) *verb.* 1. To write or engrave (letters, words, numbers) upon a surface: My identification bracelet is *inscribed* with my name and address. 2. To write a brief message in a book, on a photograph, etc. 3. To make a lasting impression, especially on the mind: The scene of the accident was *inscribed* on her memory. **inscribed, inscribing.**

in•scrip•tion (in-SKRIP-shən) *noun.* Words, usually only a few lines or less, written or carved on something like a memorial stone.

in•stance (IN-stənss) *noun.* 1. A sample. 2. One part or point in many parts or points.

in•stinct (IN-stingkt) *noun.* 1. An inner force that moves one to action: *Instinct* guides animals to places where they can find food and water. 2. A natural inner trait: an artistic *instinct.*

in•tro•duce (in-trə-DOOSS or in-trə-DYOOSS) *verb.* 1. To make known or acquaint, as one person to another: Sally *introduced* me to her cousin from Detroit. 2. To make (someone) aware of for the first time. 3. Insert; include. 4. To begin; start off with:

The minister *introduced* the sermon with a reading from the Bible. **introduced, introducing.**

in•ves•ti•gate (in-VESS-tə-gayt) *verb.* To look into or examine closely. **investigated, investigating.** —**investigation** *noun.*

itch (ICH) *noun.* 1. A prickling sensation of the skin that makes one want to scratch. 2. Any of various skin diseases that make one want to scratch. 3. A restless urge or feeling: Bill had an *itch* to do something. —*verb.* To feel an itch.

jag•ged (JAG-əd) *adjective.* Rough; having sharp points: I cut my foot on the *jagged* rocks.

jag•uar (JAG-wahr or JAG-yoo-ahr) *noun.* A large wildcat found in the jungles of South America.

jew•el•er (JOO-ə-lər) *noun.* A person who sells, makes, or repairs jewelry.

jos•tle (JOSS-l) *verb.* To move or push aside in a clumsy or rude way. **jostled, jostling.**

jo•vi•al (JOH-vee-əl) *adjective.* Joyous, merry. —**jovially** *adverb.*

la•goon (lə-GOON) *noun.* A body of salt water surrounded by sand bars or coral reefs that separate it from the sea.

land•slide (LAND-slighd) *noun.* 1. The sliding of a mass of earth and rocks down a mountain or hillside. 2. A great victory, especially in an election. **landslides.**

lark (LAHRK) *noun.* 1. Any of several types of songbirds. 2. (Informal) Something done just for fun; a carefree adventure.

mam•mal (MAM-əl) *noun.* Any animal, including a human, that has a backbone and some hair and, in the female, feeds its young with breast or udder milk.

mam•moth (MAM-əth) *noun.* A type of huge elephant, no longer existing, that had a hairy body and very long, curved tusks. —*adjective.* Huge; gigantic.

man•da•rin (MAN-də-rin) *noun.* 1. A high official in the former Chinese Empire. 2. (Capital M) A major dialect of the Chinese language.

marsh (MAHRSH) *noun.* A swamp or bog. **marshes.**

mass *noun.* 1. A shapeless lump: a *mass* of clay. 2. A large number of things considered as a whole: a *mass* of people. 3. The greater part or majority: The *mass* of the residents favors the new playground.

mas•sive (MASS-iv) *adjective.* Solid, large, or heavy: *massive* legs of the dinosaur. —**massively** *adverb.*

med•i•ta•tion (med-i-TAY-shən) *noun.* Deep thought, often as a kind of prayer.

mer•ri•ment (MER-i-mənt) *noun.* Mirth; fun or laughter; celebration.

midge (MIJ) *noun.* A small insect, as a gnat or fly. **midges.**

mile•stone (MIGHL-stohn) *noun.* 1. A stone or marker by the side of a road that shows the distance in miles to a particular place. 2. An important event: a *milestone* in space exploration. **milestones.**

mi•ser (MIGH-zər) *noun.* A greedy person who loves money for its own sake. —**miserly** *adjective.*

mod•el (MOD-l) *noun.* 1. A small copy of a larger object: a *model* of an airplane. 2. Someone or something regarded as an example to be followed or imitated.

mon•as•ter•y (MON-ə-stehr-ee) *noun.* A building in which monks live. **monasteries.**

mor•sel (MOR-sl) *noun.* A small piece or quantity.

mor•tal (MORT-l) *noun.* A human being. —*adjective.* 1. Causing death; fatal. 2. Certain to die. 3. Lasting until death. 4. Causing death of the soul or spirit.

mu•si•cal (MYOO-zi-kəl) *adjective.* 1. Having to do with music: The piano is a *musical* instrument. 2. Having a pleasant sound: a *musical* voice. 3. Being accompanied by music: a *musical* comedy. 4. Fond of or skilled in music. —*noun.* A play with music and dance. —**musically** *adverb.*

musk (MUHSK) *noun.* 1. A strong-smelling substance taken from a gland in the musk ox and used for making perfume. 2. The smell of musk. —**musky** *adjective.*

na•tion•al•i•ty (nash-ə-NAL-ə-tee) *noun.* 1. The state of being part of a nation; citizenship: My *nationality* is French. 2. Existence as a separate nation or country. 3. A group of people organized under the same government and usually within the same country. **nationalities.**

nat•u•ral•ly (NACH-ər-ə-lee or NACH-rə-lee) *adverb.* 1. In a natural way: pose for the picture *naturally*. 2. By or through an inborn talent; by or through nature: Pat is a *naturally* good athlete. 3. Of course, surely.

no•bil•i•ty (noh-BIL-ə-tee) *noun.* 1. Nobles as a class. 2. The noble rank. 3. Generosity; greatness of character. **nobilities.**

none•the•less (nuhn-the-LESS) *adverb.* However; nevertheless; in spite of that.

nu•mer•ous (NOO-mər-əss or NYOO-mər-əss) *adjective.* Many in number: Stanley has *numerous* friends. —**numerously** *adverb.*

ob•sti•nate (OB-stə-nit) *adjective.* 1. Stubborn; pigheaded; unwilling to change one's mind or do what someone else wants: The *obstinate* dog won't obey. 2. Hard to treat, remove, or bring under control: an *obstinate* pain. —**obstinacy** *noun.* —**obstinately** *adverb.*

of•fend (ə-FEND) *verb.* 1. To insult; annoy: The speaker *offended* the audience. **offended, offending.**

out•come (OWT-kuhm) *noun.* The result; the way a thing comes out.

pack•et (PAK-it) *noun.* 1. A small package. 2. A boat that carries passengers or goods on a regular schedule, usually on a river.

pa•go•da (pə-GOH-də) *noun.* A temple, common in Oriental countries, that is shaped like a tower of many tiers.

pa•le•on•tol•o•gist (pay-lee-on-TOL-ə-jist) *noun.* A scientist who studies fossils and ancient forms of life: The *paleontologist* discovered a dinosaur bone in the cave.

pan•ic (PAN-ik) *noun.* Sudden and powerful terror that often spreads rapidly to others. —*verb.* To cause or be affected by panic. **panicked, panicking.**

par•tic•u•lar (pər-TIK-yə-lər) *adjective.* 1. Of or belonging to one person or group: Ruth is a *particular* friend of mine. 2. One apart from all others: I do not like that *particular* garment. 3. Careful, exact: He was *particular* about his appearance. —*noun.* (Plural) Details: The *particulars* of a trip. —**in particular.** Especially.

pas•sage (PASS-ij) *noun.* 1. A corridor or hallway; a means of passing through or around something. 2. A voyage; a going across. 3. A section from a speech or from a written or musical work. **passages.**

pas•ty (PAYSS-tee) *adjective.* Like a paste; moist and thick, often with a lumpy or grainy texture.

pa•tient (PAY-shənt) *adjective.* 1. Calm, kind, tolerant. 2. Willing to keep on trying: *patient* training. 3. Long-suffering, willing to put up with: We have been *patient* too long with our enemies. —*noun.* One who is under a doctor's care. —**patiently** *adverb.*

pe•cu•liar (pi-KYOOL-yər) *adjective.* 1. Odd; strange: a *peculiar* look. 2. Belonging solely to; distinctive. —**peculiarity** (pi-kyoo-lee-AIR-ə-tee), *noun.* —**peculiarly** *adverb.*

ped•dler (PED-lər) *noun.* One who moves from place to place in order to sell something.

pee-vish (PEE-vish) *adjective.* Easily irritated. —**peevishly** *adverb.*

perch *noun.* 1. A place for a bird to nest. 2. A place to rest. **perches.** —*verb.* To sit, rest, or alight on a particular place. **perched, perching.**

phy•si•cian (fi-ZISH-ən) *noun.* A doctor; one who is duly qualified to practice medicine: The *physician* examined her patient and said he was in good health.

plait (PLAYT or PLAT) *noun.* 1. A braid. 2. A fold of cloth; a pleat. —*verb.* 1. To braid. 2. To fold into a pleat or pleats. **plaited, plaiting.**

pli•ers (PLIGH-ərz) *noun, plural.* A tool, hinged somewhat like scissors, that is used to hold, twist, or cut small objects and wire.

plough *verb.* 1. To cut into and turn over soil with a plow. 2. To push aside or lift snow, dirt, or some other substance. **plowed, plowing.**

por•tion (POR-shən) *noun.* A part or section of a larger whole. —*verb.* To cut or divide into sections or shares. **portioned, portioning.**

por•trait (POR-trit or POR-trayt) *noun.* A painting or photograph of a person.

pos•ses•sion (pə-ZESH-ən) *noun.* 1. Something that is owned or controlled. 2. Ownership or control: *possession* of wealth.

pov•er•ty (POV-ər-tee) *noun.* 1. The condition of being poor or in need. 2. A poor or small quality, amount, or degree: a *poverty* of ideas.

pre•his•tor•i•ans (pree-hiss-TOR-ee-ənz) *noun.* Scholars who study the earth's distant past, or the time before human beings left written records.

pre•his•tor•ic (pree-hiss-TOR-ik) *adjective.* Referring to a time before events were written down.

pre•serve (pri-ZERV) *verb.* 1. To keep from harm or injury. 2. To keep whole, free from damage. 3. To keep from spoiling or decaying by applying a solution or other material. **preserved, preserving.**

pre•text (PREE-tekst) *noun.* A false reason; an excuse.

prey (PRAY) *noun.* 1. A hunted animal sought for food: The tiger stalked its *prey*. 2. A victim of an attack (by a person or misfortune). —*verb.* 1. To seize (animals) for food. 2. To rob or attack. 3. To worry, preoccupy: *prey* on the mind. **preyed, preying.**

prim *adjective.* Overly proper or demure. **primmer, primmest.** —**primly** *adverb.*

pris•on•er (PRIZ-n-ər or PRIZ-nər) *noun.* A person who is locked up in a prison or is kept somewhere against his or her will.

pro•ces•sion (prə-SESH-ən) *noun.* A group that moves along in an orderly way: graduation *procession*.

pro•file (PROH-fighl) *noun.* 1. A view of a person's face from the side; a picture of such a

view. 2. The outline of anything seen from the side. 3. A short article about a person. **profiles.**

pros•per (PROSS-pər) *verb.* 1. To gain success or wealth, etc. 2. To grow or live vibrantly; to thrive. **prospered, prospering.**

pro•test (prə-TEST, proh-TEST or PROH-test) *verb.* 1. To oppose or resist with strong statements; to object. 2. To state strongly; declare: The man *protested* his innocence. **protested, protesting.**

quiv•er (KWIV-ər) *verb.* To shake or cause to shake slightly; tremble: The leaves began to *quiver* in the breeze. **quivered, quivering.** —*noun.* 1. A slight shaking. 2. A case used to hold arrows.

rave (RAYV) *verb.* 1. To speak in a wild and senseless manner. 2. To speak about very favorably or with great enthusiasm: Dave *raved* about the new movie. **raved, raving.**

re•cov•er (ri-KUHV-ər) *verb.* 1. To get well. 2. To get back something taken away or lost. 3. To make up for: Can the time I spent away from school be *recovered?* **recovered, recovering.** —**recovery** (ri-KUHV-ə-ree) *noun.*

reed *noun.* 1. A tall straight grass with a hollow stem, found in marshy places. 2. A musical pipe made from a reed.

reef *noun.* A strip of sand, rocks, or coral that is at, or close to, the surface of the water.

re•gard (ri-GAHRD) *verb.* 1. To look at with attention. 2. To think about in a special way. 3. To like; admire: *regard* someone highly. 4. To consider; heed. **regarded, regarding.**

re•gret (ri-GRET) *verb.* To feel sorry about; be disappointed about: "I *regret* that I have but one life to lose for my country." (Nathan Hale). —*noun.* 1. A feeling of distress, disappointment, or sorrow. 2. (Plural) A message that one will not accept an invitation: I sent my *regrets* that I could not attend the play.

re•lease (ri-LEESS) *verb.* 1. To free; *release* from jail. 2. To give up: Vera *released* her claim to the property. **released, releasing.**

re•lieve (ri-LEEV) *verb.* 1. To ease or make less, as pain or worry. 2. To give aid or assistance.

re•new (ri-NOO or ri-NYOO) *verb.* 1. To restore, make like new. 2. To start (efforts) again: He *renewed* his attempt to force the door open. 3. To continue or get again: *renew* a magazine subscription. **renewed, renewing.** —**renewal** *noun.*

res•cue (RESS-kyoo) *noun.* Deliverance from danger. **rescues.** —*verb.* To save from danger. **rescued, rescuing.**

res•er•va•tion (rez-ər-VAY-shən) *noun.* Land set aside by the government for a special purpose, for example, for people to live on.

re•spect (ri-SPEKT) *noun.* 1. Honor; regard, consideration: *respect* for the rights of others. 2. (Plural) A polite expression of regard or honor: I'd like to pay my *respects* to your parents. —*verb.* To show or have regard or consideration for: The students *respected* the excellent teacher. **respected, respecting.**

re•spon•si•ble (ri-SPON-sə-bəl) *adjective.* 1. Having an obligation or duty regarding: Parents are *responsible* for their children. 2. Being the cause of: The broken machine was *responsible* for the loud noise. 3. Able to accept duties; worthy of trust: The manager gave the important job to the most *responsible* worker. **—responsibly** *adverb.*

rest•less (REST-liss) *adjective.* 1. Not able to relax or be still: The *restless* man paced up and down the hall. 2. Without rest or sleep: The tourist spent a *restless* night in the noisy hotel. **—restlessly** *adverb.*

re•strain (ri-STRAYN) *verb.* To control; keep from (acting or doing). **restrained, restraining.**

re•ward (ri-WOHRD) *verb.* To give something in return for an action or service. **rewarded, rewarding.** **—noun.** 1. Something earned or given in return for an action or service. 2. Money or something else of value offered for the capture of a criminal.

rheu•ma•tism (ROO-mə-tiz-əm) *noun.* A disease that affects the muscles and joints with stiffness and pain.

rhi•noc•er•os (righ-NOSS-ər-əss) *noun.* A very large mammal, found in Africa and Asia, that has thick folds of skin and one or two large horns on its snout. **—rhinoceros** or **rhinoceroses** *plural.*

ro•bust (roh-BUHST or ROH-buhst) *adjective.* Healthy and vigorous; sturdy. **—robustly** *adverb.*

rock•er (ROCK-ər) *noun.* 1. A rocking chair. 2. A curved section on which a rocking chair or cradle rocks.

rug•ged (RUHG-id) *adjective.* 1. Sturdy; tough and strong: *rugged* fullback. 2. Having a very rough, uneven surface: *rugged* mountains. 3. Difficult; harsh: *rugged* voyage. 4. Not smooth: a *rugged* face. **—ruggedly** *adverb.*

ruin (ROO-in) *noun.* 1. (Often plural) The remains of something that has decayed or been destroyed: the *ruins* of an old castle. **ruins.**

saber-toothed tiger (SAY-bər-toothd TIGH-gər) *noun.* A prehistoric animal with long and sharp canine teeth or fangs.

sap•ling (SAP-ling) *noun.* A young tree.

sar•dine (sahr-DEEN) *noun.* A small fish, of the herring family, that can be eaten.

sat•is•fy (SAT-iss-figh) *verb.* 1. To fill (a need or wish): The ice cream *satisfied* my hunger. 2. To give assurance to; to answer. 3. To pay or fulfill. **satisfied, satisfying.**

scuff (SKUHF) *verb.* 1. To scrape or drag the feet when walking. 2. To cause a scraped or rough spot on: Tim *scuffed* his new shoes when he tripped. **scuffed, scuffing.** **—noun.** A scraped or rough spot.

sel•dom (SEL-dəm) *adverb.* Not often.

shaggy-coated (SHAG-ee-KOHT-əd) *adjective.* Having long or coarse hair.

sha•man (SHAH-mən) *noun.* A member of an early tribe who practiced magic by means of spells, dances, and so forth.

sher•bet (SHER-bit) *noun.* A sweet frozen dessert made with fruit juice, milk or water, and gelatin or egg white.

474

shield (SHEELD) *noun.* 1. A large piece of metal or wood held in front of the body to protect it in combat. 2. Anything that serves to protect. 3. Something shaped like a shield, as a police officer's badge. —*verb.* To defend or protect. **shielded, shielding.**

shim•mer (SHIM-ər) *verb.* To shine with a faint unsteady sparkle; gleam faintly. **shimmered, shimmering.** —*noun.* A faint gleam or sparkle.

ship•ment (SHIP-mənt) *noun.* 1. The act of shipping or delivering goods: Pack the goods for *shipment.* 2. The things that are shipped: We received a big *shipment* of flowers.

shrine (SHRIGHN) *noun.* A place considered sacred because of a person or event associated with it: The Lincoln Memorial is an American *shrine.* **shrines.**

shrink (SHRINGK) *verb.* 1. To make or become smaller or less. 2. To draw back; shy away (from): *shrink* from a dog. **shrank** or **shrunk, shrunk** or **shrunken, shrinking.**

sift *verb.* 1. To separate big or coarse parts from little or fine ones by passing through a sieve: *sift* flour. 2. To pass (through): The sunlight *sifts* through the branches. 3. To examine with care: I must *sift* all he tells me. **sifted, sifting.**

site (SIGHT) *noun.* A place where something is, will be, or was: Gettysburg was the *site* of a great Civil War battle. **sites.**

skull (SKUHL) *noun.* The part of the skeleton that forms the head.

sky•line (SKY-lighn) *noun.* 1. The line where the earth and the sky seem to meet; horizon. 2. The forms of buildings as seen against the sky. **skylines.**

slaugh•ter (SLAW-tər) *verb.* 1. To kill (animals) for food. 2. To kill in large numbers. **slaughtered, slaughtering.** —*noun.* Killing.

smog *noun.* A mixture of smoke and fog. —**smoggy** *adjective.*

snork•el (SNOR-kəl) *noun.* 1. A tube or tubes permitting a submarine to take in fresh air while it is under the water. 2. A tube used by a swimmer to get air when his head is under the water. —*verb.* To swim under the water while using a snorkel. Also called "snorkel dive." **snorkeled, snorkeling.**

snuf•fle (SNUF-l) *verb.* To sniff repeatedly, as when one is crying or has a cold. **snuffled, snuffling.**

snug•gle (SNUHG-əl) *verb.* To cuddle; press close or lie close (to) in a loving way. **snuggled, snuggling.**

so•ber•ness (SOH-bər-ness) *noun.* The state of being quiet or serious.

so•cial stud•ies (SOH-shəl STUHD-ees) *noun.* The study of history, geography, and other social sciences.

spear-head (SPIHR-hed) *noun.* 1. The pointed end of a spear. 2. The forward line of a military attack. —*verb.* To lead a military attack or any movement or project. **spearheaded, spearheading.**

spec•ta•cle (SPEK-tə-kəl) *noun.* 1. A show or display; something unusual to look at. 2. (Plural) Eyeglasses.

splotch (SPLOCH) *noun.* A smear or spot of a color or material different from that of the surface or background.

stab *verb.* 1. To wound or pierce with a knife or other pointed object. 2. To offend deeply; hurt the feelings of. **stabbed, stabbing.** —*noun.* 1. A wound made by stabbing. 2. A thrust; a poking into. 3. (Informal) A quick try; attempt: Janet took a *stab* at water skiing.

stain (STAYN) *noun.* 1. A spot or mark. 2. A liquid used to dye or color something. —*verb.*   1. To spoil or make a spot or mark on.   2. To blemish or spoil, as one's honor or character; dishonor.   3. To color, as with a dye. **stained, staining.**

sta•lag•mite (stə-LAG-might or STAL - əg - might) *noun.* A mineral deposit that is built up from the floors of caves. **stalag-mites.**

stam•pede (stam-PEED) *noun.* A sudden and widespread rush or running. —*verb.* To run suddenly in a large group. **stampeded, stampeding.**

stif•fen (STIF-ən) *verb.* To make or become thick, rigid, or tense. **stiffened, stiffening.**

strain (STRAYN) *verb.*   1. To injure by too much effort: Ralph *strained* his back when he lifted the log.   2. To make a great effort: The movers *strained* to lift the piano.   3. To force through a sieve or screen to separate small from large pieces or solid from liquid parts. **strained, straining.**

streak (STREEK) *noun.*   1. A narrow stripe that is different from the surrounding area: Mother's hair has *streaks* of gray.   2. A particular quality: a mean *streak.*   3. A series of events: a winning *streak.* —*verb.*   1. To make lines or streaks.   2. To move quickly. **streaked, streaking.**

stroll (STROHL) *verb.* To walk slowly. **strolled, strolling.** —*noun.* A slow walk.

stub•by (STUHB-ee) *adjective.*   1. Short and thick: *stubby* fingers.   2. Covered with or made up of stubs. **stubbier, stubbiest.**

stu•di•o (STOO-dee-oh or STYOO-dee-oh) *noun.*   1. The workshop of a painter, musician, photographer, or other artist.   2. A place for broadcasting radio or TV programs, or for making movies. **studios.**

sulk•y (SUHL-kee) *adjective.* Sullen; quiet because of bad temper. —**sulkily** *adverb.*

sum•mit (SUHM-it) *noun.* The highest point; peak; top.

sum•mon (SUHM-ən) *verb.*   1. To command to come: The President *summoned* his Cabinet.   2. To order to appear in court.   3. To call up; rouse: *Summon* our courage. **summoned, summoning.**

swamp (SWAHMP or SWAWMP) *verb.*   1. To sink; flood; fill with water: A big wave *swamped* our boat.   2. To put into deep water; to cover with water.   3. To overcome; flood: Molly's new shop is *swamped* with business. **swamped, swamping.** —*noun.* A marsh; soft, wet land. —**swampy** *adjective.*

sweet•meat (SWEET-meet) *noun.* A candy.

Swiss *adjective.* Having to do with the country of Switzerland.

tangy *adjective.* Having a sharp, biting flavor or odor.

tart (TAHRT) *adjective.*   1. Sour; sharp: Cherries have a *tart* flavor.   2. Cutting, biting, as a sharp remark. **tarter, tartest.** —*noun.* A small open pie. —**tartly** *adverb.*

tem•per (TEM-pər) *noun.*   1. The state of one's feelings or attitudes: a gentle *temper.*   2. A state of anger; rage.   3. Control of one's feelings: The coach lost his *temper.* —*verb.*   1. To treat a metal to make it hard or flexible.   2. To modify, make less severe. **tempered, tempering.**

tempt *verb.* 1. To encourage to do something, especially something unwise or improper. 2. To dare; to test: *tempt* your luck. 3. To be inclined: *tempted* to quit the team. **tempted, tempting.** —**temptation** (tem-TAY-shən) *noun.*

ten•sion (TEN-shən) *noun.* 1. The act or condition of stretching or being stretched: When a fish bites, there is *tension* on the fishing line. 2. Mental strain; nervousness. 3. An uneasy, unfriendly feeling or state.

three-fourths (three-FORTHS) *noun.* A part of a whole, when the whole is considered to be four fourths.

thresh•old (THRESH-ohld) *noun.* 1. A doorsill. 2. The beginning: the *threshold* of adventure.

throb *noun.* A quivering feeling or movement, as a strong beat of the heart. —*verb.* To move, beat, or vibrate in a steady, pulsing way. **throbbed; throbbing.**

throng *noun.* A crowd; large group. —*verb.* 1. To gather in a crowd. 2. To crowd into; to cluster. **thronged, thronging.**

tid•al (TIGHD-l) *adjective.* Relating to a tide or tides.

tilt *verb.* 1. To tip, lean, slant: Don't *tilt* your hat; put it on straight. 2. To charge or fight on horseback with a lance. **tilted, tilting.** —*noun.* 1. State of tilting or being tilted: The flagpole has a slight *tilt.* 2. A *tilting* contest, as between knights.

tired•ness (TIGHRD-ness) *noun.* The state of being tired; weariness.

tis•sue (TISH-oo) *noun.* 1. A very light, thin fabric or paper. 2. (Biology) Similar cells in a part of the body or plant: muscle *tissue.*

tol•er•ance (TOL-ər-ənss) *noun.* 1. The ability to be fair to those whose views, customs, or actions are different from one's own. 2.

(Medicine) The natural or acquired ability to resist the effect of (an element, as a drug).

tomb (TOOM) *noun.* 1. A grave or burying place. 2. A special building or monument for the dead.

tom•fool•er•y (tom-FOOL-ə-ree) *noun.* 1. Foolish or silly behavior. 2. Nonsense.

torch *noun.* 1. A flaming light, usually carried by hand. 2. (British) A flashlight. 3. A tool that burns gas to produce a hot flame, used to melt metals and remove paint; a blowtorch. **torches.**

tor•rent (TOR-ənt) *noun.* 1. A rushing stream of water. 2. Anything flowing swiftly and wildly like a torrent: a *torrent* of criticism.

trag•e•dy (TRAJ-ə-dee) *noun.* 1. A very sad event; a piece of extreme bad luck. 2. A serious play, novel, or other work with an unhappy ending; such writing in general.

tri•al (TRIGH-əl or TRIGHL) *noun.* 1. A trying or testing. 2. (Law) An examination of facts, conducted in court, to determine the truth of charges or claims. 3. A person or thing that causes hardship.

tu•pe•lo (TOO-pə-loh) *noun.* A large tree that grows in swamps. Its soft, light wood is used for making wooden shoes, and pieces of its root are used to float fishing nets.

tur•ban (TER-bən) *noun.* 1. A Moslem head covering made by winding a long cloth or scarf around the head. 2. A hat that looks similar to a turban.

tur•moil (TER-moil) *noun.* State of agitation or commotion; confusion.

tusk (TUHSK) *noun.* A long, curved tooth (usually one of a pair) of an animal such as the elephant.

ty•rant (TIGH-rənt) *noun.* 1. A ruler who exercises complete control or authority; a cruel ruler. 2. Anyone who dominates other persons cruelly or unfairly.

un•pop•u•lar (uhn-POP-yə-lər) *adjective*. Not well liked; not favored or approved of. —**unpopularity** (uhn-pop-yə-LA-rə-tee) *noun*.

un•rea•son•a•ble (uhn-REE-zn-ə-bəl) *adjective*. 1. Not having or showing sense or clear thought. 2. More than is right or sensible. —**unreasonably** *adverb*.

urge (ERJ) *verb*. 1. To encourage earnestly; to push (someone) to action: We *urged* Dad to buy a new car. 2. To present (an idea, plan, or such) strongly; to recommend strongly. 3. To push or drive forward: The farmer *urged* the oxen into the field. **urged, urging.**

ven•ture (VEN-chər) *verb*. 1. To risk; take a chance. 2. To take the chance of going: *venture* into the cave. 3. To dare (to give an opinion): I *ventured* to tell Augustus that he was wrong. **ventured, venturing.** —*noun*. An enterprise that is risky or unsure. **ventures.**

vi•brate (VIGH-brayt) *verb*. 1. To move or make move up and down or back and forth quickly. 2. To make a wavering sound: Tarzan's voice *vibrated* when he pounded his chest. **vibrated, vibrating.** —**vibration** (vigh-BRAY-shən) *noun*.

vic•tim (VIK-tim) *noun*. 1. One who is hurt or killed. 2. One who is fooled, cheated, or hurt: the *victim* of our pranks. 3. An animal offered as a sacrifice. —**victimize** *verb*.

vul•ture (VUHL-chər) *noun*. 1. A bird in the hawk family that lives by eating the carcasses of dead animals. 2. A person who feeds on or profits from the mistakes or bad luck of others.

waft (WAHFT or WAFT) *verb*. To float or move gently through the air or on the water. **wafted, wafting.** —*noun*. A gentle puff of air.

ware•house (WAIR-howss) *noun*. A large storage building. **warehouses.** —*verb*. To store or put into a warehouse. **warehoused, warehousing.**

wa•ver (WAY-vər) *verb*. 1. To sway; move back and forth. 2. To incline first toward one thing and then toward another. 3. To lose strength. **wavered, wavering.**

wheeze (HWEEZ) *verb*. 1. To breathe with a whistling sound, usually because of sickness. 2. To make a whistling sound. **wheezed, wheezing.** —*noun*. A high, whistling sound. **wheezes.**

whiff (HWIF) *noun*. 1. A puff or light current of air. 2. A sniff or quick breath, as of an odor. 3. The odor itself, moving through the air: a *whiff* of newly cut grass.

wilt *verb*. 1. To droop or cause to droop: Cut flowers *wilt* without water. 2. To weaken; lose courage or strength. **wilted, wilting.**

wince (WINSS) *verb*. To pull back, as if in pain. **winced, wincing.** —*noun*. The act of drawing back.

woo *verb*. 1. To try to gain the love of. 2. To seek: Both candidates will *woo* the labor vote. **wooed, wooing.**

wor•ri•some (WUHR-ee-səm) *adjective*. 1. Causing worry or concern. 2. With a tendency to worry.

ABCDEFGHIJ 08543210
PRINTED IN THE UNITED STATES OF AMERICA